On Meaning

D1603762

Theory and History of Literature
Edited by Wlad Godzich and Jochen Schulte-Sasse

For other books in the series, see p. 238.

On Meaning

Selected Writings in

Semiotic Theory

Algirdas Julien Greimas

Translation by Paul J. Perron and Frank H. Collins
Foreword by Fredric Jameson
Introduction by Paul J. Perron

Theory and History of Literature, Volume 38

University of Minnesota Press, Minneapolis

The University of Minnesota Press gratefully acknowledges translation assistance provided for this book by the French Ministry of Culture.

Published by the University of Minnesota Press
2037 University Avenue Southeast, Minneapolis MN 55414.
Published simultaneously in Canada
by Fitzhenry & Whiteside Limited, Markham.
Printed in the United States of America.

Chapter 1, "Comparative Mythology," was first published under the title "La Description de la signification et la mythologie comparée," *L'Homme* (Sept.–Dec. 1963):51–66; chapter 2, "Toward a Semiotics of the Natural World," was first published under the title "Conditions d'une sémiotique du monde naturel," *Langages* 10(1968):3–35; chapter 3, "The Interaction of Semiotic Constraints," was written in collaboration with François Rastier and was first published in *Game, Play, Literature, Yale French Studies*, no. 41(1968):86–105; chapter 4, "Elements of a Narrative Grammar," was first published in *L'Homme* 9(1969):71–92; chapter 5, "A Problem of Narrative Semiotics: Objects of Value," was first published in *Langages* 31(1973):13–35; chapter 6, "Actants, Actors, and Figures," was first published in Claude Chabrol and Jean-Claude Coquet, eds., *Sémiotique narrative et textuelle* (Paris: Larousse, 1973); 161–76; chapter 7, "Toward a Theory of Modalities," was first published in *Langages* 43(1976):90–108; chapter 8, "On the Modalization of Being," first appeared as a prepublication in *Le Bulletin du Groupe de recherches semio-linguistiques* 9(1979); 9–19; chapter 9, "On Anger: A Lexical Semantic Study," first appeared as a prepublication in *Documents de recherche du Groupe de recherches sémio-linguistiqes* 3(1981), and English translation by Gary Phillips was published in *Monographs, Working Papers, & Pre-publications*, Paris School of Semiotics, ed. Paul J. Perron (Toronto 1983); chapter 10, "Knowing and Believing: A Single Cognitive Universe," was first published in *Du sens II* (Paris: Le Seuil, 1983):115–33; chapter 11, "Semiotics and Social Communication," was first presented as a paper entitled "Stato e tendenze attuali della ricerca sulle communicazioni di massa" at a conference held in Milan in October 1970 and was published in the *Annuario 1970* of the Instituto Agostino Gemelli, Milan; chapter 12, "On Theoretical Models in Sociolinguistics," was presented at a conference during the *Journées internationales de socio-linguistique* organized by the Instituto Luigi Sturzo in Rome in September 1969 and was published in a volume entitled *International Days of Socio-Linguistics*; chapter 13, "On Evenemential History and the Deep Structures of Historiography," is a revised version of a paper submitted for a symposium on the theme *Geschichte und Geschichten*, held in Constance in 1970. These papers were published in R. Koselleck and W. D. Stempel, eds., *Geschichte: Ereignis und Erzälung* (Munich: Fink, 1973); chapter 14, "Reflections on Ethnosemiotic Objects," was presented to the First International Congress of European Ethnology in August 1971.

Library of Congress Cataloging-in-Publication Data

Greimas, Algirdas Julien.
  On meaning.
  (Theory and history of literature; v. 38)
  Includes index.
  1. Semiotics. 2. Discourse analysis, Narrative.
I. Title. II. Series.
P99.G67 1987   001.51   86-12326
ISBN 0-8166-1518-7
ISBN 0-8166-1519-5 (pbk.)

Contents

Foreword
Fredric Jameson

A. J. Greimas is the last of the great thinkers and theoreticians of French structuralism and poststructuralism to be translated into English and presented to the
American public, and perhaps in many ways the most difficult and forbidding—
bristling with scientificity, as these texts are, and breaking out at all points into
that graphics of formalization (equations, schemata, nonverbal symbols of variables and invariables) that always seems to the "humanist" to draw a boundary
across which one looks with frustration at the forbidden promised lands of
mathematics or symbolic logic, or of musical theory. We need, not one, but
many, introductions to this "semiotics"; this volume, which richly and substan-
tially covers the whole range of Greimas's interests and practical work, is already
endowed with an excellent account of the theory, as it were from the inside and
on its own terms: an account that makes it clear that Greimas's pastures belong
to us, that they are not on the far side of some hard-scientific discipline but occupy
a whole terrain of narrative, meaning, discourse, ideological connotation, which
is scarcely distinct from the privileged areas of study of any responsible literary
or cultural criticism today, nor either from those areas of the contemporary social
sciences and philosophy that have followed us into the great new problematic of
representation itself.

What a rather different kind of introduction needs to show, however, is how
the interested outsider can navigate this conceptuality and occasionally beach and
camp with profit and stimulation within it; my own testimony is that of a fellow
traveler of Greimassian semiotics, with a deplorable nonchalance toward its or-
thodoxies, but also a passionate interest in the ongoing development and dy-

namics of this new "discipline," whose capacity to produce fresh problems, and urgent, exciting problems at that, is not the least sign of the deeper truth and rightness of its starting point. Indeed, we have reached a paradoxical moment in the development of this particular semiotics (there are of course many other kinds), in which, some twenty years after the inaugural texts of a kind of research sometimes denounced as ahistorical and universalizing in some bourgeois analytic scientistic fashion, has now begun not merely to reflect on its own history but also and above all to discover the deeper historicity of its own inner logic of development and of the dynamic whereby a local concept, modified at its saturation point and at the moment of diminishing returns, in its turn proves to demand the enlargement and subsequent modification of the entire conceptual field of which it was a part. The consequence is that in Greimassian semiotics, in some intense and original new way, concepts bear a date and are historical in their very essence—not, to be sure, in the crude and multiple chronologies of calendar years, but on the intrinsic calendar of the unfolding of the semiotic problem field itself; and this is something very different from the older "periods" of a philosopher's thinking (the thoughts of some younger Hegel or Marx, or of the Heidegger before and after the *Kehre*, etc.). Nor is the matter of the inner date, the inner chronological mark, merely to be thought in terms of some vague provisionality, later, more "rigorous" formulations taking the place of earlier hypotheses: In Greimas's work all the formulations—early and late—are interesting and in some sense "valid" in themselves; only their intelligibility is incomplete without a keen awareness of the "moment" of each, of the time of the problematic as a whole, of the shape and point in the life cycle of this particular exploding galaxy in which that technical term pulsates with its brightest life.

I will put this in a different way and in a different language by saying that the "genius" of Greimas—the privileged form of his intelligence—has always seemed to me to lie in his extraordinary sense of precisely this tendential development of the problem field itself, and in those magisterial "lessons" in which he situates this or that concrete or local analysis, shows what it solves and how it modifies things, and above all designates the directions in which "future work is to be done," in which future work is *now* to be done—this extraordinary perpetual present of the problematic itself. Not all theory, nor all philosophy, surely, works in this way (although Metz was able to occupy a similar position and do something analogous for a certain extraordinarily productive moment in film theory), and it is not a matter of prophecy either, nor of the fatalistic and hyperlucid sense of limits ("we're eventually going to have to confront the problem of *nature* again, or base and superstructure, of what used to be called 'consciousness' "). It would also, in my opinion, be incorrect to detect Authority, and authoritarianism, at work in this "master's" surveillance of the multiple fields of research and his staying on top of the multiple tempos of research and the minutiae of the various laboratories under supervision. It is not exactly a matter of the inventive parceling out of new thesis topics; nor any willful and arbitrary channeling of the disciples' energies into the byways closest to the ideologue's heart (and least menacing for his project). What reigns here, at its best, is what Hegel called *die Sache selbst* and its objective dynamics and tendencies: Greimas's superintendence is an effacement of self before those and a watchful patience, a nurturing alertness, for their moments of ripeness and their specific, uneven, "semiautonomous" temporalities.

This narrative reading of the semiotic record is thus obviously for me the most exciting way in which to use it. But for most beginners it will equally obviously not be the first one. I must therefore propose more accessible alternatives and will suggest that we bracket the whole question of science and scientificity in Greimas, and think of the body of texts that follow, as we do for other "structuralisms" or "poststructuralisms," as a code, an idiolect, a theoretical private language among many others resonating through the airspace of the contemporary public sphere. Let us therefore initially think of the "concepts" of Greimassian semiotics rather as a specific nomenclature, as a fresh and idiosyncratic, arbitrary, violent, often unlovely renaming of a whole space and collection of objects already familiar to us under other names and in different installations or perspectives: actants, narrative contracts, narrative programs, isotopies, modalizations, cataphora, and finally that peculiar act of nomination (the semiotic square) that is less a name than a visual articulation, a new hieroglyph (which then carries its terminology within itself like so many articulated organs: deixis, the complex term, the neutral term, and so on). I will be so bold as to suggest that, besides trying to grasp the conceptual links between all these terms as signs and moments of a whole project, we outsiders or interlopers—who resist the invitation to join the discipline and to "become semioticians," that is, to *convert* to the entire Greimassian code (and to abandon the other ones as so many false religions and false gods)—should also feel free to *bricolate* all this, that is, in plainer language, simply to *steal* the pieces that interest or fascinate us, and to carry off our fragmentary booty to our intellectual caves. The dishonesty of the suggestion (in our current penal code it bears the name "eclecticism") is not as fundamental as it may at first seem for we will find ourselves obliged, in the fullness of time, to return to the central laboratory complex for conceptual spare parts and missing tools or instruments.

I have omitted, from my list of key terms or favorite neologisms, what is apparently the basic concept of them all, the inaugural terminological complex, the founding nomenclature, the very language of the sign: that bewildering proliferation of syllables that, beginning with the "seme," fans out into "sememes" and "lexemes" and seems to describe some central space around the initial program of a "structural semantics." But just as I believe that the early book bearing this title is absolutely the wrong place to begin one's exploration of Greimas, so also I think that the scholastic problems turning on the seme itself—although constituting both the absolute presuppositions of Greimassian semiotics and its highest and most self-conscious moment of reflection on its own procedures – are also best postponed or suspended, and this, not only on account of their philosophical complexity (and their polemic and intradisciplinary relationship to other contemporary linguistic theories), but also for other reasons, which can be, I think, fairly clearly specified. (As for the matter of a starting point, the more practical one would be the initial text or object of study of this semiotics, which is Propp's *Morphology of the Folk Tale*, and the process of "semiotic reduction" to which Greimas, following a classic critique by Lévi-Strauss, subjects it.)

Whereas the philosophical point of departure of this semiotics and the problem of the sign itself are paradoxical in their very nature, something that has been splendidly formulated by Jean Petitot-Cocorda in an excellent recent book: "Greimassian epistemology is a direct consquence of the fact that its object is the form of meaning and that, in its very presence, meaning is by definition nonobjectifiable. Meaning is not a phenomenon available to the senses. *Qua* meaning it is imperceptible. This veritable 'foundational aporia' demands the conception of a conceptual-descriptive theory, one that is metalinguistic and a construction, and that is based on undefinables" (p. 273).[1] This is to say that a "semiotic reduction" (as I will call the central operations of Greimassian analysis) aims at rewriting a verbal or linguistic text into more fundamental mechanisms of meaning, as, for example, in the analysis of "modalizations," which *reduce* – a word I wish to use here strongly and positively – which reduce, then, a given text to the more primary "modes" of wanting, knowing, or doing (*vouloir, savoir, pouvoir*). When such reduction has been achieved, however, all we have are other words and other meanings, another text, a set of terms that, although redolent of an apparently more primary everyday speech and of simpler and more ultimate verbal gestures, are open to all the drift and force fields of philosophy and psychology, that is to say, of texts and linguistic and conceptual operations if anything even more complex than the original verbal object to be thereby "reduced." This infinite regress of the metalanguage across its fatal intertexts is only too well known and is normally "solved," that is, arrested, by the reification of the words we find remaining in that "explanation with which we agree to stop" (Wittgenstein), in other words, by the creation of some new and privileged philosophical or theoretical code or system. This is not, I think, exactly what Greimas does, although it can certainly look that way and Greimassian semiotics can very easily be misread or misunderstood as one more "system" of some kind. Yet it is not "by means of words that one gets out of words," to paraphrase Ponge. On the other hand, if it helps, we can certainly think "semes" and "sememes" in terms of the slack traditional notion of "thematics," clusters of deeper themes within a conceptual complex, a more subatomic logic of subconcepts at work in the official "thought," which then itself finds embodiment (or "manifestation") in some discursive entity of a verbal kind, which may be a page from a philosophical treatise, but just as easily a cookbook recipe or a short story, or a scientific textbook or whatever. The notion of thematics, however, is unsatisfactory — even if provisionally practical — because it marks a regression from linguistic terminology to a terminology of consciousness and ideas, and also because that mythology of a non- or prelinguistic consciousness then fatally positions us in a "world" in which the subject is divided from the object, and the "themes" from their referent, and in which, therefore, texts, and in particular the texts of culture, are optional and subjective: everyone knows the guilty relief afforded by the discussion of the "themes" of Faulkner, say — the word conveniently sets them all back inside his head like so many private obsessions, comfortably recontained and emptied of their "meaning" (again that problematical word!), transformed into mere psychological projections. It is therefore permissible to begin to grasp this semiotics in terms of the more familiar notions of the various kinds of thematic criticism, provided we ultimately reach that later stage in which we see it rather as a powerful substitute and alternative for such psychologizing methods, with which it is radically incompatible: The semes indeed actively organize the world itself, which is unthinkable in any independence from them.

To put it this way, however, is to find ourselves back in the philosophical and metaphysical perplexities we began by trying to bracket, to avoid, or to postpone. Petitot's discussion, however, from which I quoted, moves in a different direction by designating the crucial passage in which Greimas himself effects and describes his own decisive swerve: "The production of meaning is meaningful only if it is the transformation of a meaning already given; the production of meaning is consequently a signifying endowment with form [*Mise en forme*] indifferent to whatever content it may be called on to transform. *Meaning, in the sense of the forming of meaning, can thus be defined as the possibility of the transformation of meaning*" (*Du sens*, p. 15). These pronouncements can now be paraphrased as follows: We can ignore the static or philosophical problem of meaning and its relationship to language, along with the infinite regress of metalanguages that seems to result whenever we try to isolate the meaning of a certain verbal complex, only to find ourselves producing yet another text in its place; and the reason we can ignore this problem is that that static moment of the apparent presence of meaning in a text is a mirage or an optical illusion. Meaning is never there in that sense, or rather it is an "always-already-given" (to borrow a different metalanguage) in the process of transformation into another meaning. It is now this process of transformation — of the *production* of meaning — that is the object of semiotics, and its only possible object (meaning as such having proved to be a reification or a deceptive afterimage of some kind). With this step, however, not only has a decisive reformulation of the very problematic of semiotics and signs been made, but a new problem generated, and along with it a whole new field and conceptuality come into being, which is none other than that of *narrative* and narrative theory. (But in this first step, "narrative" merely registers the phenomenon of change — transformation, production, modification, etc. — which, falling out of the objects registered by static modes of thought and analysis, is here identified as the scandal of the event, of temporal originality, or even of "catastrophe" [in René Thom's sense].)

Greimassian semiotics will then become preeminently that school of contemporary theory that argues for something like a primacy of narrativity. Narrativity is here something a little more than a new object of study, or even a privileged, or the privileged, object of study; were this a question of philosophical or metaphysical propositions, the implication would be that of the primacy of narrative as a mode of thinking, or of a claim as to the profound narrativity of all thinking, including the apparently cognitive or specialized-abstract. Such propositions, which find their inspiration in Lévi-Strauss's path-breaking work on the structure of myth and the nature of *pensée sauvage* (or preconceptual, perceptual "science"), are not the appropriate form in which to characterize the interest and originality of narrative semiotics. Indeed, were one to assimilate such philosophical assertions to semiotics, it might easily by observed that in that case they only seem to hold for early Greimas and that in recent years this semiotics has tended (quite explicitly and programmatically) away from narrativity in the direction of "modalization" (evidently a more cognitive or grammatical, but at any rate, a more abstract focus than that of the whole problematic of events, actors, exchanges, and transfers, which obtained throughout what one may therefore call the "narratological" period of semiotics).

It is better, therefore, to underscore a more complex dialectic in this work between the narrative and the cognitive: In effect, each is used to undermine the seeming primacy or priority of the other, when this last is dominant, either by virtue of the nature of the text under study or of the drift and tendencies of some dominant methodology. Thus paradoxically, what has been loosely called the priority of narrative was at first staged—in narrative analysis proper, in Lévi-Strauss, in Propp and Greimas's fertile and inaugural rewriting of Propp, and then later in a host of small studies, culminating in the comprehensive and monumental *Maupassant*[2]—as a *reduction* of a properly narrative surface (myth, fairy tale, short story) to a complex interaction of cognitive traits. Narrative is thereby triumphantly demonstrated to be a form of thinking, but at a heavy price, namely, its rewriting, reduction, or transformation back into abstract thinking and its tokens or counters. To be sure, in these forms of semiotic analysis, the articulation of cognitive features and their interplay and implication is far more detailed and complex than anything we had hitherto possessed in traditional literary criticism, where the status of the cognitive was at best allowed to include the opinions of the author, the prejudices of the age (including its readership), the operation of enormous and vague *Weltanschauungen*, the association with some equally vague conception of the "history of ideas," or the intervention of this or that novel "concept" (most frequently drawn from the history of the sciences, e.g., "entropy"). Rhetorical criticism (Kenneth Burke) elaborately decoded the surface moves of the text, but in a nonnarrative fashion, which failed to integrate the extraordinary intuitions of its conception of deep structure (Burke's "dramatism" in hindsight has much in common with Greimassian "actantial" and "positional" analysis). Meanwhile, although Frye's archetypal criticism was historically epochmaking in its reassertion of the centrality of narrative as such, one cannot say that cognitive content, as such, emerged as a central problem for this approach. An older Marxist criticism, finally, sought to enlarge the narrow literary conception of "ideas" to include political and social positions (progressive/reactionary, class ideologies), but in spite of the extraordinary narrative self-consciousness of Marx himself (in *The Eighteenth Brumaire of Louis Bonaparte*), it is clear that most of these studies (even those of Lucien Goldmann) worked with a naive view of the dynamics and structure of narrative proper. Of the entire older tradition, therefore, one wants to say — using the language of theater people — that for all its intermittent philosophical brilliancies, it "lacked technique," and it is precisely this analytic technique that Greimassian semiotics at last triumphantly unveiled and made available.

Still, as I have suggested, the reduction of narrative to an intricate microscopic play of semes and sememes (couched in what remains a cognitive language of abstract themes) — far from securing the triumph of some universal metaphysics of narrativity — might well be said to do the contrary and to absorb the last remnants of some seemingly irreducible narrative discourse back into the cognitive. For example, the two seemingly ultimate atomic units of "pure" or primary narrative — that stubbornly anthropomorphic remnant that is the "character" or the "actor," and that abstractly unthinkable "fact of the matter" that is time, change, event, act, catastrophe — to these ultimate narrative strongholds Greimassian semiotics lays elaborate seige; and virtually the most interesting moment of the semiotic adventure is this particular engagement, which at length — by way of conceptions such as the *actant* and exchange — "reduces" these subjects and verbs, these last bits of narrative grammar, to "effects" of a microsemiotics of a radically different, cognitive order. (As we shall see shortly, the "semiotic square" emerges as the unified field theory of this rewriting procedure.)

Yet it is a two-way street: If narratives are transformed back into something that still distantly resembles a cognitive dynamic, overtly cognitive texts — philosophy, science, and the like — are thereby opened up and made vulnerable to a now more properly narrative analysis. This is the other pendulum swing of the dialectic of Greimassian semiotics, which will now decode and unmask the seemingly abstract, in its various disciplinary discourses, as the covert operation of narrative programs and schemata of all kinds, so that the movement of an abstraction or a concept through rigorous philosophical argument becomes readable and visible as the procession of a "character" through multiple trials and perils, menanced by its conceptual adversaries and aided and abetted by "magical helpers" who are no less mythic than those of Propp's peasant stories: Kant thereby becomes the first great modern novelist. Even the humble cookbook is unmasked as the locus, not merely of storytelling, but also of alchemical transmutation; and at this point, the very concept of narrative expands to become coterminous with the entire universe of texts itself, without thereby in any way undermining the specificity of the cognitive. For the operation is not to be confused with a (sometimes necessary) work of demystification, wherein a set of ostensible abstractions is shown to be myth or irrational figuration (in all the bad senses): To demonstrate the narrativity of philosophical thinking is not to discredit its conceptual or intellectual claims, if only because, as we have seen, that very deeper narrative structure can then itself in turn be rewritten as a new form of microthinking or of cognitive microphysics. The essentials of the semiotic position lie, not in some ultimate metaphysical choice between the narrative and the cognitive, but rather in the constant process whereby the one is ceaselessly displaced by the other, until this last, become dominant in its turn, is ripe for its own inverse and reciprocal humiliation. (This accounts for my own reluctance to feel that the swing away from narrativity to theories of modalization represents anything like a final victory, in Greimas's work, of the cognitive over the narrative.)

Yet this dialectic is visible only if we vigilantly bear in mind the bracketing of the ultimate philosophical problems with which we began—the suspension of the question of a final metalanguage, and the operative "fact of life" of this semiotics that must use a seemingly cognitive language to identify and name "semes" that are, however, neither cognitive nor narrative, but best described, in Petitot's language, as "nondefinables." Dialectical language, however, seems to me to offer another practical way out of this philosophical impasse in the concept of the *mediation*, for the process I have been describing would seem most adequately characterized by a ceaseless two-way mediation between two types of language, neither of which can be permitted to become dominant or to take on metaphysical priority. This is why I have also felt that some enlarged version of the traditional concept of *ideology* (which plays only the most limited and mechanical role in Greimas's texts) might well be appealed to at this point, both as a way of specifying the nature of these semiotic analyses and operations and also as an occasion for evaluating them and suggesting their wider implications. To this end, indeed, I have suggested that ideology, in some more comprehensive sense, be grasped as a twofold or amphibious reality, susceptible of taking on two distinct and seemingly incompatible forms at will, which are very precisely our old friends the narrative or the cognitive. That "ideology" in the narrower sense is a mass of opinions, concepts, or pseudoconcepts, "worldviews," "values," and the like, is commonly accepted; that these vaguely specified conceptual entities also always have a range of narrative embodiments, that is, indeed, that they are all in one way or another buried narratives, may be less widely understood and may also open up a much wider range of exploration than the now well-worn conceptual dimension of the ideology concept. Yet it was not to replace the cognitive by the narrative that my proposal was made but rather to coordinate both by way of a definition that insisted on their necessary alternation: Ideology is then whatever in its very structure is susceptible of taking on a cognitive and a narrative form alternately.

The relevance of these proposals for Greimas's work turns on the whole matter of the so-called elementary structure of signification, or, in other words, the famous "semiotic square," for many of us the supreme achievement of Greimassian semiotics. Here finally we find opened up the "black box" through which narrative is somehow "converted" into cognition and vice versa: Finally we have the equations, we can witness the processes of transfer, which need no longer be posited mystically since it is "visible" before us (I will return to this matter of the visible and of space at the conclusion of the present remarks). How this can be so, however, obviously demands yet another simplified exercise in the explanatory capacities of the "square," whose canonical form is herewith reproduced:

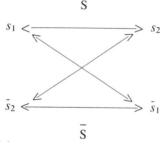

The enumeration of the advantages of the square can begin at once with the observation that it is a decisive enlargement on the older structural notion of the binary opposition: s_1 versus s_2 is clearly just such a binary opposition, or in the language of philosophical logic a "contrary," that is, a strong opposition (white versus black, male versus female), but one that the square now reveals to encompass far more than two available positions. It immediately implies, for example, the two supplementary slots of what logic calls a "contradictory," where $\bar{s}_1$ and $\bar{s}_2$ are the simple negatives of the two dominant terms, but include far more than either: thus "nonwhite" includes more than "black," "nonmale" more than "female." Meanwhile, the two compound or "synthetic" positions of S and $\bar{S}$ offer still greater conceptual enlargements, S standing as a complex or utopian term, in which the opposition of "white" and "black" might be transcended (mestizo, for example), whereas $\bar{S}$ stands as the neutral term, in which all of the privations and negations are assembled ("colorless," for example). Finally, the transversal axes map the place of tensions distinct from the principal or binary one, while the synthesis hypothetically proposed by uniting the two sides of the square ("white" plus "nonblack") designates alternative conceptual combinations. The entire mechanism then is capable of generating at least ten conceivable positions out of a rudimentary binary opposition (which may originally have been no more than a single term, e.g., "white," which proves to be internally defined by a hidden opposition we articulate by promoting the concealed pole "black" to visibility). I have suggested that other traditions may find this schema interesting if they entertain the hypothesis that it constitutes a virtual map of conceptual closure, or better still, of the closure of ideology itself, that is, as a mechanism, which, while seeming to generate a rich variety of possible concepts and positions, remains in fact locked into some initial aporia or double bind that it cannot transform from the inside by its own means.

However this may be, it seems appropriate to conclude this introduction with an outsider's observations on the multiple uses and interests of this mechanism. A few initial remarks ought to concern its "proper use," that is, to offer some warnings about what it can and cannot do. The square does offer, I believe, a kind of "discovery principle," but of a special type, and it cannot be guaranteed to replace intelligence or intuition. Indeed, insofar as it can often be called on simply to map thoughts and interpretations arrived at in other (seemingly less technical) fashions, it is appropriate at the outset to stress its initial pedagogical function: One can, in other words, very properly use this visual device to map out and to articulate a set of relationships that it is much more confusing, and much less economical, to convey in expository prose, and these humbler pedagogical capacities of the semiotic square may not be the least index of its importance.

As for its heuristic value, however, experience testifies that you must blacken many pages before you get it right and that a number of key decisions intervene in the process. One lists a variety of entities to be coordinated; it is a list that must never be considered final, nor should the nature and nomenclature of the entities be foreclosed. It is desirable (even, on my view, necessary) that seemingly aberrant or marginal, minor, eccentric entities be enumerated, since it is their place in the scheme of things, and their very presence, which is the most interesting of the problems the square can be called upon to solve.

As for operative decisions or moments, I will mention three that seem to me crucial. The first is the inaugural decision, not merely about the terms of the binary opposition to be expanded and articulated in the square as a whole, but also, and above all, the very order in which those terms are arranged; it makes a fundamental difference, in other words, whether the founding binary is ordered as white versus black, or as black versus white. The square is in that sense not symmetrical but "temporal" or positional, and the placement of the terms (obviously this initial formulation will already imply something like dominant/subordinate, center/margin, self/other), like that of mathematical equations (or the lobes of the brain, or right and left hand), is not indifferent but actively determinant in astonishing ways (that very astonishment playing its own part in the unexpected lessons we find ourselves learning in this process).

The second important recommendation is that the four primary terms (s_1, s_2, $\bar{s}_1$, $\bar{s}_2$) need to be conceived polysemically, each one carrying within it its own range of synonyms, and of the synonyms of its synonyms—none of them exactly coterminous with each other, such that large areas of relatively new or at least skewed conceptuality are thereby registered. Thus, for example, in Hayden White's conception of "metonymy,"[3] two relatively distinct "semes" are encompassed—that of reduction (scientific or mechanistic explanation, determinism) and that of separation; this term thus includes a fruitful terrain for dialectical slippage, such that its "reductive" aspect may allow it to stand in opposition to the visionary and representational plenitude of "metaphor." Its other "identity"—as sheer disjunction or separation—then allows it unexpectedly to be coordinated with (or against) "synecdoche" as the reintegration of the separated and the construction of new wholes. This will to embrace the slippage within terms is here a practical recommendation, like handicraft rules of thumb or inherited wisdom, but it also opens up a dizzying perspective of the subatomic universes, a prospect of what a very different semiotician, Umberto Eco, following Peirce, calls "infinite semiosis," in which each of the four primary terms of the square threatens to yawn open into its own fourfold system, down into the infinite divisibility of semiotic nature.

A final warning must be directed to the peculiar nature of the fourth term, the negation of the negation: $\bar{s}_2$. This must be (when the operation is successful) the place of novelty and of paradoxical emergence: It is always the most critical position and the one that remains open or empty for the longest time, for its identification completes the process and in that sense constitutes the most creative act of the construction. Once again, it is simply a matter of experience that the first three terms are relatively "given" and demand no great acts of intellection, but the fourth one is the place of the great leap, the great deduction, the intuition that falls from the ceiling, or from heaven. Yet this is something that here can be only mythically conveyed, as in that system of apocalypses foretold by Mayan religion, which, fourfold in a relatively universal fashion, only springs apart from Western paradigms unexpectedly in its fourth moment. The world, for the Mayans, will end in fire, as for us; a second time around, the world will be destroyed by water, as for us; yet a third time, and it will be destroyed by air (hurricanes). And it will also be destroyed a fourth time . . . by jaguars! (which, formerly the stars in the heavens, take on their new carniverous form and drop upon the earth to devour the human race). So also with J. G. Ballard's early and haunting end-of-the-world tetralogy: by water (*The Drowning World*), by fire (*The Burning World*), by air or hurricane (*The Wind from Nowhere*), and then . . . by turning into crystal (*The Crystal World*)!

The semiotic square is thus not static but dynamic: The significance of positionality within it is only one index of the way in which it can just as easily be considered to map a temporal process as to register a conceptual blockage or paralysis; indeed, the latter can most often be grasped as the very situation that motivates the former, namely, the attempt, by rotating the square and generating its implicit positions, to find one's way out of the conceptual or ideological closure, out of the old or given – into which one is locked – somehow desperately to generate the novelty of the event, or of breakthrough, or of the *Novum*. Yet to see the square as the very image of closure itself tends to encourage some pessimism about the possibilities of escaping from it in any other way than the Hegelian one: One does not resolve a contradiction; rather, by praxis, one alters the situation in such a way that the old contradiction, now dead and irrelevant, moves without solution into the past, its place taken by a fresh and unexpected contradiction (which may or may not be some advance on the older aporias or ideological imprisonment).

Yet the very gestalt properties of the square – its capacity to be indifferently static or dynamic – are what accounts for its powerful mediatory capacity: It can, in other words, "reduce" a narrative in movement to a series of "cognitive" or ideological, combinatory positions; or it can rewrite a cognitive text into a desperate narrative movement in which new positions are generated and abandoned, and in which terms ceaselessly amalgamate in order to achieve the release of this or that ideal synthesis, and release from their warring and antagonistic, structural-fragmentary nature.

I have offered elsewhere[4] illustrations of possible "applications" of the square to problems of narrative analysis: these unorthodox efforts may serve to suggest ways in which the two planes of narrative – "characters" or, better still, *systems* of characters, and cognitive complexes or contradictions – can be coordinated and transcoded into one another. Here I will briefly sketch a sample of the analysis of a "cognitive" or theoretical text, Hayden White's *Metahistory*, which is to be sure in a way pre-prepared, insofar as this text is itself already organized around a fourfold set of categories: the four tropes of Metaphor, Metonymy, Synecdoche, and Irony. This first system of categories is then multiplied by three more: a typology of worldviews, drawn from Stephen Pepper (Formism, Mechanicism, Organicism, and Contextualism); Frye's "emplotments" (Romantic, Tragic, Comic, and Satirical); and finally Mannheim's categories of ideology (Anarchist, Radical, Conservative, Liberal). In practice, it may be suggested that this set of, as it were, vertical layers in fact tends to amalgamate into two groups of coordinated features: The tropes and Pepper's "world hypotheses" function as alternate languages for the same characteristics, whereas the "emplotments" and the "modes of ideological implication" also tend to function synonymously. Yet within each of the two groups (which roughly correspond to the structure of a given history and to its metaphysical connotation, or reception, respectively), we already find that creative slippage I have referred to, the possibility of passing from one term to another by way of a shift in these levels (the earlier example of Metonymy illustrates a shift from the tropological sense of this "term" to its conceptual, or world-hypothetical, sense). What remains an open question is whether the two groups of categories need always function in unison, or whether one might not imagine a dissonance, that is, a contradiction, between say, the tropological mechanism and the emplotment or ideological message. This is something White seems to foresee[5], without, however, drawing any explicit conclusions from the possibility.

White's book seeks to do (at least) two things: first, to reassert the historical and cognitive claims of the so-called philosophers of history (Hegel, Marx, Nietzsche), who have, in the traditional canon of historiography, been assigned a lower and more amateurish status by the historians themselves, in contrast to "real" or practicing historiographers, of whom this book deals with four (Michelet, Ranke, Tocqueville, and Burckhardt). What Metahistory in fact achieves is a good deal less modest than this, since the thrust of the argument tends toward the assertion that in fact the philosophers of history are *better* historians than the historiographers. How the text generates this position will then be one of the questions an articulation by the semiotic square needs to answer.

The other function of *Metahistory* (which is specifically limited to the nineteenth-century "historical imagination") is to demonstrate not merely the relevance of the conceptual typologies already enumerated but their *cyclical* function, in a rhythm that begins in naive Metaphor or Romanticism, passes through the negative or Metonymic, Mechanistic stage of reduction, begins to reclaim a larger totalizing construction in the new unities of Synecdoche, and finally, in the moment of Irony, comes to a self-consciousness of its own linguistic or tropological procedures that signals a new crisis of the historical imagination and may be expected, by way of the great Viconian *ricorso*, to swing around again into a fresh belief, a fresh Metaphoric or Romantic moment with which the cycle can begin all over again on a heightened level. Indeed, it is this rebirth of historiographic belief that White calls for in his concluding pages, which speak out of the moment of Irony and its crisis. What is peculiar, however, is that the moment of Irony, *Metahistory*, takes two distinct forms: The crisis of the nineteenth century reaches as it were two distinct paroxysms simultaneously – the "bad" Irony of Burckhardt, serene and aestheticizing (the "philosophy" of Croce is in effect a more elaborate double of this position), and the "good" or strong Irony of Nietzsche from within which Hayden White clearly speaks (even though Hegel and Marx were to have been "rehabilitated" more or less on equal grounds with the author of the *Genealogy of Morals*). These intricate moves are, however, not random ones, nor are they in any way the "mere" results of the personal opinions or ideological predilections of the metahistorian; the pattern is indeed a very logical one, which can be clarified and articulated by the operation of the semiotic square as the various possible terms and positions of *Metahistory* are mapped onto it.

The diagram attempts to respect as much as possible the combinatory richness and intricacy of the text, very specifically including what I have called the slippage within the terms, that is their multiple semic content or the copresence of various levels and codes within each.

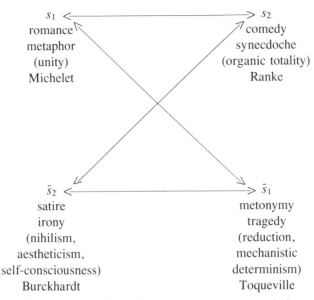

s_1
romance
metaphor
(unity)
Michelet

s_2
comedy
synecdoche
(organic totality)
Ranke

$\bar{s}_2$
satire
irony
(nihilism,
aestheticism,
self-consciousness)
Burckhardt

$\bar{s}_1$
metonymy
tragedy
(reduction,
mechanistic
determinism)
Toqueville

What should be clear from this initial mapping onto the semiotic square is that the four historians each present, in all their differences, the spectacle of unison between all the levels, and that indeed it is this very absence of inner tension or contradiction that accounts for the author's evaluations of them: itself a form of irony, not to say contempt, save in the case of Toqueville, where a certain tragic honesty carries conviction, but where, it should be noted, this univocal position also ultimately disintegrates under its own momentum into a Burckhardt-type irony and nihilism, which itself—as yet another univocal ideological position—then is subjected to the full force of the metahistorian's Irony. This last must therefore be of a different type, and it is precisely the advantage of the semiotic square to hold open other conceivable positions, which have not yet been secured in our diagram, and which are the so-called compound terms, the complex and neutral terms S and $\bar{S}$, and the deictic axes in which the lateral sides of the square also designate possible syntheses. Before demonstrating those, however, it is worth noting the strategic function, already referred to, involved in the choice of an initial binary opposition. The story, as anyone would naturally tell it, and as Hayden White himself initially maps it in his diagram of the levels on page 29 of *Metahistory,* is one in which an initial Metaphoric consciousness disintegrates into a Metonymic or negative moment of determinism and random mechanistic causality. That negative crisis is then—on anyone's stereotypical narrative paradigm—slowly overcome by Synecdochic reconstruction, only to be sapped and vitiated by a new kind of disintegration and a new kind of crisis—that of Ironic self-consciousness, and of the sense that even the Synecdochic solution was itself only fictional and linguistic — at which point as I have already said, the entire system turns over and swings back into a new cycle of Metaphoric reaffirmation.

But this corresponds, neither to the order of the chapters, nor to the combinatory logic of the work itself, in which Romance is followed by Comedy, and Metaphor by Synecdoche, rather than by Metonymy. Thus, we have mapped the semiotic square around a quite unexpected binary opposition, not the familiar one of Metaphor versus Metonymy, but some new constitutive tension between Metaphor and Synecdoche — a tension that must necessarily be conceptualized as the antagonism between two forms of *unity*, an intitial Metaphoric or representational one (Michelet's great ecstatic moments of national unity in the the Revolution and more specifically of the "fêtes de la Fédération" of June 1790) and a Synecdochic one, the construction of more "artificial" social unities, built up from their separate parts, in the form of Ranke's *institutions* (church, nation, etc.). The point I wish to stress is that the square *will not work* any other way (the reader may now wish to test this assertion by experiment) and that only this arrangement of the terms will generate the essentials of *Metahistory*, a book about which we have therefore learned something new, namely, that its deepest subject, the fundamental contradiction it is concerned to resolve, is not that of meaning versus non-meaning, or belief versus causality (Metaphor versus Metonymy: the traditional way of mapping the nineteenth-century "crisis of faith"), but rather the tension between two incompatible visions of the social, neither of which (ecstatic revolutionary spontaneism and the slow permanency of the great social institutions) seems satisfactory.

I must also add a word about the question of the "fourth term," also raised earlier. It is clear that, although the word itself is scarcely fresh or surprising, Irony is the great magical term on which the text turns and that its combinatorial mechanisms aim fully as much as *producing* this extraordinary "position" from across a wide range of meanings and uses (the slippage in this fourth term is far greater than in any of the others) as they simply register it as an object of study and one attitude among others.

We may now rapidly conclude the mapping of the square, whose complex and neutral terms can be loosely designated as historical Optimism and Pessimism respectively, a language whose slackness need not detain us long, since both are clearly logically impossible positions that the movement of the work rejects (S is a conceivable but impossible synthesis, $\bar{S}$ is merely the empty wiping out of that content and the place of the global, mechanical negations of both terms of the initial opposition). It is therefore to the lateral (or deictic) syntheses that we turn our attention. Here indeed the great "philosophers of history" find their positions, which have been generated by the inner logic of the square itself. Both Hegel and Marx, White tells us, achieved syntheses of Tragedy and Comedy: History is a comedy, all of whose individual moments are tragic. Nietzsche, meanwhile, begins with an identification of Tragedy and Comedy, which luminously eclipse each other and in their indistinction give rise to something else, which will be an Ironic sense of the powers of language that now once again releases the great Metaphoric energies. (Note how it is very precisely the semiotic slippage between Romance and Metaphor that enables this ultimate moment to be something more than a mere synthesis of Romance and Satire.) With this, the combinational movement of the book is exhausted and a message emerges: the priority of Hegel, Marx, and Nietzsche over the "univocal" historians, and after that, perhaps, the more tentative priority of Nietzsche over the other two positions insofar as Nietzsche "includes" their moments of Tragedy and Comedy and then projects further new and original possibilities, Metaphor and Irony (properly linguistic or reflexive moments), out of the earlier pair.

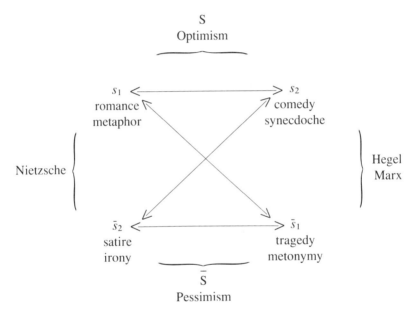

Returning now to the nature of the semiotic square itself, it seems clear that its emergence from the dynamic of Greimassian semiotics betokens some profound spatiality in the system in general. This is something that has been recognized by Petitot in the book already mentioned, which sets out indeed to achieve nothing less than a grounding of Greimassian semiotics in the spatial (he calls it positional or topological) premises of René Thom's catastrophe theory. What interests me is not the viability of that enterprise, nor how one might resolve this persistence of the irreducibly spatial within semiotics in some new and enlarged philosophical system, but rather the historical fact of its emergence in our society, where it is by no means the only example or symptom of a period intellectually given over to space in a way radically different from the preceding generation of the modernists, in thrall to temporality. All the structuralisms are deeply spatial in one way or another, and not merely in their rhetoric or modes of presentation (although the fact, previously mentioned, that we find these diagrams today more pedagogically convincing and persuasive than the corresponding linguistic expressions and developments of them is surely not insignificant either). Alone of the great philosophers, Henri Lefebvre, has posited a genuine new philosophy of space, and this on a historicist basis, namely, the tendential spatialization of late capitalism (and, one might wish to add, using a concept not foreseen in Lefebvre's work, of the *postmodern*). That Greimassian semiotics should be "true" in some sense (or at any rate, pragmatically, richly usable and full of practical development) and at the same time stand as a profound historical symptom of the nature of the age I find no difficulty in reconciling: the latter — the structure of the late capitalist global system — constituting something like the conditions of possibility for the conceptualizing and articulation of the new theoretical system. Perhaps this may also offer yet another new and unexplored terrain for the development of semiotics itself: not the semiotics of space, already a local region of Greimassian semiotics in which work is currently being done, but the space and spatialization of semiotics itself and the dynamics of this new positional or topological horizon of meaning and of our thought. At any rate, it is an honor for me to be associated with this first panoramic view of the semiotic adventure to be presented to the English-speaking public.

Translators' Note

The well-worn but ever-valid cliché "traduttore tradittore" was always present in our thoughts as we worked on and revised these translations. Our task was to make a selection of Professor Greimas's writings accessible to anglophone readers for whom the original French is too difficult. Although these are technical translations, we did not feel we had to concentrate exclusively on communicating the content, as is so often the case in technical and scientific translation. Our author is a scientist/humanist and to ignore the idiomatic and stylistic aspects of our final version would indeed have been a "betrayal" of the source texts. Yet these texts pose real problems for the translator. One major problem, that of the translation of technical terms, was solved by adopting as our authority, *Semiotics and Language: An Analytical Dictionary*. In this we were steadfastly consistent. The second major problem had to do with a sentence structure encountered frequently in Professor Greimas's work: the complex sentence par excellence. These are great, long sentences with embedded clauses that, in some ways, make us privy to the thought processes of the author as he fits together the pieces of a complex demonstration or argument. We frequently had to break them down into shorter sentences. However, just as often, we tried to be faithful to our author's style, using, as he does, commas, dashes, and parentheses to reproduce his sentence structure in translation. Highly attentive reading may be required as a result, but we believe that this is no more so than is the case for readers of the original texts.

In all aspects of our work, we have been guided by a conviction as to the importance of these texts and by our admiration and affection for the author.

Introduction
Paul J. Perron

The intention of this introduction is not to retrace the development of semiotics in Europe, or to situate in every detail all of Algirdas Julien Greimas's works within the intellectual tradition of his times. J.-C. Coquet, in his lengthy and informative introductory chapter in *Sémiotique – l'École de Paris* (1982) and his "Éléments de bio-bibliographie" (1985), provides us with a detailed overview of the fundamental role played by Greimas in the history of semiotics as well as a complete bibliography of his numerous works. In addition, Herman Parret and Hans George Ruprecht in their perceptive introduction to *Recueil d'hommages pour/Essays in honor of Algirdas Julien Greimas* (1985) not only discuss some of the salient features of the theory but also sketch the intellectual horizon in which it was elaborated. The essays in this volume of translations have been selected from three major works: *Du sens* (1970), *Sémiotique et sciences sociales* (1976), and *Du sens II* (1983a), both to provide the English reader with the founding texts of Greimassian semiotics and to highlight the heuristic value of narrativity theory as applied to literary, historical, ethnological, sociological, psychological, and scientific discourses.

Beginnings

The essays appearing in *Du sens* (1970), which opens with the cursory remark "It is extremely difficult to speak about meaning and to say something meaningful about it" (p. 7), explore and set into place the first two phases of Greimassian semiotics. In 1956, Greimas published a programmatic article in *Le Français*

Moderne entitled "L'actualité du saussurisme," in which he examined works by Maurice Merleau-Ponty and Claude Lévi-Strauss and concluded that the "Saussurian postulate of a structured world apprehensible in its significations" (p. 193) can in fact contribute to the elaboration of a unified methodology for the human sciences.[1] At this time Greimas became aware that although structuralism in its many forms focused mainly on problems of language from a linguistic perspective (e.g., Lévi-Strauss and Georges Dumézil in anthropology, Roland Barthes in literature, and Jacques Lacan in psychoanalysis to name but a few of the dominant figures who revolutionized their respective disciplines), no structural linguists per se were striving to do the same in their own field. In France the latest word in linguistics was Leonard Bloomfield's distributionalism. Nonetheless it was apparent to Greimas that by extrapolating concepts borrowed from Ferdinand de Saussure and Louis Hjelmslev and forging new methods of investigation, great strides were being made in various domains of the human sciences.

"Comparative Mythology," chapter 1 in this volume, was written in 1962 and owes a great deal to Lévi-Strauss and Roman Jakobson in its methodological and theoretical underpinnings. Greimas's point of departure is that the investigation of meaning is by definition a metalinguistic activity that paraphrases and translates words and utterances by other words and utterances. It therefore follows that the first step in describing signification resides in the transposition of one level of language into another level, of one language into another language. Since meaning can be described as this very possibility of transcoding, the next step is to develop a new terminology and construct an adequate metalanguage that can account for the object in question. Thus, to uncover the "mythological signified," Greimas endeavors to work out a rigorous methodology based on objective criteria of analysis partially adopted from structural linguistics, which, as we noted, had at the time more or less abandoned research into signification. Dumézil's work on myth, considered in chapter 1 as the translation of "mythological language into ideological language," is "overanalyzed" much in the same way Lévi-Strauss overanalyzed the Oedipus myth. In short, a new formulation of Dumézil's analysis is proposed by which the study of myth and the structural methodology borrowed from the social sciences are used to examine the superstructures of social ideologies. This is indeed a major development from a semiotic point of view, since in Hjelmslev's terms a "connotative semiotics" is transformed into a "denotative semiotics" that is a precondition for an adequate description of a text.

By reducing the problem of meaning to its minimal dimensions, that is to say, to the transcoding of significations, scientific activity in this domain consists in establishing techniques of transposition.[2] The main feature in the analysis of Dumézil's work can be found in the conversion of the syntagmatic manifestation of myth into paradigmatic relations, or, in other words, in the setting up of correlations between a limited number of units of the mythic signified distributed throughout the narrative. As a first important methodological step a level of pertinence is defined and a discourse, based on the principle of interdefinition, is constructed on the mythological object.[3] However, it should be noted that this new formulation of Dumézil's text does not correspond *stricto sensu* to formalization as defined for example by logicians in formal theory, since, from the outset, semiotics is not considered a formal language per se but rather an intermediary stage toward explanation, toward giving a scientific account of meaning.

Yet, in spite of the real gains made in adopting the preceding methodological perspective, the conclusions of this study clearly point to the insufficiencies of Lévi-Strauss's paradigmatic definition of myth as a correlation of two pairs of units of the signified that are in significant opposition to each other and that exclude any syntagmatic relation. Indeed, Greimas does use methodological procedures borrowed from structural anthropology and even refines major constituent units by breaking them down into distinctive features called semes, or semic categories and archilexemes (sets of semic categories constituting pairs of lexemic oppositions making up the elementary structures of myth). Yet he also makes a case for the need to investigate syntagmatic structures that could be grounded in discourse analysis.

"Toward a Semiotics of the Natural World," chapter 2 of this volume, was written after *Sémantique structurale* (1966), which sketched out the initial model of the elementary structure of signification and for the first time presented a syntactic and semantic (actantial) theory of discourse (for a detailed account of this seminal work, see Fredric Jameson, *The Prison House of Language*, 1972, and Ronald Schleifer's introduction to Greimas, *Structural Semantics*, 1983b). Chapter 2 raises further questions of a metasemiotic and theoretical nature by exploring the possibilities of the description or the apprehension of signification in systems not dependent on natural languages. Paraphrasing Hjelmslev, Greimas (1970) defines semiotics as "a hierarchy that *can* be subjected to analysis and the elements of which *can* be determined by reciprocal relations (and by commutation)" (p.22). In other words, a semiotics exists only as a possibility of description and the system of relations described does not depend on the nature of the signs by which the external or internal world is manifested. Description is thus thought of as the construction of a network of relations by the identification and naming of both the observed relations and their points of intersection or disjunction.

This investigation of the gestural domain of the natural world through the description of pertinent features at the level of content, which are at the same time distinctive and significative, brings to the fore the anthropological dimension of Greimas's semiotics. "Comparative Mythology," as we have noted, focuses on the paradigmatic organization of text, whereas chapter 2 investigates the syntagmatic dimension of gesture, considered both as a "discursive structure" because it appears within the context of the subject/object relation and as an "utterance" constructed by the human subject and deciphered by another subject. The semiotic status of gestural signs, which are defined in terms of the semiotic relation between expression and content, is studied in conjunction with the fundamental problem of identifying what actually constitutes gestural units. Human beings, as bodies, are first of all viewed as figures of the world and then as complex mechanisms that, through mobility, produce differential (positional) gaps at the level of the signifier by which signification can take place. Gestural activity is explored within the framework of the project defining it. Consequently a programmed gestural project can be said to constitute the signified of gestural activity, whereas the gestural sequence can be equated with its signifier. This enables Greimas to define the semiosis of a gestural program as the relation between a sequence of gestural figures taken as the signified and the gestural project considered as the signifier. Yet when all is said and done, the analysis of gestuality raises problems as to the functional nature of gestural semiotics. In chapter 2, Greimas identifies the need to work out a level of analysis dealing specifically with the organization of content and which would be part of a general functional semiotics also encompassing the semantic dimension of natural languages and hints at the possible form it could take.

Narrative Grammar

Chapters 3 and 4, the last two programmatic essays we translated from *Du sens*, lay the groundwork for what will become the cornerstone of Greimas's semiotics. These two works openly acknowledge a debt both to Vladimir Propp, who provided the syntactic component for the deep semio-narrative grammar, and to Lévi-Strauss, who furnished the idea for the semantic component. After Propp's thirty-one functions (designating syntagmatic units that remain constant despite the diversity of narratives, and whose ordered sequence makes up the structure of folktale) were redefined in terms of a limited number of actants, it then became possible to conceive of a principle of organization underlying whole classes of narratives. And thus deep structures were posited as being the principle of organization, not only of figurative discourses, but also of abstract discourses (philosophical, political, scientific, etc.) as well as of other semiotic systems not necessarily expressed through natural languages (cinema, figurative painting, architecture, advertising, etc.). Moreover, following Jean Petitot-Cocorda (1985) we would like to suggest that these structures are lived existentially in human passions, ideology, actions, and dreams and that semio-narrative structures, to borrow a phase from Gilbert Durand, can be thought of as "the anthropological structures of the imaginary." This being so, for Greimas it became of the utmost importance to work out a means, or a grammar, that could account for such structures. Indeed, the semio-narrative grammar he elaborated establishes a specific relation between syntax and semantics, which Petitot-Cocorda describes as "the projection (or conversion) of the paradigmatic axis onto the syntagmatic axis, the understanding of which constitutes one of the central problems of structuralism, perhaps even its most central problem" (1985, pp. 48–49).

The semantic universe defined as the set of the systems of values can be apprehended as meaningful only if it is articulated or narrativized. Thus, any discourse presupposes a semantic universe hypothetically made up of the totality of significations, postulated as such prior to its articulation, and which it actualizes in part.[4] This microsemantic universe, at the fundamental level, articulates elementary axiological structures such as life/death (individual universe) and nature/ culture (collective universe). These basic structures situated at the deep semantic level are considered as ad hoc universals that serve as starting points for the analysis of semantic universes, be they individual or collective. Their meaning is never apprehensible as such, but rather only when they are manifested in the form of an articulated signification, or in other words, when they are converted into actantial structures. Petitot-Cocorda (1985) clearly perceives the theoretical import of Greimas's semiotics when he situates the semio-narrative structures within an anthropological framework: "The deep semantic categories are universals of the imaginary. We are not unconscious of them, and they exist only because they are axiologized and ideologically invested in object-values, the quest for which governs *the actions* (narrative programs in Greimassian terminology) of the subject actants. It is only through the circulation of object-values governed by actantial syntax that they can be apprehended. In other words, they cannot be subjectivized as such but instead only by means of a logic of actions. The role of actantial syntax is therefore to *convert into a narrative doing* the fundamental semantics that constitute the message of narrative and determine its anthropological function. This syntax enables one to grasp, through the simulacrum of a 'scene' that dramatizes them, the unconscious crystallizing processes of subjectivity" (1985, pp. 50–51).

Chapter 3, "The Interaction of Semiotic Constraints," suggests the possibility of a generative trajectory, beginning with a fundamental semiotic level that is then converted into an actantial syntax before ultimately being manifested through discoursivization, but focuses especially on the first domain of the global trajectory. The main object of the theory of the semiotic square is to articulate the substance of the content (in Hjelmselv's terms) and therein constitute the form of content. This elementary structure should be considered "on the one hand, as a concept uniting the minimal condition for the apprehension and/or the production of signification, and, on the other hand, as a model containing the minimal definition of any language (or, more generally, of any semiotic system or process) and of any semiotic unit" (Greimas and Courtés, 1982, p. 314). Prior to any semantic investment whatsoever, the elementary structure appears as a complex binary semic category that correlates two contrary semes by means of a relation of junction (conjunction/disjunction) and by a relation of reciprocal presupposition. Yet, as Petitot-Cocorda (1985) remarks, "As a simple logical form formalized in terms of Boolean elementary set logic, the semiotic square is trivial, and of little interest, since it only reformulates logical squares going back to Aristotle. But if we see it as a structure in the strong sense of the term, then everything changes, since it becomes an 'organic' and 'self-regulating' system of interdependent and founding relations that do not define terms, but rather in much the same way as in a phonological paradigm, *positional values*, places that are defined in a purely relational fashion." The constituent relations of contrariety and contradiction of the semiotic square, it is argued, are not logical in nature, but in the Jakobsonian sense are "qualitative oppositions and privative oppositions and must be treated as such." The formal characteristics of the semiotic square are founded on a dynamic topology of places and connections and not upon a static logic of terms and connections (pp. 51–52).

Chapter 4, "Elements of a Narrative Grammar," sets in place the various components and the interrelationships of the first two levels of the theory of narrativity, represented graphically in their entirety under the heading of Generative Trajectory in Greimas and Courtés (1982); see the accompanying schema.

Generative Trajectory			
		Syntactic Component	Semantic Component
Semiotic and narrative structures	Deep level	FUNDAMENTAL SYNTAX	FUNDAMENTAL SEMANTICS
	Surface levels	SURFACE NARRATIVE SYNTAX	NARRATIVE SEMANTICS
Discoursive structures		DISCOURSIVE SYNTAX Discoursivization Actorialization Temporalization Spatialization	DISCOURSIVE SEMANTICS Thematization Figurativization

The main theoretical problem that arises in this model of narrativity concerns the passage (conversion) on the one hand from a taxonomic morphology, or paradigmatic relation, to an operative syntax or syntagmatic one, and on the other, the passage (conversion) from a fundamental abstract syntax to a narrative anthropomorphic surface-syntax, and ultimately to a discoursive-figurative syntax. We should note, however, that there exist in the theory two types of conversions; "vertical" conversions (having to do with the relations between levels) and "horizontal" conversions (dealing with the relations between the syntactic and semantic components of each level) (See Petitot-Cocorda, 1982, p. 5). At the deep level, horizontal conversion, or the passage from the elementary morphology constituted by fundamental relations to an operative syntax, is ensured by the introduction of an actant subject: "Signification, to the extent that one seeks to find in it an object, appears as an articulation of stable fundamental relations; it can also be represented dynamically, if one considers it as an apprehension or production of meaning by a subject." In short, equivalences are established between the fundamental constituent relations of the taxonomic model and the projections of the same relations or operations by means of a horizontal anthropomorphic conversion at the deep level. And thus the relation of contradiction at the taxonomic level as a contradictory operation at the syntactic level will negate one of the terms and at the same time affirm its contradictory term.

In this transpositional model the problem of vertical conversion, or the passage from the fundamental syntax to the surface anthropomorphic narrative syntax, is resolved by the setting up of procedures that establish equivalences between these two levels. It should be noted that the equivalence posited here does not correspond to identity but rather is founded on the presupposition that "two or more syntactic forms (or two or more semantic formulations) can be referred to a constant topic" (Greimas and Courtés, 1982, p. 62). In addition, insofar as a meaning is transformed into signification when articulated, each new articulation is an enrichment or increase in meaning, so that in proceeding from the deep level to the surface levels the surface must be considered as richer than the deep level: "Consequently any conversion must be viewed as equivalence and as a surplus of signification" (ibid.). As Greimas reiterates in an interview with Ruprecht (1984), conversion is homotopic and heteromorphic; that is to say, "the forms pass from the deep structures (where operations take place on the semiotic square) to the semio-narrative level (where there exists a surface narrative grammar); both of these levels are concerned with the same thing but in a different way" (p. 14).

The conversion of the deep level into the surface level is ensured by the establishment of equivalences between syntactic operations at the fundamental level and syntactic doing at the surface level. Thus syntactic doing, having been converted from syntactic operation that was itself converted from taxic relation, provides the necessary mediation for the generation of a narrative utterance that is the major component of narrative grammar. The utterance $NU = F(A)$ is seen as a process that is composed of a function, in the Proppian sense, and an actant. Conversion thus rests on the equivalence between the syntactic operation and syntactic doing on the one hand, and between syntactic doing and an elementary utterance of the actantial doing, on the other.

The anthropomorphic actantial dimension establishes relations between subjects and objects, subjects and anti-subjects, subjects and senders and receivers. The first relation, founded on the institution of the subject as a wanting subject and the object as an object of value, can be described in terms of modal utterances. *Wanting* is the first of a series of determined semantic restrictions that specify actants as virtual operators of a doing. Other semantic restrictions, the introduction of the modalities of *being-able-to* and *knowing*, constitute the being or the doing of the actant subject. The relation of subject and object is, furthermore, syntactically describable in terms of utterances of state that are junctive in nature. The second relation between subject and anti-subjects is considered as the conversion of the paradigmatic relation of contradiction at the deep level, into an anthropomorphic syntagmatic series at the surface level. In addition, the transformation of contents, which at the surface level appear as a series of confrontations and struggles constituting the narrative units, results from operations of contrariety (negation) and presupposition (assertion). Negation is reformulated as domination and assertion as attribution, whereas performance is formulated as a syntagmatic, ordered, series of confrontation, domination, and attribution.

The third relation between subject and sender, subject and receiver, is reformulated in terms of a general structure of exchange. The attribution of an object of value is here seen as a disjunctive operation (privation) and a conjunctive one (attribution). This reformulation makes it possible to represent the previous operations as places of transfers of objects of value from one location to another and thereby to establish a topological syntax of objective values, which, since it follows the logical operations at the level of deep grammar, organizes narration as a process creating values. However, by changing focus and examining the relation between operators, subject and sender or receiver, we can see that topological syntax governs the transfer both of the subject's capacity to do, and of the values. Also, by manipulating subjects and endowing them with the virtuality of doing, the topological syntax governs the institution of syntactic operators. In a later, more complete version of the theory, the subject and sender will be characterized by a dual contractual relation, since not only will the subject actant have a contractual relation with the manipulating operator actant (sender) that institutes it as an operator subject, but also performance will be sanctioned by a final sender, whose absolute competence is presupposed.

Greimas has always claimed, and rightly so, that semiotics was not a science but rather a scientific project, still incomplete, and that what he had attempted to do was to establish theoretical principles that needed to be completed and transformed.[5] However, we should not minimize the import of the theoretical prob-

lems related to the issue of conversion and that are due to the generative conceptualization of the model according to which various components are linked together
along a trajectory that proceeds from the simplest to the most complex, from the
most abstract to the most concrete. The problem of conversion and equivalences
is raised on numerous occasions by Greimas himself, beginning with "Elements
of a Narrative Grammar." In an interview with Frédéric Nef (1976) the author
admits, "A theoretical construct, no matter how satisfying it appears at first view,
runs the risk of remaining hypothetical as long as the problem of *equivalences*
between different levels of depth is not clearly posed, as long as the procedures
of *conversion* from one level to another have not been elaborated" (p. 24). Again,
in a special issue of *Le Bulletin* (1981) devoted to the semiotic square, Greimas
once more states that one of the urgent tasks facing semioticians is to undertake
research on conversion, to conceive of and construct procedures for passing from
the deep level of semantic categorizations to the more surface ones of anthropomorphic narrative syntax and of its investments (pp. 45–46). The same awareness
of the possible weak point in the theory is demonstrated in Greimas and Courtés
(1982): "As can be expected, the elaboration of conversion rules will be one of
the fundamental tests of the coherence of semiotic theory" (p. 62).

It is especially on this very issue of conversion and equivalences within the
framework of the narrative grammar we have just sketched, that Paul Ricoeur
(1983) puts forth reservations about the actual coherence of the theory. Ricoeur
basically takes issue with the model on three counts. The first concerns the conversion of contradiction at the deep level, into polemic at the surface level; that
is to say, polemic negativity cannot be derived either from the taxonomic relations of contradiction-contrariety, or from the syntactic operation of negation.
The second is related to the fact that there exist syntagmatic supplements at the
surface level that cannot be obtained from the conversion of the fundamental
grammar to the surface grammar. The third is that the praxic-pathic dimension
of narrative sets into play a semantics of action that activates a syntax whose very
intelligibility is mixed, since it is both phenomenological and linguistic (see
Petitot-Cocorda, 1985, p. 268). In his truly original and brilliant work on the
morphogenesis of meaning, Petitot-Cocorda (in a highly innovative and insightful
discussion of the legitimacy of schematizing the structural categoriality of the
semio-narrative structures elaborated by Greimas in terms of catastrophe theory)
argues that for Ricoeur's critique to be truly pertinent, the implicit phenomenol-
ogy of the praxic-pathic semantics of action would have to be formalized so that
it could be integrated into a formal model. He also argues that polemical negativity can be schematized in terms of catastrophe theory, and thus a reformulation
of fundamental grammar, starting from the schema of conflict, should be able to
overcome the difficulty encountered because of its logical conception. He then
concludes that the hypothesis of a syntagmatic supplement that is irreducible to
the paradigmatic is tenable only if one forces Greimas's thought and views con-

version as a simple equivalence between metalanguages, and this is far from being the case (p. 268). In the final analysis, the real problem in the theory that must be addressed is the one Greimas himself has raised all along, namely, the need to establish the actual procedures of conversion.

Instead of being a simple *aide-mémoire*, the generative trajectory presented earlier provides us with a useful schematization within which we can situate the essays published in *Du sens II*, and which further refines the global semiotic model. Within this specific generative approach, each work reexamines and develops the relations between the various levels, components, and subcomponents of the trajectory.

In surface narrative grammar, the object is one of the terms of the elementary utterance that, when inscribed in a junctive relation with the subject, guarantees the latter's semiotic existence. However, the object, while "remaining unknowable in itself," exists semiotically as "a locus of fixation, a locus of circumstantial clustering of the value determinations." Values invested in the object can only be accounted for syntactically, and it is in this "syntagmatic unfolding that syntax joins semantics." Furthermore, it is only when they are converted from semantic into syntactic structures that values can be apprehended as signification. Subsequently, conversion makes it possible both to define narrativization as the syntagmatic emplacement of values and to perceive it as a discursive organization that manipulates the constitutive elements of the elementary utterance. Moreover, two broad categories of values—descriptive (consumable or storable objects, states and feelings) and modal (wanting, being-able-to, knowing-how-to-be/to-do)— can be distinguished. In turn, descriptive values can be divided further into subjective (essential values) and objective (accidental values), and, in narrative programs, base values can be distinguished from instrumental ones (see Greimas and Courtés, 1982, p. 365).

Since narrative at the surface level was defined as the transformation of a series of utterances of state (junctive utterances) by a metasubject operator (utterance of doing), this syntactic organization makes it possible to represent narrative as a series of virtualizations and actualizations of values. Values inscribed within a given axiological universe circulate in two ways. In the case of constant values between subjects in an isotopic and closed universe, they circulate in the mode of conflictual-polemic confrontation, whereas in the case of exchange, the presence of two objects of value is required, and this structure constitutes a new virtualization and a new actualization of the subject. Simple exchange can then be considered as a complex mode of value transfer at the level of surface syntax. Nonetheless, for such an operation to take place in the case where exchange values are not identical requires their preliminary identification by subjects, who, by fixing the exchange value of the said objects of value, establish a fiduciary contract between themselves. When the objects of value are objects of knowing, or messages being communicated, and when the subjects in question are competent but unequally modalized, then the polemic-contractual, which is one of the fundamental organizing structures of narrative grammar, is transposed into the very core of intersubjectivity, where, as Greimas (1983a) notes, "It seems to be able to account for the fiduciary, troubling and groping, but, at the same time, cunning and dominating, nature of communication" (p. 11).

In participatory communication the contractual dimension of exchange within a closed universe is ensured by a sender that guarantees the circulation of values, the latter corresponding to a mediating domain between an immanent universe and a transcendent universe that are manifested through the presence of actants at the surface level syntax. The sender, who is the source of the contract in discourse, is the disengaged representative of the paradigmatic system of the invested contents, or the values that are the taxonomic constituents of the fundamental grammar (Courtés, 1976, p. 99). From this it follows that the internalization of the conversion of the paradigmatic dimension in the narrative is constituted by the relation between the contractual sequence and the performance sequence. If the contractual sequence is accepted by the subject-receiver as a narrative program, it is transformed into a performing subject: "(on the condition that it acquire a modal competence) that ensures the mediation between system (paradigmatic) and process (syntagmatic), and realizes virtual values" (Petitot-Cocorda, 1985, p. 240).

Insofar as it guarantees the semiotic existence of actants, the "narrative organization of values continues to be the foundation of narrativity." The object of value, which is one of the terms of the elementary utterance previously defined as a semiotic simulacrum, representing our relation to the world in the form of a scene, is also a syntactic concept. The distinction between actants (considered initially as simple supports and then progressively invested by values through junctive relations) and actors (which can syncretize several actants) enables us to explore the relations between elementary narrative structures and discoursive structures (see chapter 6).

As an actant progresses through its narrative trajectory it can assume a certain number of narrative states or actantial roles that are defined by its position within the narrative trajectory (syntactic definition) and its modal investment (morphological definition). As a necessary step toward performance, the subject actant will be endowed successively with the modalities of competence, and in this case the "subject assumes those actantial roles which manifest the subject in terms of wanting, the subject in terms of knowing, and the subject in terms of being able to do, and which then indicate the three states in the acquisition of its modal competence" (Greimas and Courtés, 1982, p. 6). Actantial roles, because they are defined morphologically by their modal content, and syntactically by the position of the actant in the narrative trajectory, are situated within narrative syntax. However, when associated with "thematic roles (which structure the semantic component of the discourse), they allow for the construction of actors as loci where narrative and discoursive structures converge and are invested" (ibid.).

What first of all distinguishes an actantial role from an actor is that at the level of discourse "an actor's semantic content is defined by the presence of the semes that are (1) *figurative entity* (anthropomorphic, zoomorphic order), (2) *animated*, and (3) subject to *individuation*." At the same level the actantial role is "manifested, as a qualification, as an attribute of the actor. From a semantic point of view, this qualification is no more than the denomination subsuming a field of functions (that is to say behaviors actually noted in the narrative, or simply implied). Consequently, the minimal semantic content of *role* is identical to the concept of actor, despite the *exception of a seme of individuation*, which the former does not possess. The role is an animated figurative entity, albeit anonymous and *social*. In turn, the actor is an *individual* integrating and assuming one or several roles" (Greimas, 1970, pp. 255–56). From this it follows that there are three distinct levels of narrative interplay: roles, which are elementary actantial units corresponding to coherent functional domains, are related to actants (elements of the narrative) and to actors (units of discourse) (ibid., p. 256).

The actor is thus seen as the point of investment of both syntactic and semantic components. To be designated as an actor, a lexeme must have both an actantial and a thematic role. And thematic roles in turn, "in order to realize their virtualities, call into play the lexematic level of language and are manifested in the form of figures that are extended into discoursive configurations." Thus the figurative level of discourse, which is the final domain of the narrative trajectory, is characterized by the investment of themes and values in figures. Figures, defined as "figures of content which correspond to the figures of the expression plane of the natural semiotic system" (Greimas and Courtés, 1982, p. 120), when strung over sequences, constitute their discoursive configurations. The procedures of figurativization, the first of which can be described as figuration and the second as iconization, invest these figures with specificities that produce a referential illusion. And one of the basic components of figurativization is the onomastic one. Figurativization specifies and particularizes abstract discourse "insofar as it is grasped in its deep structures and by the introduction of anthroponyms (corresponding respectively, on the plane of discoursive syntax, to the three procedures constitutive of discoursivization: actorialization, spatialization, and temporalization) that can be inventoried as going from the generic ("king," "forest," "winter") to the specific (proper nouns, spatio-temporal indices, dates, etc.)" (Greimas and Courtés, 1982, p. 119).

Toward A Grammar of Modality

The semiotic square and the actantial model worked out in *Du sens* have often attracted the attention of critics who have been quick to seize the import of their heuristic value without necessarily being aware of the general structure of this hypothetico-deductive theory of narrativity.[6] In Greimas's own words, the third phase of his semiotic project, while continuing to evolve a theory of narrativity, focused on constructing a semio-narrative grammar developed as a modal and aspectual grammar.[7] Sensing the need to construct a better-articulated elementary syntax, he abandoned the Proppian formulation of narrative in order to free the theory from concepts that remained too close to the manifest level of discourse.

The first step consisted in reformulating surface narrative syntax in terms of modalities (chapter 7). Starting with the definition of modality as "that which modalizes a predicate of an utterance," modalization is then considered as the production of a "modal utterance which over-determines a descriptive utterance" (Greimas and Courtés, 1982, p. 193). Defined in terms of the structure of the elementary utterance whose end terms are actants, utterances of doing or utterances of state can be considered as the transformation of a junctive state. However, a reformulation of the act as "that which causes to be" permits its redefinition as a hypotactic structure combining competence and performance, with performance presupposing competence, but not vice versa.

Transitive relations defining the descriptive predicate between the subject and the utterance of doing are distinguished both from veridictory relations established by a subject and an utterance produced by another subject, and from factitive relations between the subject and object that are already an utterance of doing. These last two relations, which appear between two hierarchical, distinct subjects—a cognitive subject and a pragmatic subject—constitute the simple modal structure. The advantage of reformulating the act in these terms is that a theory of performance can be developed in the direction of a semiotics of manipulation (or the manipulation of the subject by the sender), a semiotics of action (the acquisition of competence by the subject), and a semiotics of sanction (judgments on self and on other subjects).

When considered at the level of the organization of pragmatic competence, four fundamental modalities were identified: the modalities of having and wanting, which virtualize the process, and the modalities of being able and knowing, which actualize it. Yet the fact that this canonical representation of competence does not always correspond to what happens at the level of manifestation pointed to the need to construct a model that could account for the fundamental modal structure by subsuming its diverse articulations through a series of interdefinitions: "The criteria of interdefinition and classification of modalities should be simultaneously syntagmatic and paradigmatic; each modality would be defined on the one hand as a hypotactic modal structure and, on the other hand, as a category which could be represented on the semiotic square" (Greimas and Courtés, 1982, p. 195).

After having analyzed the modality of doing, Greimas turns in chapter 8 to the modality of being. As Coquet (1985) notes, this analysis completes the study of the actions of the subject (modal competence) with the study of their passions (modal existence) within the context of a modal grammar reformulated along the lines of surface narrative syntax (p. lxxviii). Thymic space, which at the deep level represents the elementary manifestations of a living being in relation to its environment (animated), at the surface level is converted into modal space appearing as an overarticultion of the thymic (human) category. Yet, in any utterance, the subject's semiotic existence is determined by its relation to the object of value and the modalizing of being considered as the "modifications of the status of the *object of value*. The modalities affecting the object (or rather the value invested therein) [are] said to be constituents of the subject of state's *modal existence*." A taxonomic network for modal syntax is elaborated by projecting the modal utterances onto the semiotic square (wanting-to-be [desirable for the subject of state] having-to-be [indispensable], being-able-to-be [possible], knowing-how-to-be [genuine]). The same interrelations discovered when analyzing the modalization of doing are encountered here and a syntax of modalized values is suggested, based on elementary narrative syntax.

It has been shown that thymic values are converted from the deep level when invested with syntactic objects defined by junctive relations with subjects. As Parret and Ruprecht perceptively remark, this conversion profoundly affects value by placing it under subjectivity and its intentionality. As a theoretical consequence of this the possibility for the pragmatization of Greimas's semiotics by the introduction of *tensivity* and *graduality* in the deep structures themselves is opened up, "thus freeing us from the notion that at the deep level values are economical (in the Saussurian sense) and at the surface level they are graduated and tensive" (p. xlvii). In this way the introduction of modality theory and the working out of conversion procedures constitute decisive steps toward an integrated theory of narrativity.

We have suggested that the problematics of passions are linked to the study of the modal existence of the subject, and more precisely to the modal component of the actantial structures. Whether the object of investigation happens to be a lexeme-passion such as anger — considered as a virtual narrative trajectory — or, on the contrary, passional stories that are realized narrative syntagms, as Landowski (1979) remarks, the exploration of the "passional field" closely involves "all of the levels of the articulations of the theory of narrativity: not only the semio-narrative structures proper (instances of passions being identifiable by their underlying modal and actantial structures), not only the discursive structures (aspectualization, actorialization, semantization of the underlying syntagms), but also the deep level abstract structures" (p. 8).

In contradistinction to action, which can be defined as a syntagmatic organization of acts (Greimas and Courtés, 1982, p. 6), passions (chapter 9) can be considered as the syntagmatic organization of states of mind, or the discursive aspect of the modalized being of narrative subjects (Greimas and Courtés, 1986, p. 162).

Passions, which are either simple or complex (a syntagmatic intertwining of states and of doing), are expressed through actors and, along with actions, determine the roles (actantial and thematic) they realize. Thus the opposition between action and passion represents the "conversion on the discursive level of the deeper and more abstract opposition between *being* and *doing*, or more specifically between modalized being and modalized doing" (ibid.).

The being of the subject, whether, for example, in simple or in fiduciary expectation, is first of all modalized by the modality of wanting, which actualizes (wanting-to-be-conjoined) in order then to be realized (i.e., to be conjoined with the object of value). It is this very conjunction that guarantees the subject's semiotic existence. Whether at the semiotic or at the discursive level the notion of value, which we also saw with regard to the doing of the subject, is at the very heart of the theory. Thus, parallel to the trajectory of the subject of doing made up of the acquisition of competence and the accomplishment of performances, there exists a comparable trajectory of the subject of state, presented as successions of "feeling states" made up of highs and lows. Consequently the modalization of the being of the subject has an essential role in the constitution of the competence of syntactic subjects, and the concept of passion is closely linked to the concept of actor. Passion thus becomes "one of the elements that contribute to actorial individuation, able to offer denominations for recognizable thematic roles ('the miser,' 'the quick-tempered,' 'the unconcerned,' etc.)" (Greimas and Courtés, 1986, pp. 162–63). Moreover, the linking of passions to actors and the investigation of relations between thematic roles and actantial roles have opened up a new domain of research into passional typologies.

Another area of investigation mapped out within the confines of a theory of modalities is related to procedures leading to the epistemic act (chapter 10). When situated at the level of surface narrative (manipulation, action, sanction) both persuasive and interpretative doing are defined as cognitive procedures "that, in the first case, end up as causing-to-believe and, in the second, as an act of believing, that is, as an epistemic act." The epistemic act is then defined as a transformation that, when articulated on the semiotic square (to affirm, to refuse, to admit, to doubt), at the level of surface syntax is manifested as a series of hierarchically linked narrative programs. Epistemic modalizations can also be represented as modalities and junctive operations, and before becoming act, or operation (which is of the order of doing), a modal competence or the being of the doing is presupposed on the part of the subject. A further step is taken after noting that since transactions engage the subjects in a fiduciary contract, communication can be defined in terms of contract propositions, which in fact is a presupposition to communication. Situated within a semiotics of manipulation and sanction, cognitive space becomes the locus for a manipulation according to knowing, in which a subject transforms another into a convinced subject, and submits it to judging epistemic activity on the part of a final subject.

However, since the initial definition of epistemic act converted the elements of the square onto the surface syntax, not as contradictions, but as linear gradations, Coquet (1985) notes that "this type of semiotic square represents an important development of 'syntagmatic rationality' " (p. lxxxii). Technical thinking, of an algorithmic nature "founded on objective modal necessity (= on a /not-being-able-to-not-be/)," is opposed to practical thinking, "of a stereotypical nature [which] depends on the co-occurrence, in temporal contiguity, of acts—or the utterances that describe them—whose successivity can be considered predictable and therefore plausible or even necessary ('subjectively,' according to the mode of /having-to-be/)." At the surface level of discourse causal reason, or syntagmatic rationality, is further defined in terms of technical thinking and practical thinking. Yet, parallel thinking leads us to discover a bi-isotopic nature of discourse based on the seeming of the implicit characterizing figurative discourses that, when dereferentialized, create a new referent or thematic level. Parallel discourse, by projecting a double reference ("one that *moves deeper* and creates a more abstract thematic isotopy, and one that *moves laterally* and develops a new parallel figurative isotopy"), constitutes an original type of syntagmatic articulation. Figurative models such as parables, allusive in nature, are given as an example of figurative reasoning. These models, projected by the sender, fiduciary by definition and of the order of subjective /having-to-be/, are opposed to homological thinking, which "introduces mathematical proportion into the evaluation of the relations between isotopies that are presumed to be parallel." Thus, in this chapter, further refining the theoretical foundations of modal grammar, the relations between the fiduciary and the logical within a cognitive universe defined as a network of formal semiotic relations from among which the "epistemic subject selects equivalences it needs in order to receive veridictory discourse" and thereby demonstrates that believing and knowing "are part of the same cognitive universe" are outlined.

Semiotics and Social Sciences

Although modal grammar does constitute a breakthrough in the theory of narrativity, we have pointed out that this grammar was a reformulation and a refinement of the general semiotic grammar worked out in chapter 4, "Elements of a Narrative Grammar." We also have noted that at all levels this grammar sets in place refined significative articulations that correspond to an augmentation or increase in the production of meaning, since signification is indeed defined as articulated meaning. Moreover it has been argued that meaning can be grasped only when articulated or narrativized, narrativity being "the very organizing principle of all discourse, whether narrative (identified in the first instance, as figurative discourse) or non-narrative" (Greimas and Courtés, 1982, p. 209). The theoretical task of semiotics, considered as the science of signification, was to set in place models that could account for the articulation of content and for the trajectory of meaning, from the fundamental domains where semantic substance receives its first articulations, to the final domain where the signification manifests itself through discourse. This has led to the elaboration of hierarchized fundamental and surface semantics and grammar (taxonomy and syntax) establishing formal models able to organize and manipulate contents.

The essays translated from *Sémiotique et sciences sociales* (1976) must be situated within the preceding theoretical context and can be seen as different formulations, different instances, of the fundamental problematics posited by Greimas from the very outset. Specifically, what are the conditions for the production of meaning and how can the transformation of meaning into signification be described? In itself this would have remained trivial had Greimas not defined his project in terms of the elaboration of a scientific discourse, starting from a limited number of concepts (*relation, description, system, process, conversion*) and the construction of models that are hypothetical representations that can be confirmed, invalidated, or falsified within a general semiotic theory controlling their homogeneity and coherence.

Greimas has stated on numerous occasions that semiotics and, in this particular case, a semiotics of the social sciences, cannot claim to have the status of a science that might be described in terms of a "completed organization of knowledge" (Greimas, 1976, p. 9). Knowledge about human beings is so uncertain and contested that at best a semiotics of the social sciences could be characterized as a scientific project in the process of elaborating a scientific discourse.[8] If this is the case, it is legitimate to investigate the scientific status of such discourse by examining its modes of manifestation and "the conditions of its production, as well as the criteria that distinguish it from other forms of knowledge" (ibid.). Such a stance amounts to abandoning the idea that science is a system and adopting the notion that it is a process; that is, in the domain under investigation, science in fact corresponds to a scientific doing.

In chapters 11 through 14, the same procedures are adopted, beginning with an investigation of the claims to "scientificness" of four important disciplines in the social sciences (communication, sociolinguistics, history, and ethnology). This is followed by a reformulation of each discursive practice, within a coherent theory of narrativity. The purpose here is not only to describe criteria for scientific discourse in general but also to describe scientific doing and thereby investigate how each discipline in question, which does indeed claim to have some sort of scientific status, might better evaluate its own practice and more rigorously organize its doing within a global theory of narrativity. The constructed subject of such discourse, totally independent from its ontological status, as a syntactic actant is described in terms of its virtual and actualizing role as manipulating operator. The taxonomic and syntactic components of this linguistic doing can be examined, the function of the veridictory apparatus can be founded on coherence, and the knowing of the subject can be described. The referentialization of this discourse, the enunciative contract, and the actantial structure of scientific communication, are seen as dominant features of such discourse, which is said to be objective in nature. It is also recognized that "the ideological model of the social sciences—some of which do not seem to have gone beyond the doxological state" (Greimas, 1976, p. 38)—because they are defined by their scientific project and by a scientific doing exercised in the name of this project, is inevitable, "since this project, like any human project, can only be ideological" (ibid.).[9]

Starting from the observation that most definitions of media, or communication, are concerned with means rather than articulated contents, Greimas argues in chapter 11 that the traditional communication model, sender-code-receiver, does not offer any guarantees of methodological homogeneity. Sender and receiver constitute an interpersonal structure and are endowed with emissive and receptive competencies needed to control performance. Approaching communication from the angle of media necessitates the introduction of channels and codes. This makes analysis unduly complex and, indeed, the only way to confer a homogeneous status on research in the cultural dimension of societies is to posit the unicity of signification manifested through the codes used. One should not lose sight of the fact that the reason for research into this domain is to study the relation between society and individuals. This being so, the interpersonal verbal-exchange model is adapted to the social dimension of semiotic phenomena.

The opposition language (coextensive with grammar)/speech (free use of the lexical thesaurus), leads to the positing of a common language, a common semantic store between members of a linguistic community. The lexemes of this common thesaurus, which is of a metaphorical and axiological nature, constitutes a fundamental semantics that the individual manipulates as a necessary condition for participating in language communities. Social groups are defined semiotically, on the one hand as restricted groups characterized by the competence of all individuals in the group, and on the other, in terms of a typology of a semantic universe and socialized discourses such that "the same individual can participate in several *semiotic groups* and take on as many *sociosemiotic* roles as there are groups into which he or she is integrated." The figurative dimension of discourse is considered as the level at which the involvement of individuals of a society manifests their general adhesion to the ensemble of value systems making up their culture. Greimas proposes a discursive sociosemiotics able to "take on all social discourses, independently of all substances, the channels, or *media* through which they appear (television, film, collective sports, entertainment, picture books, etc.), if only because they all refer back to the very same signifying universe and because their forms of discursive organization are comparable," and suggests specificity criteria for distinguishing between narrative objects produced by social discourse (i.e., relative nonintervention of a narrator, absence of semantic codes).

In chapter 12, "On Theoretical Models in Sociolinguistics," Greimas defines the area of study that focuses on languages having social connotations as being part of the broader field of a socioeconomics delineated in chapter 11, which includes the investigation of the social connotations of nonlinguistic semiotic systems (gestural, alimentary, dress semiotics, etc.). In an attempt to describe natural languages from a sociolinguistic perspective, Greimas explores scientific and ethnological taxonomies, and since they cannot account for how languages are inscribed in their social contexts, he discards them in favor of sociolinguistic taxonomies, which, contrary to the typology of cultural spheres, can indeed be said to establish methodological boundaries within a single domain of investigation.

For sociolinguistics to become a scientific project of a general nature it is necessary to postulate a homogeneous level of research and description. Consistent with the theoretical program elaborated for the analysis of sociosemiotic discourse, Greimas proposes a general model that is both hypothetical and operational. It has three types of connotative categories and taxonomical models that could embrace the domain of sociolinguistics: proxemic, morphological, and functional. These categories and models can be used to distinguish archaic societies from industrial ones. In addition to morphological models, a sociolinguistic syntax, along the lines of a strategy of communication, completes this sociolinguistic grammar, which, as such, could account for the hitherto ill-defined domain of social connotations.

The thrust of chapter 13, "On Evenemential History and the Deep Structures of Historiography," is both to demonstrate the need to construct general models that could account for the production of history and to elaborate the conditions under which a historical knowing-how-to-do, scientific in nature, could be set in place. True to procedures worked out in his general theory of narrativity, Greimas establishes a fundamental deep level where taxonomic organizations and structural transformations take place, a mediating intermediate domain organized by means of surface narrative syntax, and a surface dimension where historicity is manifested. The need to set up such a global, integrated, hierarchical model stems from the nature of historical studies on the whole. Although, for instance, the *Annales* School and Marxist tradition have proposed adequate models for the analyses of deep structures, no coherent models, as such, exist that could link these deep structures to the "conjectural structures of historicity" made up of an "infinite number of microevents happening together at each moment and everywhere."

The deep structures (taxonomic component) would be part of a sort of grammar of history having restrictive rules as well as "rules governing the organization of the syntactic strings that can be inscribed in historical discourse." The intermediate surface syntax would organize the events of history, and it is at this level that procedures for recognizing historical events from among daily facts would be established. It is at this intermediate level that the utterance of doing enables

the formulation of all historical events in a univocal manner. However, the specificity of historical discourse necessitates the introduction of the concept of the collective subject considered as the agent of a programmed doing and defined as a
modalized actant governed by presupposed virtualizing and actualizing modalities. In addition to the preceding preconditions, the historical collective subject
is not a collective actant as such, but a hyponymic subject, for example, a social
class. To avoid giving the historical project an intentional ideology, historical
syntax, when establishing strings of utterances, should start from "the ends and
not the beginnings of historical programs" and make use of "a logic of presuppositions that would found the constituent relations of the strings."

Questioning the aims of ethnology is not a trivial matter since in chapter 14,
"Reflections on Ethnosemiotic Objects," Greimas suggests that the identification
of specific objectives can bring about not only a reevaluation of approaches but
also the elaboration of new methods for bringing together poetic, musical, and
gestural facts within a given culture. If considered from a discursive perspective, then these heterogeneous facts can be seen as complex semiotic objects of
a syncretic nature. Extrapolating the schema elaborated in investigating sociolinguistic categories (archaic societies with morphologically stable "languages" vs.
modern societies with a mobile sociolinguistic syntax) and applying the same
principle of transformation, "complex semiotic objects, recognizable at the level
of ethnosemiotics, break apart and give rise to a stylistics of multiple variation
at the sociosemiotic level."

To study the passage of societies from an ethnosemiotic state (archaic) to a sociosemiotic state (developed) corresponds to analyzing the passage from a "global
discourse to disjoined and autonomous discourses (poetry, music, dance), from
a discourse having a sacred function, to discourses having ludic or aesthetic functions; from a collective dimension, to an individual dimension" (Coquet, 1985,
p. lxv). Thus, for instance, the passage from sacred poetry (collective axiological
system) to folk poetry (absence of a specific semantic code) can be considered
as a form of desemantization, whereas the passage from the latter to modern poetry (individual values) could be characterized as a reactivation of signification
(reintegration of semanticism within its formal structures). When situated within
the context of communication, at the ethnosemiotic level, mythical objects are addressed by a sender to a mythical receiver and not to a passive human listener
as is the case within the sociosemiotic context where poetry is recited, music
heard, and ballet seen. Ethnosemiotic communication, which is a making-to-do
and never a making-to-see, has a cohesive function, since it integrates the individual subject within the group by constituting the social group as a collective
subject. It is these very integrative social systems of communication that are seen
as one of the main features underlying participatory folk manifestations.

* * *

Throughout this introduction, in which we have traced the salient features of Greimas's semiotic from a developmental or historiconotional perspective, we have attempted to stress the constructed and hypothetico-deductive aspect of a theory in which concepts are interdefined and hierarchically ordered. We also have emphasized the anthropomorphic dimension of the global theory, conceived of as an ongoing scientific project founded on internal coherence as a precondition to formalization. Further, we have identified three major phases: formulation, narrative grammar, and modal and aspectual grammar. We also have identified the manner in which research began on deep structures, then explored semio-narrative structures, before concentrating on surface (discoursive and figurative) structures. However, we should not conclude that the transpositional semiotic theory presented here is in any way a fully completed theory, since research is currently being carried out on the pathemic, ethical, and aesthetic dimensions of discourse. This should complete the construction of the semio-narrative grammar, and further work on aspectualities should lead to the development of an integrated and complementary discourse grammar. As Greimas himself says, "These two tasks should occupy the next generation of semioticians."[10]

References

Coquet, J.-C. 1982. *Sémiotique – l'École de Paris.* Paris: Hachette.

——. 1985. "Éléments de bio-bliographie," In *Recueil d'hommages Pour/Essays in Honor of Algirdas Julien Greimas.* Edited by H. Parret and H. G. Ruprecht. Amsterdam: John Benjamins.

Courtés, J. 1976. *Introduction à la sémiotique narrative et discursive.* Paris: Hachette.

Culler, J. 1975. *Structural Poetics.* London: Routledge & Kegan Paul.

Greimas, A. J. 1956. "L'actualité du saussurisme," *Le Français Moderne* 3:

——. 1966. *Sémantique structurale.* Paris: Larousse.

——. 1970. *Du sens.* Paris: Le Seuil.

——. 1976. *Sémiotique et sciences sociales.* Paris: Le Seuil.

——. 1981. "Contre-note." *Le carré sémiotique. Le Bulletin du groupe de recherches sémio-linguistiques* 17:42–46.

——. 1983a. *Du sens II.* Paris: Le Seuil.

——. 1983b. *Structural Semantics.* Introduction by R. Schleifer. Translated by D. McDowell, R. Schleifer, and A. Velie. Lincoln and London: University of Nebraska Press.

——. 1984. "Universaux et narrativité," unedited paper presented at a colloquium on the universals of narrativity, University of Toronto.

Greimas, A. J., and Courtés, J. 1982. *Semiotics and Language: An Analytical Dictionary.* Translated by L. Crist, D. Patte, and others. Bloomington: Indiana University Press.

——. 1986. *Sémiotique: dictionnaire raisonné de la théorie du langage, II.* Paris: Hachette.

Greimas, A. J., and Landowski, E. 1979. *Introduction à l'analyse du discours en sciences sociales.* Paris: Hachette.

Jameson, F. 1972. *The Prison House of Language.* Princeton: Princeton University Press.

Landowski, E. 1979. Introduction. *Sémiotique des Passions. Le Bulletin du groupe de recherches sémio-linguistiques* 9:3–8.

Nef, F., ed. 1976. "Entretien avec A. J. Greimas." In *Structures élémentaires de la signification.* Brussels: Ed. Complexe.

Parret, H., and Ruprecht, H. G., eds. 1985. *Recueil d'hommages pour/Essays in Honor of Algirdas Julien Greimas*. Amsterdam: John Benjamins.

Patte, D. 1982. "Greimas' Model for the Generative Trajectory of Meaning in Discourses." *American Journal of Semiotics* 1:59-78.

Petitot-Cocorda, J. 1982. Introduction. *Aspects de la conversion. Actes sémiotiques: Le Bulletin du groupe de recherches sémio-linguistiques* 24:5-7.

——. 1985. *Morphogenèse du sens I*. Paris: PUF.

Ricoeur, P. 1983. "Greimas' Narrative Grammar." In *Paris School Semiotics*, P. Perron, ed. *Toronto Semiotic Circle Publications* 3: 91-114.

Ruprecht, H. G. 1984. "Ouvertures meta-sémiotiques: Entretien avec A. J. Greimas." *Recherches Sémiotiques/Semiotic Inquiry* 4:1-23.

On Meaning

Chapter 1
Comparative Mythology

To Georges Dumézil

The interest linguists or semioticians – since the linguistic system is just one privileged system among so many other semiotic structures – can have in mythology is twofold.[1]

For them a mythology is a "natural" metalanguage that structures itself using an already existing human language as its object-language. Linguists or semioticians then try to identify and describe the functioning of the "forms" of this new complex signifier that is being used to realize mythical significations.

Mythological research also attracts these scholars because of the obvious and compelling way in which the description of the signification of metalinguistic forms shows itself to be imperative in that research. Being less indissolubly linked to its signifier than is the case in ordinary language, the mythological signifier is there to be discovered and identified through a slow and often very subtle explicative process that requires an exact methodology based on the constant search for objective criteria of analysis. As we know, for a long time structural linguistics, for reasons of principle, did not allow itself to become engaged in any research into signification, and it is only recently that it has begun to be able to envisage with less horror the analysis of substance, be it phonic or semantic.

Historians can observe the manner in which pre-Socratic philosophy emerged from mythology. It is exciting to follow mythologists as they carry out their twofold task. We see how the interpretation of myths brings into being a new "ideo-

logical" language, because this is indeed what happens: An analysis of signification must necessarily lead to a new "terminology," a new metalanguage. In other
words, mythologists translate mythological language into ideological language.
This movement is inescapable: A "connotative semiotics" is transformed, if we
use Hjelmslev's terminology, into a "denotative semiology." Whoever can read
the greater of these can read the lesser of them: Thus mythological research could
serve as a model for the study of superstructures and for the description of social
ideologies.

Given the diversity of the levels where mythological signifiers are found,[2] and
the multitude of forms they take, one's attention is quite naturally attracted by
myths, stories of various lengths in which, in a syntagmatic chain that is more or
less coherent, theologemes and mythemes marked by redundancies and repeti-
tions, as well as other interlinked units of the signified, are linked paradigmatically even though the story may make it appear otherwise. The remarkable structural study of myth carried out recently by Claude Lévi-Strauss[3] leaves no doubt
on this subject: One must not read myth syntagmatically in a way that is dictated
by the story line; it is instead a grasping, in a way that is often unconscious on
the part of the member of the community in which the given myth prevails, of
the relation between the various units of the signified, distributed throughout the
length of the story. These units of the signified, despite the richness of the signifiers, are of a very limited number in the story, and thus the expression of myth
can be reduced to a mathematical equation. Lévi-Strauss formulates the Oedipus
myth in the following way:

$$\frac{/overestimated\ familial\ relationships/}{/underestimated\ familial\ relationships/} \simeq \frac{/autochthonous\ human\ nature/}{/negation\ of\ autochthonous\ human\ nature/^4}$$

Such a formulation of myth presupposes two conditions:

1. At the point at which one believes the analysis of the mythical signifier to have been completed, the information that signifier is able to
   encompass should be reducible to a small number of units of the signified.
2. These significative units should organize themselves into a twofold relational network:
   a. Each pair of units of the arithmetic relation constitutes an opposi-
      tional *couple* characterized by the presence or absence of a distinctive
      feature (or features) of the type:

      A vs. non-*A*.

b. The two couples are globally linked by a *correlative*. The very simplified formula for myth will then show the following equation:[5]

$$\frac{A}{\text{non-}A} \simeq \frac{B}{\text{non-}B}.$$

By way of example, we propose to take a number of stories analyzed by Dumézil to see if these stories fit the unique formulation suggested by Lévi-Strauss. Despite the lengthy nature of his presentation, a result of the polemical nature of part of his work as required to convince and answer his critics—reasons no longer valid—Dumézil's analysis is so rich and to the point that our task will consist not so much in innovating as in giving another formulation, using a terminology that is sometimes a little different.

We are also attempting to see if a more rigorous analysis of significative units, as defined by Lévi-Strauss, which would break them down into *distinctive features* (the usual practice in phonology), is possible: The use of such an analysis in the structural description of semantic substance might eventually be generalized.

The difficulties of this twofold analysis—into units of the signified and distinctive features—will have to be confronted when we come to its application in a comparative study.

The "Myth" of the Social Contract

Those to whom Dumézil's work is familiar will know the Indian tale of the accession of King Prthu, a story to which mythology has subsequently, through a slow process of modification, added the parallel stories of the "election" of the censorking Servius and the deposal of the Irish king Bress. Even though it is debatable, for reasons we will return to later, this example has the advantage of simplicity: The fact that the units of the signified and the distinctive features are identical in the Indian and Latin stories allows us to show progressively, one by one, the difficulties of the comparatist method.

Dumézil does a good job demonstrating how this story metaphorically signifies the twofold contract set up, at the time of his succession, between the king and his people. The story, which can be divided almost symmetrically into two equal parts, first tells of the way in which the people qualify the king and then of the way the king qualifies them. This qualification is seen as reciprocal, situated within the linguistic category of the exchange of messages: The king is qualified through praise; in return he distributes gifts (which are qualifying), or vice versa. However, two particular cases have to be distinguished from each other: If the gifts (and/or favors) precede the qualification, we call this simple qualification;

if, on the other hand, the qualifying praise precedes the distribution of gifts, this is valorizing qualification (*çams-*) and gives new power to the thing or person qualified, since the anticipating *parole* has been turned into reality. Once again, this new power is next designated symbolically by possession of the Cow of Plenitude.

The contract the Indian king sets up with his people can then be formulated in the following way:

$$\frac{king}{people} \simeq \frac{qgV}{gq}$$

in which q = qualification, g = gifts, and V = valorization or overvalorization.

The first phase of the contract does not merely consecrate the king, it invigorates him (French, *vigorise*); the second is no more than a simple symbolic exchange that consecrates the rights and duties of the people. We see that what distinguishes a simple qualification (gq) from the valorizing qualification (qg) is, in the first instance, the syntagmatic order of the first exchange:

$$(q \rightarrow g) \quad \text{vs.} \quad (g \rightarrow q);$$

and in the second instance the sequence of the story that has to do with the Cow of Plenitude (which the king captures following his qualification), this being a redundant way of underscoring his new power. If, given the fact of overvalorization, we set aside this syntagmatic ordering, the relationship between the qualification of the king and that of his people would seem to be a relation between two terms of which the first is characterized by the presence of the distinctive feature V, while in the second V is absent. The category of the signified that is thus identified can be formulated as follows:

$$V \text{ (marked) vs. non-}V \text{ (not marked).}$$

The reconstruction, which Dumézil carries out with the aid of pseudohistorical facts and sequences from the life of King Servius, in turn allows us to formulate the Roman symbolic mythification as follows:

$$\frac{king}{people} \simeq \frac{gq}{qgV}.$$

In Rome it is the people, not the king, who are qualified in a valorizing manner: Servius, elected king thanks to his largesse (gq), sets up the *census* (q), which qualifies the citizens according to rank and wealth. Of course this will create an inflow of taxes (g); here the Cow of Empire replaces the Cow of Plenitude and the story of its acquisition and sacrifice is chronologically placed after the qualification of the people (and not of the king), thus confirming the praises sung of the Roman people by the king.[6] We can see that the same valorizing category here sets up the relation between the two symbolic exchanges and constitutes a doubly sealed social contract.

One might ask if such a formulation, which allows us to give an equational form to the comparison of the Indian and Roman stories:

$$\text{India vs. Rome} \simeq \frac{V}{\text{non-}V} \text{ vs. } \frac{\text{non-}V}{V}$$

sheds new light on Dumézil's analysis according to which the qualifying praise (*çams-*), in India, qualifies and valorizes the king whereas in Rome, this happens to the people and not to the king, thanks to the institution of the *census*.

Certainly nothing in the basic aspects of the analysis is changed: Far from being enriched, this analysis can, in fact, seem to have been weakened by such a reduction. But the same cannot be said about the methodological refinements attained: Thanks to the discovery that the two stories have the exact same symbolism, the conditions for comparison are now self-evident, where before they seemed only to be implied; as opposed to what was for so long the teaching here, the comparison is far from being just a simple catalog of similarities and differences and is instead a juxtaposition of identical phenomena, an establishing of a common base that alone will allow us to measure and compare differences.

The Myth of Good and Evil

Our second example is no less well known: It is the famous Scandinavian *Götterdämmerung* myth viewed alongside the Indian *Mahabharata* and reinterpreted by virtue of this parallelism. In both stories two kinds of eras, good and bad, unfold for humans according to the two different kinds of combat that the gods engage in — the one unfair and rigged, the other fair. In both cases the myth can be formulated in the following way:

$$\frac{/\text{unfair combat}/}{/\text{fair combat}/} \simeq \frac{/\text{worse world}/}{/\text{better world}/}.$$

This identical formulation for the two myths is possible only because they share many elements — the same concept of life as combat, the same moral view of the human world — with this making explicit of what is identical being necessarily accompanied by a provisional setting aside of those categories of signification with features that differentiate between the stories.

The description of the units of the signified that we next analyze into distinctive features, through successive consideration of each of the relations of the equation, reveals, in effect, appreciable structural differences that although they are sometimes difficult to identify if each of the two mythical structures is taken individually, become fully obvious when the two myths are compared.

Thus, taking into consideration only the opposition

/worse world/ vs. /better world/ ,

we note:

1. That the moral judgment made of the world is linked to a category of
   time that involves not two but three terms:
   /past/ vs. /present/ /future/ .

2. That we are dealing not with the dichotomy of /good/ vs. /evil/ but in
   fact with the relative category of /better/ vs. /worse/, which also contains a third term, this one complex:
   /better/ <-----------------------> /worse/

   /positive/ vs. /complex/ vs. /negative/ .

If we now bring these two categories together, we see that the complex term
is, in the final analysis, no more than the time that is now present to human beings
and which is being judged as either better or worse vis-à-vis the past or the future.
A larger schema, which will include our two categories and in which interpretation of the oppositions between the Indian and Scandinavian myths is included,
can be set out as follows:

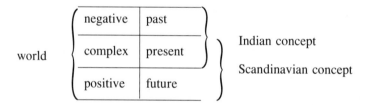

We can see that neither of the categories (each one including three terms) is fully
realized in either the Indian or Scandinavian myths taken separately. A wider unit
of signification, belonging to the new analysis and of which the two myths manifest only incomplete realizations, must thus now be postulated: It alone can give
our description its structural framework.

The first part of the relation /unfair combat/ vs. /fair combat/, which brings
into play the /fair/ vs. /unfair/ category, appears at first sight to be the stable element in the equation. However, analysis reveals a complementary feature in the
signified that would not be noticed unless the comparison were made: If the signified /combat/, organized into /fair/ vs. /unfair/, is found in both myths, the category /good/ vs. /evil/, which determines the instigating agent of the combat, is
not distributed in the same way:

India

combat	{	unfair		instigator:	evil
		fair		instigator:	good

Scandinavia

combat	{	unfair		instigator:	evil
		fair		instigator:	good

In the Indian case the symmetry of the two correlative categories that qualify the combat partially camouflages the distinction between two value judgments, one concerning the origin of the combat, the other its unfolding: The combat can be, as to its source and its causes, good or bad, and its unfolding, that is, the manner of its taking place, fair or unfair.[7] On the other hand, in the Scandinavian version the symmetry is broken and the combat, be it fair or unfair, is always provoked by the agent evil. The good and evil category that is realized in the Indian myth is *neutralized* in the Scandinavian version, and this is to the advantage of its unmarked term /evil/. Hjelmslev would say that this term is under the dominance of /combat/, which, as we shall see later, is the negative term in the Scandinavian category of signified /war/ vs. /peace/, which is in close correlation with the /evil/ vs. /good/ category. War and combat, for the Scandinavians, are always caused by evil, which in the event, is redundantly underscored by the story of Balder.

The Myth of Excess

The third example, which is somewhat more complex than the first ones, involves the parallelism between the Scandinavian Kvasir myth and the episode in the *Mahabharata* in which Mada, the Indian counterpart of Kvasir, briefly appears.

Both appear in a war situation: Kvasir, who incarnates wisdom, is produced by the gods in order to seal the agreement for peace; Mada, a symbol of superhuman drunkenness, obliges the gods by simply appearing before them to bring about peace. Because each of them is "larger than life" for a situation of peace, both are in the event destroyed. Kvasir is turned into poetry and Mada into four male passions: drink, women, hunting, and gambling.

The Scandinavian myth can be formulated as follows:

$$\frac{/excess/}{/moderation/} \simeq \frac{/better\ world/}{/worse\ world/} .$$

The episode from the Indian myth is quite similar:

$$\frac{/\text{excess}/}{/\text{moderation}/} \simeq \frac{/\text{worse world}/}{/\text{better world}/} \; .$$

As we move from one version to the other, we see, as in the case of the social contract "myth," an inversion of the relation making up the second half of the equation. Given that the units of the signified at play in both cases are the same, the inversion can be viewed as one of the modalities of the structure of myth.

Moving to a second-degree analysis, we see that the relation

/excess/ vs. /moderation/ ,

is at first interpreted as the relation

/whole/ vs. /part/ .

Indeed, we can remember that Mada, as well as all that remains of Kvasir, is symbolically *divided* into parts. Nevertheless, though Mada is "really" divided into four parts/passions, Kvasir reappears in the form of poetry, not as a fraction of his initial condition, but as a reduction of it. We thus are dealing with two different concepts of *totality* and, therefore, two different articulations of totality: One original, harmonious totality finds its counterpart in a conception of totality as an arithmetic sum of its parts. This opposition can be formulated as follows:

Scandinavia		*India*	
/integral/	vs. /partitive/	$\simeq$ /universal/	vs. /cardinal/ .

Other distinctive features apply to this fundamental opposition of the two conceptions of totality, and they give us two diametrically opposed conceptions of excess. We can add nothing to the list of distinctive features established by Dumézil; we will simply reproduce it schematically:

Scandinavia	*India*
/integral/	vs. /universal/
/beneficent/	vs. /maleficent/
/spirit/	vs. /matter/
/peace/	vs. /war/ .

The last three features, which are distinctive for Kvasir and Mada, are articulated into dichotomous categories within what we will define later as an archilexeme.[8] We see it as a remarkable proof that the analysis is complete when the same categories meet in the same way as they did in the first part of the relation:

Scandinavia (poetry)	*India* (divided passions)
/partitive/	vs. /cardinal collection/
/beneficent/	vs. /maleficent/
/spirit/	vs. /matter/ (drink + women)
Poetry /peace/	vs. /war/ (hunting + gambling)

As for the second half of the equation, we already know which categories qualify it. Although the /better/ vs. /worse/ category is established here in the same way as in the preceding myth, the category of time that is correlative to it is present only with the two symmetrically posed terms of past and present.

Furthermore, the terms of the two categories, that of time and that of /better/ vs. /worse/, are not linked in the same way in the two myths: The past is viewed as worse by the Indians and better by the Scandinavians, and inversely, in relation to this past, the present is better for the Indians and worse for the Scandinavians. What appeared as an inversion of relation at the stage of formulation of the units of the signified now is integrated, within the archilexeme, into a scheme that, although somewhat different from that of the preceding story, can account for the distribution of distinctive features in both myths:

world $\left\{ \begin{array}{|c|c|} \hline \text{negative} & \text{past} \\ \hline \text{complex} & \text{present} \\ \hline \text{positive} & \text{future} \\ \hline \end{array} \right\}$ Indian concept

Scandinavian concept

Since both myths, that of good and evil and that of excess, present series of correlatives in which the same categories of signification are involved, comparing them might be instructive, if only to identify the basic elements for typology of myth and of those "ideologies" that, in the final analysis, are the object of all studies of Indo-European mythology.

What strikes us, at first sight, is the identical way in which the two Indian myths judge the world. In both we find, in opposition to each other:

/past negative world/ vs. /present complex world/ .

Evil, in Indian mythology — if our extrapolations are not too daring — is situated in the past. The present seems to represent an amelioration of the common lot of human society. The philosophy of Indian history is, one might say, that of the *least present evil*.

On the other hand, the Scandinavian myths use three dimensions of time and situate the reign of good, in relation to the complex present, either in the past or in the future. If we compare both myths in these terms, we find:

/positive past world/

In the myth of excess:

/complex present world/

/complex present world/

In the myth of good and evil:

/positive future world/

If we allow ourselves an extreme generalization, we can say that the first myth is that of the *fall of the world*, whereas the second is that of the *salvation of the world*. From this point of view, Scandinavian mythology presents a striking parallelism with Christian philosophy.

Mythical Story or Ritual Story?

It is now time to return to our first example, the story that recounts the concluding of the social contract. We had knowingly simplified it by at first considering only Indian and Roman variants, provisionally setting aside the Irish stories concerning the deposing of King Bress.

An analysis of the whole group of these Irish stories, following again the methods of Dumézil, can now be carried out in two ways. The *deposing* of the king obviously is the counterpart to his *accession to the throne*, and we can ask ourselves whether this Irish variant might not allow us to reconstruct the Indian and Roman schemata of the deposing of a king, versions that have been handed down to us in a fragmented and incomplete way and that concern the deposing of the predecessors of Prthu and of Servius. One might also try to see whether the story of the deposing of the king of Ireland might not furnish us with the schema for royal accession in the Irish context; in other words, if the comparative series

$$\frac{\text{Vena}}{\text{Prthu}} \sim \frac{\text{Tarquin}}{\text{Servius}} \sim \frac{\text{Bress}}{X}$$

might not have valid heuristic possibilities.

Roman Jakobson, a supporter of distinctive-feature analysis in linguistics, clearly distinguishes between two types of opposition that allow us to view the terms of a given relation as distinctive. We can have on the one hand the relation

a vs. non-a ,

in which a is considered to be *marked*, because it possesses an extra distinctive feature that *non-a*, an *unmarked* term, lacks. A completely different relation is set up between

a vs. $-a$,

in which $-a$ is the negation of a.

When we analyzed the social contract that is concluded when a king accedes to the throne, we first distinguished between valorizing qualification (V) and simple qualification (non-V). The Irish variant that is a negation of the social contract should, in the archisemic analysis now so familiar to us, set up the opposition

$$V \text{ vs. } -V$$
$$\text{non-}V \text{ vs. } -\text{non-}V ,$$

thus allowing the formulation of the abolition of the social contract:

$$\frac{people}{king} \simeq \frac{-\text{non-}V}{-V} .$$

This simply means that since the people have not been qualified in a suitable manner, the king finds himself, for his part, disqualified, and he loses his initial vigor.

Reconstruction of the ascension schema, within the framework of the Irish ideology, can thus be conceived of as a twofold operation: The negation signs are done away with and the relation *king* vs. *people* is inverted. We can thus say that

$$\text{India vs. Rome vs. Ireland} \simeq \frac{V}{\text{non-}V} \text{ vs. } \frac{\text{non-}V}{V} \text{ vs. } \frac{V}{\text{non-}V} ,$$

and this permits us to say that the Irish ascension schema is identical to the Indian one.

Although the passage from negation to affirmation is quite normal, inversion of the relation, which is necessary in order to include Ireland in the equation that subsumes the Indian and Roman schemata, can, from one point of view, be rather disquieting. Indeed we note not only that

$$\frac{deposing}{ascension} \simeq \frac{negation}{affirmation}$$

but that there further exists between the two terms of the relation a syntagmatic relation (the king is qualified first, then the people; first the people are disqualified by the king, then the king finds himself disqualified and dispossessed). Additional analysis shows that the inversion of the syntagmatic relation is also found at a lower level. Using the symbols already used, the detailed Irish deposing schema appears in this way:

$$\frac{people}{king} \sim \frac{g(-q)}{(-g)\,(-q)\,(-V)} \ .$$

Because the king has refused to qualify his people, each according to his rank, the following episode relates, in order of succession, the satirical disqualification of the king by the poet and, finally, the wasting away of the king because of his having drunk the false milk of the false Cow of Plenitude (whose features distinguish it from the true Cow, such as /nature/ vs. /artifice/, /vigor/ vs. /illness/). The negation of hospitality precedes the disqualification of the king. Once more the two signifiers contract a syntagmatic relation that is the inverse of the relation they have in the ascension stories.

This intrusion of the syntagmatic element is troubling because it contradicts the definition of myth we presented along the lines of Lévi-Strauss's definition: a correlation of two pairs of units of the signified that are in significant opposition to each other. This definition is essentially paradigmatic, excluding any syntagmatic relation and at the same time explaining, which is very important, the atemporal character of myth.

As a consequence, it must be one or the other: Either the definition given for myth is not extensive enough, or the story that contains the symbolic expression of the social contract is not a myth. Several reasons incline us toward the second solution.

We have simplified Dumézil's description of the ascension story, of course, for use as a demonstration. To an even further extent, we wanted to highlight, in the Indian story, the oppositional couple

/qualification of the king/ vs. /qualification of the people/ ,

and thus we knowingly ignored the episode that precedes it. This episode, for which Dumézil found parallel elements in the story of Servius, appears to be a communication that, before the social contract, is established between the gods and human beings:

/the sending/, by the gods	/recognition/, by man
/of the signs of predestination/ vs.	/of these signs/
/sending out/	/reception/ .

When we remember that the rest of the story establishes *sovereignty at the human level*, the idea of setting it into a possible correlation with the concept of *sovereignty of divine origin* quite naturally suggests itself. The opposition between two types of sovereignty, that of Varuna (the "other world") and that of Mithra ("this world"), thus appears in our story, which at one moment presents a granted sovereignty, one by divine right, and at another moment, contractual sovereignty, a human right. Thus:

$$\frac{\text{Varuna}}{\text{Mithra}} \simeq \frac{/\text{granted sovereignty}/}{/\text{contractual sovereignty}/} \; .$$

Would it be too daring to push the comparison further and thus to see in the two sons of Mithra, Aryaman (king and protector of the people of Arya) and Bhaga (each one's share), the other two terms of the correlation:

$$\frac{\text{Aryaman}}{\text{Bhaga}} \simeq \frac{/\text{qualification of the king}/}{/\text{qualification of the people}/} \; ?$$

Whatever one might say about this last supposition, the parallelism between the two levels—theological and "mythical"—appears sufficiently convincing.[9] Characterized by the presence of syntagmatic relations and by the correlation of these units of the signified with the series of theological units, the story we are studying no longer corresponds to the definition of myth. Quite the contrary: Are these two criteria not enough for us to be able to say that what we see here is a *ritual story*, which is different, in terms of its structural type, from a *mythical story*?[10]

Let us now recapitulate the methodological insights gained by this study. It goes without saying, and we have emphasized this from the beginning, that this study, as undertaken by a nonspecialist, cannot be justified unless one postulates a priori that all descriptions of semantic substance are methodologically identical. Only if this is so can we extrapolate from and generalize on what we acquired from our mythological research.

In favor of the argument that the methods are identical is not only the fact that mythology belongs to the domain of language but rather, and above all, the similarity in point of departure for all such research. In effect, one must develop one's "terminology" for any description of content. One must develop a coherent system of references. This terminology is a metalanguage that has a "scientific" character. Although the terms of this system are in a way arbitrary (that is, they have no necessary relationship to reality) and as such can be refined when further work is directed at them from a higher level of research on the whole phenomenon of terminology, they possess, for that reason, a universal value. And it is this very universality of semiotic terminology that makes it of use beyond the frontiers of linguistics, in all research on signification and, more particularly, in the study of comparative mythologies.

A given mythology, considered as a metalanguage, cannot be described unless one first chooses the *units of measure*. When these are manipulated — when they are placed in relation and correlation with each other — this allows one bit by bit to reconstruct much greater structural ensembles, and eventually the entire mythological system. Lévi-Strauss, in the study we have already mentioned several times, recognizes these *constitutive units* in the signifieds that correspond to the sequences of the mythical story and that subsequently appear as the main terms of the mythical equation:

$$\frac{A}{\text{non-}A} \simeq \frac{B}{\text{non-}B}.$$

We have seen that these "greater constitutive units" can then, in turn, be analyzed into *distinctive features*. If, for example, we were to agree to designate distinctive features by the term *seme*, the terms in mythical equations, groupings of semes (of which only part is analyzed in each concrete case), could be called lexemes.[11]

Distinctive features, in turn, are relevant only because they are part of a relation of opposition made up of two or more terms. Semes thus constitute *semic categories*. Lexemes, for their part, become *archilexemes* if, instead of considering only their distinctive features, we take into account the whole group of semic categories that construct the lexemic oppositional couples. Semes and lexemes, semic categories, and archilexemes — these, it would seem, are the four principal "units of measure" mythologists and linguists use in analyzing content.

Their combinations, their elementary structures can show much variation. The placing in correlation of archilexemes (or of semic categories in more cases) constitutes myth. Other structures are probably possible, above all those in which the syntagmatic regains preeminence: It is up to mythologists to judge.

Chapter 2
Toward a Semiotics
of the Natural World

Once the arbitrary nature of the sign was posited, considerable advances in knowledge related to the internal structure of what are commonly called natural languages became possible. Nonetheless, initially this had unpredictable consequences as it inevitably led to a broadening of the problematics of the status of language. Because of this, linguists became aware of the possibilities of a generalized semiotic theory that could account for all the forms and manifestations of signification. Since the relation between the signifier and the signified is arbitrary at the level of sign, that is, at the level of the word or of any syntagmatic unit, it is also arbitrary at the level of *all* types of discourses through which language appears. In other words, language is a *form* — or better yet, an interlacing of two forms — *irrespective of the substance* in which it happens to appear.

If this point of view is reversed, it becomes obvious that the only conceivable presence signification can take on in the world is through its manifestation in the "substance" surrounding human beings. From this perspective the sensible world as a whole becomes the object of the quest for signification. As long as it takes on form, the world appears, as a whole and in its various articulations, as potential meaning. Signification can be concealed behind all sensible phenomena; it is present *behind* sounds, but also behind images, odors, and flavors, without being in sounds or in images (as perceptions).

Leaving aside the problem of variations in meaning accompanying variations of the signifier, certain linguistic theories influenced by behaviorism and that have integrated elements of communication theory have suggested that the diversity of signifiers could be interpreted as a problem of multiple encoding. Moreover, in these theories the large number and relative autonomy of the *codes of expression* come under a typology of *transmission channels*, which in turn are based on perception being distributed between five, six, or seven senses. Nonetheless the hypothesis according to which these codes of expression could be substituted one for the other—the content remaining invariable, and often unidentified—even if one admits that in switching over from one code to the other there can be a narrowing or a widening of the domain of the signified, did not seem sufficiently to take into account the complexity of the phenomenon.

First, if we admit that the *substances* of expression can be classified according to the channels of transmission by which signification reaches us, nothing tells us a priori that the *codes* organizing these different manifestations themselves can be *classified* according to the same criteria (i.e., along the lines of channels of transmission), nor that these forms of expression can be *described* in each case, by simple analogy, according to models constructed from *natural languages*.

Second, linguistic experience *stricto sensu* already points to the diversity of approaches related to the linguistic signifier, which can be apprehended and codified (that is, be given a metalinguistic interpretation by means of a new scientific language) at the "physiological" level proper to phonation as well as at the "acoustic" or "perceptive" levels. Without raising the as yet unresolved difficulties of the correlation and transposition of the various interpretations of the same linguistic code, nothing tells us a priori when examining the substances of manifestations that the appropriate codes of expression do not correspond to such and such a level of apprehension of a same linguistic phenomenon rather than to another. We will return to this problem later.

Finally, if we refuse to take up the behaviorist problematics and to accept all of its implications, we can see that the *problem of semiosis*, that is to say, *of the semiotic relation between expression and content* (which constitutes meaning and which is inherent to the axiomatics of every theory of language), is omnipresent as soon as the status of the codes of expression other than the linguistic ones is examined.

Although it is almost impossible to reconstruct archaeologically the process of the invention of writing (i.e., precisely, the transposition of a code using a sonorous substance into a visual kind of code), the slowness of that hesitating process and the complexity of the problems to be resolved—the elaboration of the implicit phonology necessary for such a transposition—suggest, and not without reason, that it is perhaps not the horse but writing that is the noblest human conquest. It could also be said that this discovery corresponds to a rapid, qualitative mutation of human thought. In the same way, the present-day effort to go beyond a linguistics limited to natural languages and to work out a general semiotics is perhaps the sign of another revolution that is equally hesitating and difficult. Obviously this is only a metaphor that is part of didactic discourse and that attempts to dissociate semiotic research from the fluctuating vagaries of fashion. It also designates the ambitions and the modest means of the following demonstration.

Recent progress in linguistics has followed that of logic. Together both have attempted to construct a coherent language that would enable them to speak with proficiency about other languages. Yet although they shared a concern with the coherence of their own language, they soon parted ways because of their differing aims. On the one hand, Saussure's discovery of the arbitrary nature of the sign enabled him to proclaim the autonomy of the linguistic object, and thus scientific discourse, in order to correspond to its object, could be satisfied simply with internal coherence. On the other hand, logical discourse, while testing the coherence of its own judgment, in addition had to be appropriate to what it was not, that is, in relation to the extralinguistic world.

This is how the concept of *reference* was introduced into linguistic debate. The position of neopositivistic logicians who affirmed the existence of the reference of "proper names" to objects of the world could only annoy linguists, who were aware that language partook in constructing the world of objects. They were also aware of relativity, associated with the diversity of human societies and with the segmentation of the universe of signification. At the same time, logicians, uncomfortable in the closed and self-sufficient world of language, tended to hypostasize it and often even went so far as to identify the world with it.

The development of semiotics, which we can consider the theory of all languages and of all systems of signification, can probably end the debate on where to situate language. It should be situated at the level of scientific epistemology and no longer at the level of its philosophical presuppositions. To do so all we have to do is to consider the extralinguistic world as no longer being the *absolute* referent, but as the place where what is manifested through the senses can become the *manifestation* of human meaning, that is to say, of signification. In short, all we have to do is consider the referent as a set of more or less implicit semiotic systems. While recognizing the privileged status of the *semiotics of natural languages* – these have the distinct property of being able to accommodate the other semiotic systems – it is necessary to postulate the existence and the possibility of a *semiotics of the natural world* and to think of the relation between ("natural") signs and linguistic systems, on the one hand, and signs and systems of signification of the natural world, on the other, not as reference stemming from the symbolic to the natural, from the variable to the invariable, but as a *network of correlations between the two levels of signifying reality*. In the same way as the natural sciences have done, the human sciences can also assert their autonomy, which comes not from the "nature" of the objects of investigation – words or things, nature or culture – but *from the method of approach that constitutes them all into human objects, into signifying objects*.

The Natural World and Its Signification

By limiting our reflection on the natural world to the *visual*—because the theme of this discussion demands it, but also because the manifestation of meaning through the visible seems the most important one quantitatively and even qualitatively—we will initially investigate in a preliminary fashion various modalities of the manifestation of the visible. This investigation leads us immediately to recognize that the visible world, instead of being projected before us as a homogeneous screen of forms, appears rather to be made up of several superimposed, or even sometimes juxtaposed, *layers of signification*.

Natural Signs

We are compelled to recognize a first level of objective reality, a world of common sense made up of mobile and immobile objects. As such, it is made up of word-objects and verb-processes, and according to the priorities laid down, lends itself to interpretation either as the result of constructive and categorizing linguistic activity, or as the source of linguistic symbolism. In both cases, though only in an a posteriori fashion, this allows us to establish equivalences between words and things, between processes and functions.

But after having accepted these equivalences, when we wish to draw the conclusions and thus consider things and processes as signs—that could even be designated as *natural signs*—we cannot be satisfied with the routine observation that things *are*, or that they are what they are. Consequently we must raise the question of their *semiotic status*. Indeed, if it is, so to speak, in the nature of signs to signify, it is not enough to say that the object *table* has "table" as content—this would only refer things back to words; but it is necessary to investigate the status of the natural sign *as sign*. It then becomes apparent that natural signs refer back to things other than themselves, but that this referential relation—although it can be defined in structural terms and therefore can be considered as an invariant relation—has different articulations, or *variables* according to the cultural communities envisaged.

Consider eighteenth-century Europe, which established the notion of natural sign and also thought of it as a reference to another natural sign: The sign *cloud* refers to the sign *rain*. Two points must be raised in this respect. First, once the referential relation has been established, it can be seen that it functions as a relation of cause to effect; thus the relation of effect to cause, which can be found, for example, in medical diagnostics (knee-jerk reflex —> good health), is simply the inversion of the former. Second, as reference the relation refers to another sign, but it is situated at the same level as the former; as François Rastier justly remarks, if *cloud* refers to *rain*, *rain* can in turn refer to *autumn*, and so on, without at any moment breaking out of the causal string of the level of sign phenomena.[1]

The interpretation of this type of civilization, which thinks of the natural world as the only level of reality but organized according to the syntactic laws of discourse, is opposed by other interpretations of natural signs that, in positing a second level of natural reality, a deeper level so to speak, interpret the sign as a reference to this second-order reality, and at the same time attribute a variable structure of metaphor, metonymy, or antiphrasis (i.e., a paradigmatic or systematic order) to this relation.

From this it follows that one could attempt to work out a typology of cultures based on a typology of the structural relationships defining natural signs (Yuri Lotman).

Two conclusions can be drawn from these preliminary remarks. First of all, the hypothesis according to which the natural world can be treated as a semiotic object seems to have been reinforced: Natural signs, because of the existence of a semiotic relation, and regardless of their articulations, have the status of signs. However, this approach in no way informs us about the nature and internal organization of the signs themselves. Since it must take into account the interpretation of the semiotic relation that is, as was seen, a variable, this approach is, in fact, a metasemiotic reflection on these signs—a semiotic connotation that transforms in various ways natural signs into cultural signs.

The Figures of the Natural World

In the study of natural languages the nonpertinence of the word as a meaningful unit has become more and more evident. Yet, in spite of what some think, it does seem obvious that it is not possible to construct a semiotics of objects by taking natural signs as a starting point. It would therefore seem necessary to locate another level at which a deeper and less evenemential vision of the world might be situated.

Gaston Bachelard thought he had found such a level when he put forth the notion of the *figurative* projected horizon into which humans delve when establishing inventories of forms and moving configurations.

Without actually raising the thorny issue of the schematism related to a person's perception and the conceptualization that one would like to derive from it, according to the most classical linguistic procedures, it can be said that to obtain the natural sign *table* as an invariant, it is necessary to carry out a twofold reduction that involves (1) reducing all the table occurrences to an invariant table, which would take on the form of a relatively simple geometrical figure; and (2) bracketing off the functional signification of table (to eat, to write, etc.), and within the inventory of other figures obtained in the same way, searching for identical or equivalent examples of the figure *table* that had been arrived at previously. A level of *figures* of the world, part of a finite inventory and giving a first idea of what the signifying world considered as form and not substance could be, therefore will have been substituted for the evenemential and accidental world of *objects*. In other words, it is exactly this cataloged set of static and dynamic figures that makes up the corpus from which a semiotic code of visual expression could be constructed.

The Categorization of the Natural World

Several objections can be raised to the Bachelardian project of a repertory of forms that attempts to account for creative imagination: (1) It is far from certain that such a repertory has a universal character—at the very least it should have the necessary articulations to account for the cultural diversity of mankind; (2) primary figures such as *water* or *fire*, although they may appear to be quasi-universal, do not refer to constant signifieds; the solution of homographies can be envisaged in two ways only: either by reference to context (and this posits a "natural" syntax) or by breaking up the figures into their constituent elements. It is the latter solution that Bachelard seems to have chosen in his final works.

An analogous solution would consist in recognizing, behind the visible figures, the existence of a *categorial* vision of the natural world, of a grid made up of a limited number of elementary categories of spatiality, whose combinatory arrangement produces visual figures and also accounts for the functioning of the visual expression code. If we insist on this it is not only because later analyses of gestuality refer sometimes to one and sometimes to the other of these two levels of visuality (*figures* and *elements*), but also because this distinction seems useful in defining the status of certain artificial languages that have been derived in relation to the natural visual code. Thus, in a recent study, A. Zemsz (*Revue d'esthétique*) showed not only how pictorial language rests on an optical code decomposed into elementary categories, but also that the diversity of optical codes can be interpreted as a different structural articulation within the same categorial space. Obviously the same could be said about architecture.

Finally, insofar as such an interpretation is correct, when attempting to extract the form of expression, it not only proposes a method of approach and a descriptive procedure to the substance of the natural world, but also enables us partially to account for the type of relations that can exist between both "natural" and linguistic semiotics and thus contributes to our knowledge of the linguistic phenomenon itself. For example, visual categories such as *high* vs. *low*, *prospective* vs. *retrospective* or *straight* vs. *curved* and *convex* vs. *concave*, which appear to make up the *form of expression* of the natural *world*, are obviously found as such when one describes the *form of the content* of natural *languages*. As a result, (1) the correlation between the sensible world and natural language must be sought not at the level of words and things, but at the level of the elementary units of their articulation;[2] and (2) the sensible world is immediately present even in linguistic form and partakes in its constitution, by offering a dimension of signification that we elsewhere call semiological.[3]

Natural and Cultural Gestuality

The preceding observations, while addressing visuality simply for didactic reasons, can be applied only to the natural world as a global given object: In linguistic terms the world is of the order of utterance and not of enunciation. As bodies, people are integrated into this world alongside other figures; they are forms comparable to other forms. We will restrict once more our area of investigation and limit it to a single human form. In this way, we will attempt to keep in mind the visual global context in which this particular form is inscribed.

The A Priori Coordinates of the Human Volume

The human body moves within a spatial context that for reasons of description must be categorized before the human volume filling it, situated in it, or moving in it can be. Three types of criteria will be retained: displacement, orientation (Vera Proca-Ciortea and Anca Guirchescu), and support (Pierre Condé).[4]

Although the utilization of *tridimensional space* in the description of human volume may seem self-evident, it nonetheless involves at least three different systems:

1. *A system of spatial coordinates*, which enables us to account for human volume itself;
2. *Spatial perspectivism*, which is introduced by the very fact that the human body as perceived object presupposes a spectator, who is also situated in a tridimensional *inclusive* space with respect to the *included* human body. In this way, from a lateral perspective, the human form would be perceived as projected onto a screen, whereas the displacement of a folk group to be grasped probably needs to be perceived from a high-low perspective;
3. *A topology*, that is, a *relativization* of space, which becomes necessary when the human form, or forms, moves in relationship to a fixed point in space (war dance) or a mobile one (fishing from a bank), or in relation to other human forms (dancing in couples or groups).

The *weight* of the human body, in a certain way, gives importance to two spatial axes:

1. *The vertical axis*, the direction in which weight is exerted, which introduces the category *contact* vs. *noncontact* of human volume in relationship to other volumes. It sometimes renders noncontact euphoric through connotations of the liberation of the body with regard to weight (ballet), and at other times it valorizes certain postures because of their deviation from the norm (walking on one's hands like an acrobat);

2. *The horizontal axis*, which in turn constitutes the solid surface (or liquid, in the case of swimming) on which "natural" displacements, in opposition to "natural" posture or the upright stance, occur. Although it is only partially motivated, the articulation *horizontal world* vs. *vertical person* is generally recognized as the inchoative position preceding mobility.

The categorical opposition between immobility and mobility, between position and movement, poses so many problems that, even bracketing off the philosophical presuppositions, it is difficult to do more than enumerate a few questions, since research on an adequate notational system has only just begun. For example, does position have a demarcation characteristic in the same way contact does, enabling us to segment the gestural text into *syntagmatic units*? Can it be described in terms of *aspect*, catching movement either in terms of its inchoative aspect, or its terminative aspect and connoting it by means of the durative, iterative aspects, etc., thus accounting for the time and rhythm of movement? Is such an aspectual description possible, and is it preferable to the description of movements considered as predicate processes?

Mobility and Motricity

The spatial context in which the human form is inscribed cannot be dissociated either from the categories of tactility or from the problematics of the dynamism of the perceived forms of the world. Nonetheless we examined them separately, since we thought that a certain categorization of the perceived – and even its approximate axiomatization while awaiting the elaboration of a semiotics of the natural world – was necessary. We did this not only to insist on the need for the description of the human body as a perceived object, but also to accentuate the separation (which has been confirmed by research on apraxia) between nonhuman space, an *elsewhere* in which human beings prolong their presence with the aid of gesture or tools, and reduced human space, a *here-there* where gesticulation takes place.

Indeed, after having reduced the area of investigation by identifying the area of perception of the human object, we can then pass on to new observations by changing the point of view: Instead of considering the human body as an *object* of perception, we can examine it as the originator of its own motor functions.

This mechanistic approach, whether it happens to be one of principle (Proca-Ciortea and Guirchescu) or simply didactic (B. Koechlin),[5] by making us see the human body as a system of levers and controls, not only enables us to circumscribe the area of gesticulation and to enclose it in a transparent geometric sphere, but also as a precondition posits a morphological disarticulation of the human body, which ceases to be a global form and appears as an organization of metonymic actors (arm, leg, head, trunk, etc.) performing so to speak by proxy, each one in its own limited space, on behalf of a unique actant.

This *morphological disarticulation* of the human body, even though it is the basis for all descriptions of gesticulation, is not an immediate and obvious fact. Like all segmentations of the body into organs, it is both natural and cultural, that is, subject to anthropological variations. This area of investigation has not been sufficiently explored. It is possible to glean precious information from visual codes of a teratological nature, such as the code that governs comic strips, in which Claude Bremond noted that the exaggeration of limbs has a gesticulatory function, or the code that could account for portraiture or caricature, or finally the code belonging to certain language of the theater.

The limitation of gesticulatory possibilities presupposed by the mechanistic approach enables us to imagine reducing human gestuality to a *general model of possibilities* related to gesticulation and posture: Each particular code is thus presented as a choice, with a limited number of possibilities in mind. It is also within such a model that we could attempt to define the limits between normal and abnormal gestuality, the latter being either a stylistic anomaly or the place where a second gestural language, of a ludic character, is elaborated.

Natural Gesture and Cultural Gesture

We can only agree with Koechlin that the work of Marcel Mauss has made it impossible to privilege this mechanistic approach to the human body and consequently, to consider human motor function as a natural phenomenon. Even though learned and transmitted gesticulation is organically limited as to its possibilities, nonetheless it is a social phenomenon just like other semiotic systems. What was said about the typology of cultures, based on the diversified interpretation of natural signs, holds true equally for so-called natural gesticulation. A typology of socialized gesticulation not only would account for diversity among cultures (e.g., techniques of kissing) or sexes (e.g., the programmed operation *taking off a sweater*), but also would explain and posit the existence of an autonomous semiotic dimension, which, if only through the differential gaps it establishes between cultures, sexes, and social groups, founds cultures, sexes, and human groups as signification.

In this way, natural gesticulation is transformed into cultural gestuality and if the expression *natural gesture* is maintained for practical reasons, just like *natural sign* it is defined only by its semiotic potentiality, that is, in fact only insofar as it is a constituting element of signification.

Because we have so defined the term *natural*, we no longer have to qualify the word it denotes each time it is used. Yet this is far from being the case with the term *gesture*, which we continue to use in too loose a fashion.

The Problem of Gestural Units

At first glance the term *gesture* seems suspect because, in current usage, it implies the exclusion of *attitudes*. However, this opposition is, as was shown earlier, far from being self-evident.

Above all we do not know to what unit of the gesticulatory text the term gesture can be applied. The disarticulation of the human body, which is justified by the need for exhaustive description, introduces what could be referred to as specific actors of motor functions. Therefore, one could think that the partial movements specified by different actor-members, could be considered simple units of expression, and simply designated as gesture. However, to be convinced that gesticulation is a *global* undertaking of the human body, in which the particular gestures of bodily agents are coordinated and/or subordinated within a global project taking place simultaneously, one has only to read carefully certain passages of Koechlin's study, related to the analogy suggested by Haudricourt between the processes of the articulation of phonemes and gestural programming.

Although the morphological division of the body is here partially rejected, it is still true that the respective distribution of the roles attributed to such and such an actor of the gesticular scene, with their predictable showcasing and backgrounding, through extrapolation and analogy can lead to the recognition of the pertinence and nonpertinence of such and such a gestural feature. Accordingly it can lead to the construction of gestural *phonemes* corresponding to the global operations of the human body, thus making the somatic actant responsible for the act of sending.

Elsewhere, Koechlin proposes an indicative list of these simple natural behaviors. It is not surprising that this list corresponds, *mutatis mutandis*, to another equally flawed list, the "Vocabulaire du français fondamental," which has been worked out on the basis of the frequency of use of French words. In this vague inventory of one thousand words, we find some three hundred verbs that can readily be reduced to one hundred, and perhaps even fewer, by means of a brief parasynonymic analysis. The similarity between these two lists does not seem fortuitous, especially if we keep in mind the previous statement according to which the elementary categories of the plane of expression of natural semiotics correspond almost word for word to those of the plane of content of verbal semiotics. In addition, if we take into account that the isomorphism, which can be postulated between the two planes of language, establishes a structural correspondence between phonemes and sememes—and we did beforehand insist on this rather unusual fact—then the parallelism between gestural phonemes, suggested by Koechlin, and sememes included in French verbs becomes more evident.

These two lists require only minimal examination. Both are verbalized and include behavior such as (1) to walk, to run, to lie down, to sleep, and (2) to take, to give, to hold, to pull, to push; clearly they suggest a very limited inventory of both simple and sufficiently general bodily activities. Because of its limited nature, this inventory in turn makes us think of the very small number of phonemes that can account for the totality of the known articulations of natural languages. This logical chain of reasoning obviously is fraught with danger, since, as Koechlin remarks, the similarities asserted only serve all the better to hide the differences. However, the arguments we are making in an attempt to establish a case for a theory of gestuality as a semiological dimension of culture, in a very broad sense, allow us to use the analogy phonemes-sememes linked here with the methodological undertaking we are using to establish an inventory of gestural phonemes. If the procedures of analysis of gesticulatory substance reducing it to figures of the plane of visual expression are applied (and these are procedures that imply bracketing off meaning attributed to these simple behaviors), it seems possible to formulate the hypothesis according to which the inventory of simple natural behaviors corresponds to various areas of gestural text. This allows for *the segmentation of this text into manifest units having minimal dimensions on the plane of expression*, minimal units whose combinatory arrangement produces gestural utterances and gestural discourse itself.

Gestural Praxis

Let us recapitulate. Starting from observations on the visible world and on the meaning it can have for humans, we investigated in succession people as bodies, considered first of all as a certain figure of the world. Then we examined individuals as complex mechanisms that because of this mobility meet all the necessary conditions for the production of differential gaps of the signifier, from which signification can arise. The next step might be to introduce a specifically human dimension in the natural world.

The Presence of Meaning

To determine the signification of the word *meaning*, all we have to do is consult any dictionary. We can see that this word is always interpreted in two irreducible ways: It is understood either as *referencing* or as *direction*. In the first case, it is seen as the superimposition of two configurations, as one code—the *code of expression*—which refers back to another code, called perhaps equally arbitrarily the *code of content*. In the second case, it appears as *intentionality*, as relation to be established between the itinerary to be covered and its end point.

We saw that the human body, as configuration, met the conditions of serving as a support for a code of expression: Artificial semaphoric gesticulation is a concrete example of this phenomenon where a natural language is the underlying code of the referential content. It is therefore legitimate to suggest that the mobile configuration of the body, transformed into a system of constraints by its inscription into a particular cultural context, can function as a sender code. However, in order for natural gesticulation to be considered as a set of encoding operations (and it is actually a question of this), the de jure if not de facto antecedence of the axis of *communication* must be recognized, and both a sender-encoder and receiver-encoder must be presupposed.

It is a little different when the second definition of meaning (*sens*) is applied to human gesticulation. We can say that a complex natural behavior corresponding to what is called in natural language *to grasp*, will be understood by a spectator—who assumes the position of receiver—as signifying "*X* grasping *Y*." It is undeniable that *X*'s behavior has meaning. We do note, however, that even though the receiver in both cases remains the same, the gesticulating actor has changed status, that is, the *sender* has become *subject*. Yet, it is still necessary to specify what this terminological distinction embraces.

In describing *grasping* we omitted mentioning the object of this behavior, which, making up a class of variables, is nonetheless necessary for the description of the behavior itself. The object makes the underlying *transitivity* of this sort of gesticulation come to light. And so, through a series of substitutions of objects, it is possible to imagine

    1. *X* grasps a stick.
    2. *X* grasps a bunch of bananas.
    3. *X* grasps a fish.

If, in the simplest case (1), the perception of the meaning of gesticulation by the spectator stems from the decoding of an elementary gestural utterance, the situation becomes more complicated in the following cases. In (2), for example, a succession of natural gestures can correspond to the content *grasping*: *X* notices a bunch of bananas at the top of a banana tree, he approaches the tree and begins to climb it, and finally grasps the bunch of bananas. In (3), the content *grasping*, supposing that the operation takes place in water and that the fish is mobile, will be embraced by apparently more disorganized and more complex gesticulation. In both cases, a series of mediating gestural utterances will be inserted between the subject's inchoative position and his terminative one. In the case of (2) it can be said that gesticulation will take the form of an algorithmic syntagm, whereas in (3) it will take that of a strategic syntagm.

Now if we investigate the status of the signification of such gestural syntagms, two series of observations come to mind.

First, everything happens as though such syntagms (= to walk in the direction of the tree, to climb, etc.), which bore meaning from the point of view of the combinatory of the natural gestures we considered, once they were integrated into larger syntagms, were *desemantisized* and retained only their status of phonemes (i.e., minimal units of the plane of expression). It can therefore be said that the gestural syntagm is a combination of these units, which are sometimes actualized as a subprogram (of the order of the syllable without meaning), and sometimes as a program (of the order of the morpheme-word, having the dimension of one or several syllables, and bearing meaning).

Second, the problem of meaning is still not resolved, however. We can even say that since it can appear or disappear during the process of the observation of gesticulation, meaning more or less escapes us. We can therefore readily understand the position certain semioticians take in excluding *practical behavior* from their field of investigation (cf. current trends in American semiotics) and focusing all of their efforts on defining within gestural praxis only "significant behavior"[6] as opposed to the former (Rastier).

The difficulty here is the apparent impossibility of segmenting the gestural text into syntagms bearing signification, except through recourse to a semantics of natural languages. This difficulty even seems insurmountable as long as one remains at the level of spectator-sender, and as long as one considers that signification stands out on a person's horizon—that it is for a person. However, this difficulty can be resolved if the person is considered at the same time as the subject of signification and also as one who is capable of producing it for himself and for the human world.

Utterance and Enunciation

The fact that certain sequences of practical gestuality (the gestures of a skilled factory worker as well as techniques for clothing the body) are initially transmitted through apprenticeship before being reduced to the level of automatic gesticulation, while demonstrating their real ability to create cultural gaps, also confirms the phenomenon of desemantisization. This could appear unusual at first view. For example, even if the programmed syntagm *to tie one's tie* could be considered as made up of nonmeaningful utterances, taken as a whole within a cultural context it has a specific signification, not only for the spectator-receiver of the visual message, but especially, and also if one can give credence to the pathology of gesticulation, for the producing subject of the program itself. What would the form of apraxia that renders the subject incapable of carrying out the program *to tie one's tie*, but not the program *putting on one's pants* signify except the possibility of segmenting the plane of content through the procedure of commutation, and of asserting the program as an autonomous "sign"? No matter whether the content of the gestural syntagm happens to be conscious or unconscious—one knows that this dichotomy is not pertinent in linguistics—if, in either case, the given gestural program *is* a demarcated signifying block for the subject.

It is the introduction of the subject into the analysis of signification and not the quest for a problematic distinction between what is significant, or is not, in gestural behavior that seems to be able to account for the different forms the latter can assume. The same is true of Koechlin's extrasemiotic classifications following Haudricourt's example, which rests on the identification of gesticulatory functions and accords genetic priority to technical gestuality.

It is necessary to take up the now classical distinction between the *subject of utterance* and the *subject of enunciation*. At the level of linguistic semiotics it is known that these two subjects, although originally distinct—the *speaker* belonging to the nonlinguistic order of the communication process, as sender of messages, and the *verbal subject* of the order of linguistic discourse—can be syncretized in utterances of the type "I am walking," where "I" is at the same time the subject in the utterance and the subject of enunciation (for the moment we are excluding the problem of the referent). At the level of natural semiotics the two subjects remain distinct. In gestural praxis, man is the subject of the utterance while being a "he" for us. He is the "I" agent of the utterance, the subject of the functions making up his behavior. However, in *communicative* gestuality, man is the subject of the enunciation. He is a "you" for us, but an "I" for himself, insofar as he desperately attempts to produce utterances. But the two subjects are now situated within the same code of expression,[7] which results in *precluding their simultaneous presence*.

The weakness of what can be called gestural language *stricto sensu* seems to stem from the impossibility of syncretism between the subject of enunciation and the subject of utterance. The code of gestural communication does not allow for the elaboration of utterances, whereas gestural praxis projects the subject only as the subject of doing. It is therefore not surprising that artificial visual codes are composite constructs that, in order to become languages, must extract the elements making up utterances through procedures of imitative description.

The Human World

In this way, the integration of gestural praxis into the domain of "natural" semiotics both limits and increases the areas of investigation. It is limiting, since a *human world* is detached from the totality of the "natural" world, which is what is specific to each cultural community. Only those events of the world having people as *subjects* are part of such a semiotics; natural events (e.g., earthquakes) are excluded. The integration also extends the area of investigation considerably. It is from this very perspective that Julia Kristeva suggests opposing *productivity* to *communication*.[8] In postulating that its procedural and interpretative approaches could eventually account for the totality of human behavior (even if we limited our investigation, arbitrarily, to their visual manifestation in the sensible world), semiotics seems to be trying to take the place of the economic and historical sciences. By stating that gestural programs are meaningful, semiotics can no longer avoid this broader definition and must interpret *gestural discourse*, in which these programs are incorporated, as just so many *kinesic practices* that can account for the process of production. In turn, in one way or another, as these practices are an attempt by human beings to transform the world and since semiotics claims to be able to describe these transformations, it does therefore seem able to deal with the historical dimension of the human world.

We are fully aware of the distance separating what is theoretically conceivable and what is actually possible. These theoretical reflections, far from being proposed as methods to be substituted for those already in existence in the human sciences, are primarily destined to broaden the problematics of this "natural " dimension of semiotics being studied. Only in this way can the diverse and multiple manifestations of meaning be understood, interpreted, and integrated into a generalized theory of semiotics. Every other approach will result only in the arbitrary, pragmatic, and enumerative inventory of gestural language and practice.

Practical and Mythical Gestuality

When, in speaking about gestural syntagms, the expression gestural *praxis* was used (for the moment gestural *communication* has been excluded, and this will be dealt with in in the next section), it was taken in a very broad sense that included the uses of a person's own body to produce movements organized into programs having a project, an ordinary meaning. Thus, within this generalized programmed activity, a specifically *practical* gestuality can be distinguished that can be opposed to *mythical* gestuality. Indeed, these two activities, while sharing the plane of expression and the very general aim (i.e., the transformation of the world), between themselves divide up the significations of the world. Yet, at first glance they do this in an extremely complex way.

And so from the start, when speaking about the possible inventory of natural gestures, we have insisted on the need, by reducing them to figures, to divest these gestures of all signification that they necessarily have when they are described verbally. The same gestural figure such as *tilting the head and bending over forward from the waist up* can signify *to bend over* on the *practical* plane and *greeting* on the *mythical* plane without our having to accept the quite commonly accepted interpretation that what we have is a practical gesture with a mythical *connotation*. It is much easier to say that the very same gestural signifier, according to the context, can be incorporated either into a practical gestural syntagm (e.g., fieldwork) or into a mythical syntagm (dancing).

We have sought to justify this distinction between the mythical and practical planes by founding it on the dichotomy of *doing* and *wanting*. Thus, an elephant hunt, as a whole, taken as practical activity, can be opposed to a village preparing for a dance, considered as mythical activity. It does not matter if in dance there exist mimetic syntagms referring to practical gestuality; dance is not a spectacle trying to *communicate* meaning to those watching it, nor is dance an *objective* doing, but an *intentionality* transforming the world as such. For example, whether we are dealing, as in a dream, with the carrying out of a symbolic murder, in which case all one has to do is to superimpose the model on the practical program of the hunt for the activity to appear as a simple effect having its cause in mythical activity, or with a simple reflection of the former, for the subjects assuming it this is only a secondary interpretative process founded on a metasemiotic typology of cultures, and not the assertion of the logical priority of the mythical, with the practical being a simple connotation. The problem of priority automatically raises the presence of two opposing metaphysical attitudes that semiotics can do without.

Therefore, mythical gestuality, which is not a simple connotation of practical activities, must not be mistaken either for communicative gestuality, or for the mimetic procedures that can take place everywhere. Mythical gestuality does not for all that make up an autonomous semiotic plane. According to the cultures being considered, the two planes, mythical and practical, do share the domain of gestural praxis. In spite of this it is obvious that magical or liturgical algorithms, ritual or ceremonial discourses, have undeniable universal characteristics.

Once this dichotomy has been accepted, one can attempt to interpret the forms of *mixed* gestuality, where the mythical has been *diffused* in the practical, and vice versa. For example, at this level, the description of kinship structures, in addition to the predominantly mythical narrative structures of ceremonies, will need to take into account the diffuse manifestations of the mythical within practical behavior (intermittent manifestations of respect, of recognition, of domination, etc.). As Rastier has noted, this added presence of the mythical seems to be nothing more than pressure from the structures of content, axiomatized at the level of societies or of social groups, which inflect the programs of practical behavior without deforming them. This is the case regarding piety in Stendhal's religious community, expressed by eating slowly and lowering the eyes at the same time. It thus seems to follow that to describe the mythical as diffused in practical gestuality, one needs preliminary knowledge of the semantic code that it is supposed to signify.

Gestural Communication

The fundamental distinctions we have made by classifying, initially, all gestural phenomena according to the dichotomy *enunciation* vs. *utterance*, and, within the latter, distinguishing *practical* gestuality from *mythical* gestuality, enable us now to introduce complementary factors. We shall therefore attempt to bring order to the domain of *gesticulation* as "language." At first glance, this domain is hazy, since various elements—gestural signs and syntagms, their programs and their codes—whether natural or artificial are most often mixed and intermingled when they appear. Although we found this attempt at classification on the *dimensions of the gestural units*, we shall try and see how these various units are reshaped when they are incorporated and integrated into the communication processes, and to what extent they can be transformed into autonomous codes or gestural languages.

Attributive Gestuality

Most semioticians agree about the relative poverty of gestural inventories listing those units we consider specifically destined for communication. We have attempted to account partially for this poverty by attributing it to the impossibility for the subject of the enunciation to be at the same time the subject of the utterance when it is the sender of communication.[9]

We are now obliged to attenuate somewhat our opinion about the weakness of linguistic communication—while maintaining that it keeps its value as distinctive criteria—by recognizing the existence of an area of signification whose content can actually be communicated because of the code of expression underlying the mobile manifestations of the human body. This area of signification covers what are commonly designated as fundamental attitudes and interior states, such as fear and anger, joy and sadness. In short, these are simply coded significations according to our first definition of *meaning*, namely, a configuration of expression that functions as a *reference to another configuration*, that of content instituting human nature as meaning. Besides the fact that human nature so signified seems to be assimilated to "the animal soul" (which, according to Chomsky, excludes the referential code from the domain where the faculty of language is operative), its mode of existence and its functioning can enlighten us about the specific properties of the code of gestural communication.

Since the human body, as signifier, is treated as a configuration, it is normal to expect that its mobility will be considered as mainly creating positional gaps and that this polarization of movements will end up in the parallel categorization of contents. In addition to the fact that on the plane of content this valorizes what are commonly called *attitudes*, at the expense of gestures (and this explains, for example, why Robert Cresswell chose the inchoative position of gesture and not movements to describe manual gestures),[10] we have also accounted for the *semiosis* that characterizes communicative gestuality. This consists in establishing a correlation between a phemic category belonging to the plane of expression[11] and a semic[12] category at the plane of content. This correlation is both arbitrary and constant. For example, there are no "natural" reasons for the relationship between *closed* vs. *open* eyes and a semantic opposition such as *ruse* vs. *innocence* (Rastier); nonetheless the relationship is necessary and restrictive in a given cultural context.

It can be noted that the contents that are so expressed are only stated as *word-phrases* or interjections, as they are also called. As the implicit subject of the utterance is always the subject of the enunciation (he is unable to recount the world and speaks in soliloquy only to himself), since (in communication) the implicit verb is one of *being* and not of *doing*, the synthetic utterance so formulated is in fact attributive, qualitative, and not predicative. What was mentioned earlier concerning the inability of communicative gestuality to produce utterances—utterances about the world or about the doing of humans—is consequently borne out by the existence of this attributive subcode.

Note: This is where *deictic* gestuality, which is attributive by nature, must also be classed.

Modal Gestuality

The acknowledgment that the correlation between the categories of expression and those of content remains constant within a given cultural context enables us to set out our observations on communicative gestuality by starting from considerations regarding content, and not, as would normally be the case for any other semiotic text, from the plane of expression.

If therefore starting from content we attempted to find the common denominator that would enable us to bring together the varied and/or redundant data presented by Paolo Fabbri, Clelia Hutt, and Rastier, and also what is known about this form of gestuality, it could be said that they all agree with respect to the status of communication and of utterance.

By *status of communication*, we mean a specific structure of content, which can be seen in gestural behaviors (sometimes concerned only with the motor function of the body, and sometimes making wider use of the ambient space), which aims at establishing, at *maintaining*, or at *breaking off communication* between human beings and which is therefore different from other gestural programs because of its specific intentionality. Clearly the linguistic or nonlinguistic type of communication defined in this way is independent of the objective conditions that establish it. The following approximative and illustrative inventory will clarify this.

1. Soviet research on ceremonials (Tatjana Tsivjan), which studies the beginning (and ending) of nonlinguistic communication, gives a perfect example of the setting into correlation of categories of *social content* such as *inferior* vs. *subordinate*, *young* vs. *old*, *man* vs. *woman* diversifying interhuman contact, with categories of *expression* such as *seated* vs. *standing*, bowing *accompanied by a smile* vs. *not accompanied by a smile*, *handshake* vs. *nonhandshake*;

2. American research in proxemics (Fabbri [13]) deals with the exploitation of *interhuman* space; the categories *near* vs. *far*, the relative position of the speaker's bodies, *face to face* vs. *back to back* or *right lateral* vs. *left oblique* (see also Proca-Ciortea and Giurchescu's study on the same problems related to the description of dancing) are set into correlation with categories on content such as *acceptance* vs. *refusal of communication*, or *euphoria* vs. *dysphoria* in which communication is initiated or continued;

3. Research carried out by Hutt [14] has demonstrated the existence (in addition to the topological structuring of space) of categories of expression such as *prospectivity* vs. *retrospectivity* of bodily movements, *opening* vs. *closing* of arm gestures, in correlation with *desire* vs. *refusal of communication* or of understanding.

By the *status of the utterance* we mean, following Jakobson, the set of the modalities of judgment that can be made about an utterance, such as *consent* vs. *refusal*, *certitude* vs. *doubt*, and *surprise* vs. *ruse*, and do not take into account their manifestation, at the grammatical level, within linguistic semiotics. It should be noted on this very point that only modal categories can make up autonomous gestural microcodes, functioning without the help of speech or gestural utterances of a mimetic order. This is the case for the microcode of *denegation* vs. *assertion* studied by Jakobson, but also for the microcode of traffic officers, *forbidden* vs. *authorized*, founded on the same category but in fact formulated differently. The reason is very simple: Their use presupposes that communication is already established and that the speakers are also interchangeable. In addition, it also presupposes that one of the speakers refuses or accepts the utterance formulated by the other.

The preceding discussion brings us to the following conclusion: The dichotomy, gestures of *accompaniment* vs. gestures of *substitution*, often used as a criterion for classifying gestuality (Cresswell), does not seem pertinent. Indeed, the type of communicative gestuality (which according to Cresswell can be interchanged) we have just outlined represents just one of the many possible complex communication programs, one of the many possible gestural practices, except that it is exclusively founded on the intention of communicating. Taken out of its programmed context, a modal category, instead of signifying acceptance or refusal, gives the idea of the effort made by a subject to chase away bothersome flies, whereas a proxemic category could make one think of an impatient child stamping about who dares neither to admit his needs nor, in the best of cases, to dance. On the other hand, when a gesture, considered inseparable from language and not interchangeable with it, is removed from its spoken context and integrated, for example into pantomime, can we be certain that it has lost all signification? The procedure of substitution that was proposed as a criterion for classification implicitly rests on a concept of the conscious apprehension of meaning, which, we well know, is not applicable in semiotics.

In regarding gestuality as programming communication, one might add that since gestuality is of the order of enunciation, utterance is, in fact, its presupposed term. Since the subject of enunciation cannot at the same time produce gestural utterances, this form of gestuality cannot happen independently and autonomously insofar as the content it is supposed to transmit must appear in another semiotic form. And this form can only be a natural language or, to a degree, an artificial gestural code.

Mimetic Gestuality

This fundamental inability of gestuality to form a semiotic code of communication that is both comprehensive and autonomous again comes to the fore when another of its manifestations, mimetic gestuality, is examined. By this we mean a certain gestural manifestation of contents, with the aim of transmitting them to a spectator-receiver. However, since this first definition is extremely vague it should be refined by reflections on the specific semiotic status of mimetic gestuality.

1. The contents, or objects, of communication have the dimension of "sememes"; they can be either nouns (*pistol*) or functions (*to asperse*).

2. In order that the contents be gestually encoded, they are taken up at the level

of their *expression*: It is not the sign *pistol* or the sign *to asperse* that is transposed, but only its signifier (Rastier).

3. Gestural transposition presupposes the existence of a semiotics having de jure and de facto precedence that has already been articulated into *signs*. This transpostion can take place either starting from a semiotics of "natural" signs (this is the case in the example of pistol given by Rastier), or from noncommunicative gestural practice (the mythical gesture of aspersion, cited by Hutt).

4. In principle, the transpositon takes place not at the level of the substance of expression (phonetic), but at the level of its *form* (phonological). As a result, this reduces the signifier to an elementary figure (the hand with index finger pointing for pistol, a long slim line to designate Cresswell's runner) and takes the elementary gesture out of its context (absence of instrument and mythical program in the case of aspersion).

5. Transposition results in *identifying the sign, by means of its signifier*, with the human body; at the same time the sign is supposed to be the subject of the enunciation and since it can produce only attributive utterances, it is *unable* to signal the articulation of the utterance, that is, *to be at one and the same time the sign and its syntax*. Hence the absence of autonomy of mimetic gestuality that always is found either accompanied by natural language or integrated, in a discontinuous fashion, with artificial codes of communication (e.g., the codes of silent monks, or pantomime).

We can take up our definition once again and say that, in fact, mimetic gestuality is simply an inventory of gestural signs that have at the level of content the dimensions of *sememes* and, at the level of expression, the dimensions of *figures*. These signs are also obtained by the transposition of the signifier taken from a preexisting perceivable substance into the gestural substance of the human body.

This transposition from substance to substance, at first glace, should probably have a number of exceptions. Yet, this does not hold up to careful analysis. This is the case with the example cited by Cresswell of the gesture *rotundity* accompanying the utterance in natural language, "It walks." The interpretation he gives of this will help us to illustrate the definition we have just given.

An identical content, the subject's confident attitude, is here manifested through two different figures: a figure of *content* representing the quick *linear progression* of walking and a figure of *expression*, mobile rotundity, probably the figurative reduction of a *wheel* or of a moving machine. Although it does confirm two of our previous observations (that the figures of expression of the natural world correspond to the figures of content of natural languages, and that gestural transposition takes place at the level of the form of expression [of the figures] and not at that of the substance), this example simply emphasizes that mimetic gestuality, even when it accompanies speech, is not a simple illustration of the latter — for if this were the case, its figures would always be isomorphic with those of the content of natural languages. Rather, mimetic gestuality actually corresponds to *the transposition of one visual semiotics into another*.

In a second example, again from Cresswell, a speaker, talking about someone's constitution, accompanies his linguistic considerations with a gesture representing a linear, lean, and mobile figure. Referring to the status of the speaker, who happens to be a physical education teacher, Cresswell justly remarks that the mediation between these two identical contents manifested in different ways must pass through the visual image of the runner whose lean silhouette, in our terminology, is only a figurative reduction. If this example lends itself to the same interpretation as the previous one—with the difference that it would be difficult for us to say, at first glance, what the *figure* of the content of the sememe "constitution" would be (for example, one can see that in the code studied by Hutt the content *God* is visualized by means of the figure of a triangle, before being transposed into gesture)—it nonetheless points to the existence of a certain *stylistic distance* between the content of a sign and its figure at the level of expression.

This immanent stylistics appears to the naked eye when, abandoning accompanying gestures, we begin to concentrate on artificial signs. Analyzing the formation of the "composite words" of an artificial code, Hutt cites the example of *bee*, the content of which is manifested by *two* figures of expression: the figure *wing* and the figure *sweet*. The first figure at the moment it takes on form passes from the content *wing* to the content *that which flies*, whereas the second one takes a much more complicated trajectory as it passes from the content *sweetness* taken as a property of sweet objects, to the content *honey*. A subject of the class of sweet objects, *honey* is considered to be result of the customary habit of that which flies. It is only as such that the figure *sweet* can act as a determinant specifying the class of beings that fly signified by the first figure, and therefore, in its canonical form, make up the definition of bee by genus and species.

If we did stop for a moment to imagine the semantic trajectory brought about by the crossing of two gestural figures, it was (1) to show the complexity of the procedures set into play in producing a gestural text, procedures that are specific to every figurative manifestation and, for example, link pantomime to poetic language; but it was also (2) to underscore the difficulties encountered with very elementary visual syntax, reduced to a simple linear distribution of figures because of the absence of demonstrable semantic universals. From this perspective this is comparable to the syntax of dreams described by Freud and analyzed by Emile Benveniste.

Ludic Gestuality

Until now we have been considering gestuality from the point of view of the possibility of *communication* by means of the gestural code. Along the way, *two types of gestural units* having different dimensions were identified: Some were of the order of phemes or semes, whereas others were of the order of phonemes or sememes. Now we must examine the possibility of integrating larger units within the process of communication, utterances or gestural discourses whose existence became apparent when examining gestural praxis.

Here the problem becomes more complicated because it seems to imply putting into question both the previous semiotic definition of very general categories such as *sacred* vs. *ludic* vs. *aesthetic*, which are not characteristic of gestural semiotics but which also arise at the level of natural languages, for example, when poetic language is opposed to sacred language or, more simply, to ludic phenomena such as witticisms or cross-words. These categories depend on a typology that is both intra- and intercultural. If we could accept these categories as data (because they are obvious or because they have already been defined within the framework of a general semiotic theory), then it would be simple to see manifestations of sacred gestuality in dances held in so-called archaic societies, aesthetic gestuality in ballet, and finally ludic gestuality in folk dance. Unfortunately this is far from being the case.

Paragenetic considerations could clarify this somewhat. We deliberately classified sacred dance as belonging to mythical gestural practice. Another form of this mythical gestuality, which appears in acrobatic acts, can be found within the framework of circus activity. The presence of the animal world and the narrative sequences of taming make it possible to interpret this form of mythical gestuality in much the same way as one would the mythical procedures of symbolic murder, that is, as an archaic universe still surviving in modern times. Within such a context, folk dance would have the same status as folktale does in relationship to mythical narrative.

This leads to the formulation of the hypothesis that *all programmed gestuality exceeding the dimensions of sememe/phoneme, insofar as it is used in communication, is mythical in origin.* Even more so, this programmed gestuality, on the axis of communication, is an actual transposition of utterances and gestural programs having an implicitly mythical content. A semiotic dichotomy will help to consolidate the previous a priori classification: (see the accompanying tabulation).

Sacred	*Ludic*	*Aesthetic*
noncommunication	both communication and noncommunication	communication
mythical praxis	e.g., folk dance	e.g., ballet

We can now say that ballet as a gestural praxis that primarily attempts to communicate and not transform the contents expressed is opposed to "archaic" dance, which is a gestural praxis without intention of communicating but with the intention of transforming the contents expressed. Folk dance occupies an intermediary position, insofar as it is both explicit communication for the spectators and for the participants, and implicitly a mythical doing. It is within this framework that the Catholic church's liturgical reform can be interpreted, since an attempt has been made to transform the Mass, which had become a pure spectacle, by reconfirming it with the same status of community participation as in a mythical doing.

What also supports the hypothesis according to which the units of ludic communication are the transposed units of mythical doing (and not of practical doing) is the often-noted fact that such spectacles have gesticulatory gaps and distortions when compared with the norms of natural or practical gestuality. Instead of considering acrobatics, but also certain aspects of aesthetic or folk dance, as being made up of stylistic gaps in comparison to "nature," it would be simpler to see them as normal manifestations of "culture" present in mythical utterances, even though they might be partially or entirely desemantisized.

The general problem, previously raised, of the meaning of utterances and gestural programs comes up at this point once again. We reexamine the specific status of *semiosis* later; it suffices for the moment to indicate how the problem can be stated when, for example, one is dealing with the interpretation of popular dance. In a restrictive manner, two approaches enabling us to circumvent the difficulties encountered now can be perceived.

The first of these approaches, as simple hypothesis, would consist in recognizing the existence of *organized gestural discourses* comparable to the narrative structures of linguistic discourses. This gestural discourse therefore could be reduced to *multiple variable formal* models that although formal, could be semantically interpreted and provide the general framework for the understanding of gestural discourse. This is the route that seems to have been adopted by the international team of scholars working on the formal description of folk dance, as long, of course, as such a description is followed by semantic interpretation. And so the description of acrobatic acts undertaken by Paul Bouissac allows us to hope that narrative syntagms comparable to those of folktale will be derived.

A second approach would be to analyze the *modal categories relative to the status of communication* discussed earlier in this chapter using a more paradigmatic type of procedure to find out the degree to which the identification of their correlated content can help understand an implicit mythical *code*. At the level of units of the phoneme/sememe type, which could be designated in this particular case as dancemes, one can then ask if the hypothesis concerning the parallelism between the figures of gestural expression and those of linguistic content, after taking all the necessary precautions, cannot be used to identify their implicit content.

Nonetheless, there remains a theoretical problem previously raised related to the desemantization that is always possible, namely, of the elements making up gestural utterance. As for gestuality having an aesthetic dimension, in ballet, for example (and we recognize the nature of its composite artificial code made up of, among other things, mimetic sequences, and in particular since the spectacle is in its entirety only an utterance produced by the subject of enunciation, the choreographer, we can now ask if the "desacralization" of mythical discourse has not brought about the desemantization of the gestural utterances, thus leaving aesthetic gestuality with only the narrative forms of discourse to signify.

Gestural Communications

We have just carried out a general survey of gestuality using a limited number of structural criteria and semantic categories. In doing so we investigated various forms of gestuality by specifically limiting ourselves to the point of view of communication. First of all we identified two types of gestuality:

1. The gestuality of direct communication and
2. The gestuality of transposition.

The first of these types, whose semiotic status is defined by the *correlation of the categories* signified/signifier, can be subdivided according to the syntactic possibility of forming utterances or of modulating utterances of the type:

a. Attributive gestuality and
b. Modal gestuality.

The second type of gestuality, which could be investigated only in the intent of communication through procedures of the *transposition of signifiers*, in turn can be subdivided, according to the dimension of the transposable units (signs or utterances), into

a. Mimetic gestuality and
b. Ludic gestuality.

The hypothetical and arbitrary nature in determining this last class of gestuality is both inevitable and important in our present state of knowledge. However, we believe that it does not excessively interfere with the general thrust of our project, which is to attempt to work out an intrinsic classification of the forms of gestuality, founded on semiotic definitions alone.

Along the way, we also tried to point out the inability of communication theory to account satisfactorily for gestural phenomena. Although they can be identified, the categories and gestural units are not autonomous since they can indeed signify attributively and modally but they cannot transfer objective contents. Nowhere are they constituted into a system of signification comparable to linguistic systems. However, they do lend themselves to the elaboration of artificial codes (mimetic and ludic) that, insofar as they are used as codes for practical communication, are simply pale reflections of linguistic communication because of their extreme weakness. When, on the contrary, they are constituted as codes of communication of mythical content, gestural forms move away from linguistic communication and take on a new consistency because of the appearance of a functional and narrative organizing principle that regulates all discourse, whether it happens to be of the order of saying or doing.

Semiosis

The preceding reflections have partially cleared the way, since what initially appeared confused now appears complex. In this last stage, it now should be possible to study the conditions of analysis and of description of gestuality, if both are subjected to a *prior investigation* on *the nature of the semiosis that can define gestuality as a presence before a signifying world*. If initially we do not ask questions about the particular status of gestuality, we run the risk of implementing only transpositions of methodological models—models we can get, for example, from the theory of communication—and simply end up with negative results about their appropriateness. Therefore, when we investigated gestural communication we concluded that in the best of cases it was only a limited and secondary phenomenon, in no way comparable to the semantic universe embraced by the entire imaginable corpus of gestural praxis.

The Production and Manifestation of Text

When one tries at this level of semiosis to imagine a possible analysis of gestural text, it is tempting to apply the well-known and tested procedures of phonological description and consider gestuality as the plane of expression of a language. Koechlin invites us to do this when he suggests that we use the program of phonation as an analogical model to interpret the complex operations of the human body producing phoneme-gestures and then, through retroanalysis, that we identify their phemic structure. Although we accept that this line of reasoning is on the whole accurate, we think, however, that Koechlin has not pushed it to its ultimate conclusion.

We readily admit that the programmed motor functions of the phonatory organs are comparable to the programmed gesticulation of the human organism. We also admit that they have the same spatial characteristics and that they appear in the same way as a network of spatial relationships. But as soon as the results of the two gesticulatory programs are compared (whether in the first case, with the production of the spoken chain articulated into phonemes, or in the second, with the production of a gestural sequence one would like to segment into gestures), the difference can clearly be seen. The same holds true for the piano player's gestural program producing an analyzable sequence of musical sounds, as well as for the speaking subject's program. In both cases, the two gestural programs— phonatory and musical—result in the *transposition* of a signifier of one sensorial order into another, the transposition of the visual order into sound. It is even possible to say that in both these cases, from the point of view of the form of expression, the two signifiers (visual and sound), as configurations of the independent relations of the manifest substance, are comparable and in certain conditions can be considered equivalent. However, no transposition whatsoever takes place in semiotic gestuality where the program of manifestation is *at one and the same time* the manifested sequence. It is possible, for example, when examining the phonological structure of a sound text, to claim that the *meaning* of the prior phonatory program is in the construction of those very phonological objects that phonemes and syllables happen to be, and that the program, as a whole, made up of sequences and concomitances along its entire trajectory, is governed by this phonological *project*. On the contrary, the observable gestural sequence (as semiotic text) is only the expressed program, without the phonological project.

It should be evident that the interpretation of certain specific gestural programs as being able to establish a new order of expression through transposition is simply a different way of considering the problem of the arbitrary nature of the semiotic function and the paralleling of the two planes of language. This makes certain languages, and notably natural languages, appear as an overlapping of two non-isomorphic algebras. In other words, it is the transposition of a sensorial order into another one that actually creates the necessary conditions for an autonomous articulation of the signifier whose figures take on independence in relation to the figures of content. And on the contrary, as long as such a transposition has not taken place, the signification of the world does not succeed in becoming completely independent of its phenomenal plane.

The Symbolic Status of Gestuality

Because at this stage it is impossible to envisage for gestuality an autonomous level of expression and at the same time the elaboration of a visual phonology, we should confine ourselves to gestural units that have been analyzed both into phonemes and sememes (cf. Koechlin's natural gestures). Moreover, for the time being at least, gestuality, according to Hjelmslev's terminology, should be considered a *symbolic and not a linguistic system*, even though nothing prevents us from postulating the existence of a gestural *form* within gestural substance, if such is the case.

We have said that this form could be obtained from the substance that the global volume of a natural gesture happens to be, through reduction to a minimal *visual figure* by varying the possible gestural contexts. A natural gesture such as *to swim* will have the meaning *swimming* at the level of practical behavior, if the subject is a swimmer and water is the environment. Yet, as Bremond remarks,[15] Superman flying through the air maintains the same gesture *to swim* as gestural predicate. Nonetheless, it is only by starting from the content of natural languages when attempting to describe the semic figure embraced by the lexeme *to swim* in the expression "I am (swimming) completely out of my depth" that one perhaps can see more readily that this figure can be reduced to an erratic movement of body limbs.

The reaffirmation that the visual figures of gestural expression correspond to the nuclear figures of linguistic content can now be incorporated into a wider interpretation. If the plane of *expression* of natural languages is made up of gestural programs (for example, phonatory) and following the transposition of the former into a different sensorial order (for example, auditory), the plane of *content* is, in part, made up by these same nontransposed gestural programs producing complex semiotic systems articulated on both planes.

Now, when establishing an equivalent between figures of the natural world and figures of content of natural languages (gestural figures must be completed by other visual figures of the world, and in turn, the latter by all the figures of all the sensorial orders by which we apprehend the world), we can, among other things and up to a point, analogically use semantic models. Thus, just as the figures of content are not in themselves sufficient to establish the linguistic text and therefore must be organized by categories, in the same way we can surmise that gestural praxis not only consists of the successive deployment of gestural figures, but indeed implies the establishment of a certain number of semantic categories, beginning with the *practical* vs. *mythical* dichotomy that, in part, formed the basis of our previous classification. On the other hand, along with the analysis of the nuclear figures of content into semes and the establishment of semic categories, we can imagine either the existence of an inventory of gestural categories, the combination of which would account for the constitution of gestural figures, or the possibility in the coupled figures of setting aside all the gestural traits in the interest of a single pertinent category, and thus explaining the makeup of the gestural microcodes of communication.

The Functional Status of Gestural Semiosis

When we raised the issue of the gestural programs of the phonatory organs, we stated that their meaning consisted in carrying out a phonological project. This observation now can be generalized and clarified. Although it is possible to imagine uncoordinated and meaningless gesticulatory activity in the same way as it is possible to emit a series of meaningless sounds taken from language, it is equally obvious that there does exist programmed, ordered gestural activity that can be apprehended and defined only by means of its *project*. We therefore shall say here that the gestural program's project is its signified[16] and that the gestural sequence embracing this signified is its signifier. Consequently the *semiosis* of a gestural program will be in the *relation between a sequence of gestural figures* taken as the signifier, and *the gestural project* considered as the signified. This rather cursory affirmation must be clarified.

The shifting of the semiotic relation that although starting from a signified having constant dimensions, ends up associating it with signifiers having variable dimensions is not surprising since in a natural language, a single phoneme (e.g., *i*) can constitute a sign, but it can also make up a syllable (*ile*) or be part of a syllabic sequence (*ilex*).

The progressive extension of the signifier is accompanied by a phenomenon designated by the term *desemantisization*. Thus if we segment the gestural program of a worker in front of a machine into textual units, we can identify gestural figures, each of which can be given a semantic interpretation and refer back to a natural gesture. Yet, this segmented motivation of the figures disappears in their programmed progression, without the figures themselves having been in any way attained, although they have been "emptied of meaning." It is in this way that following Kristeva, we can speak of the anaphoric nature of gestuality since gestural figures all refer back to a meaning that is there only in the mode of project. Because desemantisization leaves the gestural figures intact, it concerns only the semantic categories underlying the gestural text. By neutralizing the partial signifieds it transforms the immediate semiotic relation into a semiotic distance having the status of hypotactic relation, and each desemantisized gestural figure maintains its metonymic position in relation to the program's global signified.

One can therefore see that the semiosis we are dealing with here is not a simple relation between a signifier and a signified, but a relational structure designated elsewhere as *morphematic*;[17] that is, it is *both a relation between a signifier and a signified taken as a whole* (the gestural program) *and a network of relations going from the signified to each figure as a part*.

In addition to the existence of a project, the program presupposes the concept of *economy*. A gesture can be more or less economical, more restricted or more amplified, and in addition it can have interspersed subprograms. An arbitrary element, whose functional nature can be specified only after we have reached a better understanding of the organizing principles of gestural programs, is thus introduced into the already complex structure of semiosis.

These observations concerning the status of semiosis in gestural praxis must eventually be linked with questions concerning the predicative contents of natural languages, and this is normal. In addition to the correspondences already established between the figures of the gestural signifier and those of the signified of natural languages, the appearance of a new area of comparison enables us to specify the functional nature (the term function being reserved for all *nonattributive predicates*) of gestural semiotics. We have to subscribe to Kristeva's observation that the analysis of gestuality uncovers not basic units but basic *functions*, provided it is understood that the problematics of the functions (semiosis, program, project, economy, etc.), though characteristic of gestuality, also comes up as such at the level of the analysis of the content of natural languages, where a long-standing, nominalistic, reifying tradition, entirely centered on proper nouns, from time immemorial has shaded over the original semiotic status of the function by even reducing it to a simple formal relation.

It is in this very spirit that a call for a *functional semiotics* — the only possible approach to gestural semiotics, but also a dimension of the semantics of natural languages — takes on its entire signification.

Cultural Projects and Objects

We can consider gestural praxis as a transitive predication that, having humans as sole subjects, has also as its general function the carrying out of cultural projects that end up creating cultural objects.

Considered from the point of view of *cultural projects*, the different gestural programs seem to be closed discourses whose content analysis can explicate only a particular type of narrative structure. They can be represented as models of a practical or mythical knowing-how-to-do whose organization could account for a certain mode of existence of so-called economic and cultural structures.

Considered from the point of view of their results, which are *cultural objects*, gestural programs appear to be genetic definitions of things and events (a dress can be defined by the program *to sew a dress*). Moreover, semantic programs, at the level of natural languages, could be defined in the same way as literary objects (novel or poem). It should be noted that cultural objects, once they have been produced, in turn can be seen as morphomatic structures (an automobile can be reduced to parts and subparts, each having in turn a gestural subprogram from the point of view of genetic definition). Be that as it may, gestural praxis, which is by nature predicative, appears as a syntax able to produce an infinite number of utterances in the form of cultural objects and events, which are circumstantial in nature.

A cultural object can be determined by its use, that is to say, its function as helper (tool) or substitute for a subject (machine) that it can take on in a new gestural program along with its genetic and morphomatic definitions. This new functionality of objects can in turn enable one to envisage either a hierarchy of gestural programs and knowing-how-to-do or the establishment of the cultural dimensions of a given society simply defined as so many isotopies of practical and mythical knowing-how-to-do (alimentary, vestimentary, etc.). However, the introduction of these new considerations goes beyond the limited framework initially set up for this study.

Symbolic Notations

The important possibilities opened up by this reflection on semiosis in semiotic research on gesturality unfortunately remain largely unexplored and will probably remain so as long as a satisfactory graphic code of transposition has not been worked out.

The examples discussed by Koechlin of the *symbolic* notation of gestures, in spite of their cleverness, are in their infancy when compared with the importance of the problem. Koechlin seems to think that a greater degree of arbitrariness of the notational signs should help solve the problems related to the phonological description of the gestural signifier, and for him this appears to be a sufficient reason to exclude from his study the notational system proposed by American kinesics. Perhaps he is not wrong from a historical perspective, since the slow and groping elaboration of writing does point to a certain correlation between progress of the arbitrary symbolic and improvement in the transposition. Nonetheless, the slowness of the development can be explained by the necessity at the same time to invent an implicit phonology having precedence over notation. One can suppose that the existence today of comparable linguistic models must force us to reverse the terms of the inventive process and, in giving precedence to methodological reflection over notation itself, speed up the solution to the problem of transposition.

This is the very reason why we have concentrated especially on the *identification of the units* and on their semiotic status. If the new ways of preserving gestuality (film) are not adequate (in spite of recent infatuation with what is called audio-visual, which corresponds to the two recordable dimensions of the sensible world) to meet the needs of semiotics, it is because these means *register* only gestuality and do not carry out an *analysis* of text beforehand. Thus gestuality cannot be reproduced, that is to say manipulated like a scientific language. Consequently, gestural notation must not only meet the practical requirements of simplifying recordings but must be optimized to be a support for scientific investigation.

The three notations presented by Koechlin that situate description at the level of *substance* err on the side of excessive precision and detail. They are supposed to describe gestural units having the dimensions of phemic traits, yet they offer over a hundred symbols. When one thinks that phonetic writing requires only a few dozen phonemes-symbols and that the number of pertinent phemic features is by necessity much lower than that of phonemes, then it can be said that the notation of gestuality is decidedly on the wrong track. It would seem necessary to tackle the problem from another angle and begin with a simple notational system, by choosing simple gestural figures as units of description and by trying, in this way, to make phonematic writing more manageable, although it may mean complicating it later on for the purpose of specific descriptions.

The approach proposed by Bremond, which consists in starting from the known semantic functions of narrative to establish their corresponding elementary gestural invariants, seems very promising and should be generalized.

This is the direction taken by Koechlin, who asserts that the entire human body is engaged in producing gesture but nonetheless states the need to extract a small number of pertinent features from this gestural mass. One could also explore Cresswell's suggestion that the human appearance is characterized by a displacement of the center of gestural activity from the face and mouth in animals, toward the arms and hands. Accordingly one might therefore envisage using the notation of a fundamental gestuality where only hand-arm or leg-foot gestures would be considered in order to establish a provisional classification. This could be completed later by an inventory of diacritical signs that would note complementary features as well as features belonging to gesticulatory substance and that are often important as stylistic variables in the notation of inter- or intracultural differences. Otherwise, by attempting to note everything, ultimately one ends up noting nothing at all.

The task before us is not an easy one, for it is only when an appropriate notational symbolic system has been worked out that it will be possible to seriously undertake the elaboration of a semiotics of the natural world, the *sine qua non* for the success of the entire semiotic undertaking.

Chapter 3
The Interaction of
Semiotic Constraints

One should beware of believing the inventive mind operates
according to chance.

Destutt de Tracy

Explanatory Note: Perhaps out of a desire for intelligibility, we can imagine that, in order to achieve the construction of cultural objects (literary, mythical, pictorial, etc.), the human mind begins with simple elements and follows a complex trajectory, encountering on its way both constraints to which it must submit and choices it is able to make.

Our aim is to give a rough idea of this trajectory. We can consider that it moves from immanence to manifestation in three principal stages: (1) *Deep structures* define the fundamental mode of existence of an individual or a society, and subsequently the conditions of existence of semiotic objects. As far as we know, the elementary constituents of deep structures have a definable logical status. (2) *Surface structures* constitute a semiotic grammar system that arranges the contents susceptible of manifestation into discursive forms. The end products of this system are independent of the expression that manifests them, insofar as they can theoretically appear in any substance and, in the case of linguistic objects, in any language. (3) *The structures of manifestation* produce and organize the signifiers. Although they can include quasi-universals, they remain specific to any given language (or more precisely they define the specific characteristics of languages) or to any given material. They are studied by the surface stylistics of lexemes, shapes, colors, etc.

We are concerned here with only the first stage of this global trajectory.

The Structure of the Constitutional Model

The Elementary Structure of Signification

If the signification S (the universe as a signifying whole, or any semiotic system) appears, at the level of its initial apprehension, as a semantic axis, it is opposed to $\bar{S}$, taken as an absolute absence of meaning, and contradictory to the term S.

If we accept that the semantic axis S (substance of content) is articulated, at the level of the form of the content, in two contrary semes

$$s_1 \;<\!\text{-}\text{-}\text{-}\text{-}\!>\; s_2 \;,$$

these two semes, taken separately, point to the existence of their contradictory terms:

$$\bar{s}_1 \;<\!\text{-}\text{-}\text{-}\text{-}\!>\; \bar{s}_2 \;.$$

Allowing for the fact that, after its semic articulations have been set in place, S may be redefined as a complex seme uniting s_1 and s_2; in a double relation of *disjunction* and *conjunction*, the elementary structure of meaning may be represented as:

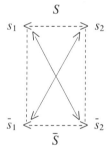

$<\!\text{-}\text{-}\text{-}\text{-}\!>$: relation between contraries
$<\!\!\longrightarrow$: relation between contradictories
$\text{-}\text{-}\text{-}\text{-}\text{-}\text{-}$: relation of implication.[1]

This model uses a small number of undefined concepts: (1) the concepts of conjunction and disjunction necessary for interpreting the structural *relation*; and (2) two types of disjunction, the disjunction of *contraries* (indicated by dashed lines) and the disjunction of *contradictories* (indicated by solid lines).

Note: The preceding model is simply a reworked formulation of the one formerly proposed by the author in *Sémantique structurale*. This new presentation makes it possible to compare the model to Robert Blanché's *logical hexagon* (see Claude Chabrol, "Structures intellectuelles," in *Information sur les Sciences sociales*, 1957, VI-5) as well as to the structures called the Klein group in mathematics and the Piaget group in psychology.

By taking into consideration only the form of the content and only simple semic terms, we can give a slightly different formulation to the same structure. It appears then as the correlating of two paired categories, the correlation itself being defined as a relation of homologized contradictions:

$$\frac{s_1}{\bar{s}_1} \simeq \frac{s_2}{\bar{s}_2} \, .$$

This new presentation allows us to see that the structure permitting an account of the mode of existence of signification, as a constitutional model of the invested contents, finds its application in extremely varied domains. This is indeed the model of myth proposed by Lévi-Strauss, in the form of the achronic articulation of the folktale, as well as the model justifying a certain number of particular semantic universes (Georges Bernanos, Stéphan Mallarmé, Antoine Destutt de Tracy). For the semiotician it is comforting to note that a deductive approach encounters empirically constructed models that can account for the limited corpora.

The Structure of Semiotic Systems

If deductive considerations thus encounter inductive descriptions, it is because *the elementary structure of signification* forms the semantic universes taken as a whole into systems. Indeed, as a semantic axis, each of the contents it defines can include others, which are in turn organized into a structure isomorphic to the next structure up in the hierarchy. Thus, the elementary structure articulates the semes and the constituent systematic instances of semiotic systems in the same way. For example, the contents *life* and *death* embrace the whole semantic universe of Bernanos's works, that is, S_1 vs. S_2. Each one is articulated into two systematic instances (negative and positive definitions) that are transcribed, respectively, s_1 vs. $\bar{s}_2$; s_2 vs. $\bar{s}_1$. They are articulated in turn into semic systems.

Let us first define the formal properties of the constitutional model; then we shall give examples of investments.

The *terms* of the model: Starting from each of the four terms, by means of the two operations—the *contradictory* and the *contrary*—we can obtain the others. Their definition is formal and prior to any investment.

The *relations*:

1. *Hierarchical*:
   A hyponymic relation is established between s_1, s_2, and S; another between $\bar{s}_1$, $\bar{s}_2$, and $\bar{S}$.

2. *Categorical*:
A relation of *contradiction* is established between S and $\bar{S}$; and at the hierarchically inferior level, between s_1 and $\bar{s}_1$, between s_2 and $\bar{s}_2$.

A relation of *contrariety* articulates s_1 and s_2 on the one hand and $\bar{s}_1$ and $\bar{s}_2$ on the other. In Hjelmslev's own terms, it may be identified as solidarity, or double presupposition.

Note: The two operations, that of taking the contradictory and that of taking the contrary, are involutive: The contrary of the contrary of s is s; the contradictory of the contradictory of s is s.

A relation of *implication* is established between s_1 and $\bar{s}_2$ on the one hand, and s_2 and $\bar{s}_1$ on the other: s_2 implies $\bar{s}_1$; s_1 implies $\bar{s}_2$, or the inverse.

The *dimensions*: By their relational definitions, the semic terms are paired and grouped in six systematic dimensions. We can distinguish:

1. Two *axes*, S and $\bar{S}$: Their relation is one of contradiction. S may be termed the axis of the complex: It subsumes s_1 and s_2. $\bar{S}$ is the axis of the contradictories $\bar{s}_1$ and $\bar{s}_2$ (of s_2 and s_1); it is therefore the neutral axis in relation to s_1 and s_2, for it can be defined as "neither s_1 nor s_2."
2. Two *schemata*: $s_1 + \bar{s}_1$ define schema 1; $s_2 + \bar{s}_2$ define schema 2. Each of the schemata is constituted by the relation of contradiction.
3. Two *deixes*: The first is defined by s_1 and the relation of implication between s_1 and $\bar{s}_2$; the second by the implication between s_2 and $\bar{s}_1$.

Thus we have the accompanying chart.

Constitutive Relations	Structural Dimensions	Semic Structures
contrariety	S axis (complex)	$s_1 + s_2$
	$\bar{S}$ axis (neutral)	$\bar{s}_1 + \bar{s}_2$
contradiction	schema 1	$s_1 + \bar{s}_1$
	schema 2	$s_2 + \bar{s}_2$
simple implication	deixis 1	$s_1 + \bar{s}_2$
	deixis 2	$s_2 + \bar{s}_1$

We can foresee the relations between the different systematic dimensions: The two axes, each constituted by relations of contrariety, are themselves in a relation of contradiction; the two schemata, each defined by relations of contradiction, are themselves in a relation of contrariety.

We propose calling the double presupposition of the two schemata *semiosis*. We reserve for later study the question of whether this twofold presupposition corresponds to that of linguistic content and expression, considered as the two schemata of a single model.

The Typology of the Rules

By definition every system has a set of rules; they may be defined positively, but they can also be defined negatively by what they are not. Let S represent the positive definition of the rules of the system, and $\bar{S}$ their negative definition. For example, everyone now agrees that a grammar system must include not only a definition of grammaticality, but also a definition of agrammaticality.

Unfortunately the concept of agrammaticality can cover several things, the rules of interdiction constituting the grammar system under consideration, as well as the infringements of its prescriptions and even the insufficient validity of the grammar in question.

We could say that with respect to the manifestation, S appears as a set of injunctions, and $\bar{S}$ as a set of noninjunctions.

By definition a system's rules of injunction describe compatibilities and incompatibilities (a system without incompatibilities would not be an ordered system). With regard to the manifestation, these rules appear as prescriptions (positive injunctions; say, s_1) and interdictions (negative injunctions; say, s_2), respectively.

Each of these two types of rules implies a contradictory systematic instance, say, $\bar{s}_2$ and $\bar{s}_1$, which are, with respect to the manifestation, noninterdictions and nonprescriptions, respectively. We can establish the accompanying diagram.

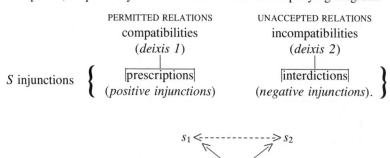

	PERMITTED RELATIONS compatibilities (*deixis 1*)	UNACCEPTED RELATIONS incompatibilities (*deixis 2*)
S injunctions $\left\{ \vphantom{\begin{matrix}a\\b\end{matrix}} \right.$	|prescriptions| (*positive injunctions*)	|interdictions| (*negative injunctions*). $\left. \vphantom{\begin{matrix}a\\b\end{matrix}} \right\}$

$$s_1 \longleftrightarrow s_2$$
$$\bar{s}_2 \longleftrightarrow \bar{s}_1$$

$$\bar{S} \text{ noninjunctions} \left\{ \begin{array}{ll} \text{noninterdictions} & \text{nonprescriptions} \\ \textit{(negative} & \textit{(positive} \\ \textit{noninjunctions)} & \textit{noninjunctions)} \end{array} \right\}$$

In traffic lights, for example, green signifies prescription (say s_1), and red signifies interdiction to proceed (say s_2). Orange sometimes signifies nonprescription (when it follows green), and sometimes noninterdiction (when it follows red), and sometimes $\bar{s}_1 + \bar{s}_2$, when it functions alone.

Insofar as the two modes of semic articulation we have distinguished are formally identical to the modes of phemic articulation[2] (at least according to Jakobson's description: For example, the feature *compact* is opposed to all the other features of the phonological system in which it is included as s_1 to $\bar{s}_1$, and opposed also to the feature *diffuse* as s_1 to s_2, by a relation of double presupposition), what we have said is also valid for the forms of linguistic expression. In a phonological system we would have:

ph_1: system of distinctive phemic groupings

ph_2: system of prohibited phemic groupings

$\overline{ph}_1$: system of nonrealized relevant groupings

$\overline{ph}_2$: system of groupings of redundant phemes constituting phemic variants.

The Investment of the Contents

The System of Sexual Relations

We shall begin by giving an example of investments of the constitutional model as shown by the study of the sexual relations of a human group, considered from a semiotic point of view.

The Social Model of Sexual Relations. It is accepted, in accordance with Lévi-Strauss's description, that human societies divide their semantic universes into two dimensions, culture and nature. The first is defined by the contents they assume and with which they invest themselves, the second by those they reject.

In the case in point, culture subsumes permissible sexual relations, and nature the unacceptable ones. Thus we have *culture* (permissible relations) vs. *nature* (unacceptable relations). The permissible relations are codified differently: Society regulates them by the prescription of matrimonial relations, accepting in other contexts yet other "normal" relations.

To these two types of relations are opposed, in the natural deixis, the prohibited relations (incest, for example) and the not-prescribed relations (nonmatrimonial). The social model may be formulated as shown in the accompanying diagram:

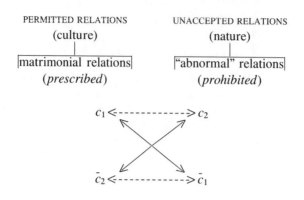

PERMITTED RELATIONS UNACCEPTED RELATIONS
(culture) (nature)

|matrimonial relations| |"abnormal" relations|
(*prescribed*) (*prohibited*)

"normal" relations nonmatrimonial relations
(*not prohibited*) (*not prescribed*)

Note: In traditional French society, for example, we have the following equivalences:

$c_1 \simeq$ conjugal love

$c_2 \simeq$ incest, homosexuality

$\bar{c}_2 \simeq$ adultery by man

$\bar{c}_1 \simeq$ adultery by woman.

Whatever the investment of the model, it is a question, in the case of nature as in that of culture, of social values (and not of the casting of nature into the realm of nonsignification).

The terms of the social model have no "objective" content. Thus homosexuality is sometimes prohibited (England), sometimes not prohibited (among the Bororo); it is always situated, however, on an axis other than that of matrimonial relations, where heterosexuality alone is permitted.

Schema 1 of the preceding model is reserved for socialized sexual relations (defined in relation to marriage); schema 2 subsumes the "natural" relations, or more precisely, nonsocialized ones, whether "antisocial" (prohibited relations) or without direct connection to the social structure (permitted relations other than matrimonial relations). Lévi-Strauss's description is confined to socialized heterosexual relations (schema 1), which define kinship; schema 2 is only defined negatively, in connection with the prohibition of incest, for example.

We shall now study the relations between the social model of sexual values and the semiotic substructures able to interact with it.

The Economic Model of Sexual Relations. The system of economic values is also a social system that regulates sexual relations. If we accept that profits come under prescription, and losses under interdiction (the consumption of wealth seems to be a ritual transgression), the system of economic values can be formulated as shown in the accompanying diagram:

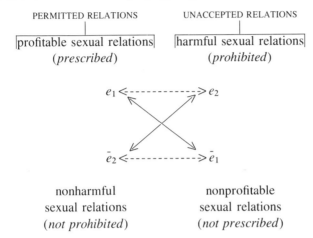

PERMITTED RELATIONS   UNACCEPTED RELATIONS

|profitable sexual relations| |harmful sexual relations|
(*prescribed*)   (*prohibited*)

e_1 <- - - - - - - - - - -> e_2

$\bar{e}_2$ <- - - - - - - - - - -> $\bar{e}_1$

nonharmful   nonprofitable
sexual relations   sexual relations
(*not prohibited*)   (*not prescribed*)

Insofar as socialized sexual relations give rise to the exchange of goods (dowries, etc.), the economic substructure conforms to schema 1 of the system of social values. Eight possible relations may be specified:

Matrimonial relations
$$\begin{cases} c_1 \simeq e_1 \text{ (profitable)} \\ c_1 \simeq e_2 \text{ (harmful)} \\ c_1 \simeq \bar{e}_1 \text{ (nonprofitable)} \\ c_1 \simeq \bar{e}_2 \text{ (nonharmful)} \end{cases}$$

Nonmatrimonial relations
$$\begin{cases} \bar{c}_1 \simeq e_1 \text{ (profitable)} \\ \bar{c}_1 \simeq e_2 \text{ (harmful)} \\ \bar{c}_1 \simeq \bar{e}_1 \text{ (nonprofitable)} \\ \bar{c}_1 \simeq \bar{e}_2 \text{ (nonharmful)} \end{cases}$$

Note: One can also foresee that relations of the type c_2 and $\bar{c}_2$ combine with the terms of the economic system, hence eight other possible combinations. For example, Balzac's Rabouilleuse has both not-prescribed and profitable relations with her master. However, in this case there is no conformity between the social system of sexual values and its economic substructure: Their prescriptions are in a relation of contradiction.

The Model of Individual Values. Let us take a hypothesis that individuals are defined, in a way analogous to society, by the assumption of contents in which they invest and that constitute their personalities, and by the denegation of other contents. Individual culture and individual nature thus define permitted and unaccepted relations, respectively; desires are included in the first group, phobias in the second. The system of individual values could be schematized as follows:

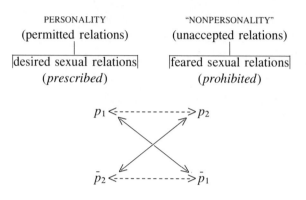

PERSONALITY
(permitted relations)

|desired sexual relations|
(*prescribed*)

"NONPERSONALITY"
(unaccepted relations)

|feared sexual relations|
(*prohibited*)

$p_1 \longleftrightarrow p_2$

$\bar{p}_2 \longleftrightarrow \bar{p}_1$

nonfeared
sexual relations
(*not prohibited*)

nondesired
sexual relations
(*not prescribed*)

The terms of this system seem to be articulated with schema 2 of social values, insofar as the individual appears outside socialized relations. This gives us eight more possible relations:

Prohibited relations
$$\begin{cases} c_2 \simeq p_1 \text{ (desired)} \\ c_2 \simeq p_2 \text{ (feared)} \\ c_2 \simeq \bar{p}_1 \text{ (not desired)} \\ c_2 \simeq \bar{p}_2 \text{ (not feared)} \end{cases}$$

Not-prohibited relations
$$\begin{cases} \bar{c}_2 \simeq p_1 \text{ (desired)} \\ \bar{c}_2 \simeq p_2 \text{ (feared)} \\ \bar{c}_2 \simeq \bar{p}_1 \text{ (not desired)} \\ \bar{c}_2 \simeq \bar{p}_2 \text{ (not feared)} \end{cases}$$

We can also expect combinations with the terms c_1 and $\bar{c}_1$, which gives us eight further possibilities.

We shall not attempt to define more accurately the structure of the combinations brought about by the interaction of the different systems. Let A and B equal the two systems; let *pr.* equal the prescriptions and *i.* the interdictions. Several types of relations can be foreseen:

Relations between homologous terms:

1. $pr.(A) + pr.(B); i.(A) + i.(B).$
2. $\overline{pr}.(A) + \overline{pr}.(B); \bar{i}.(A) + \bar{i}.(B).$

Relations between nonhomologous terms belonging to a homologous deixis:

3. $pr.(A) + \bar{i}.(B); pr.(B) + \bar{i}.(A).$
4. $i.(A) + \overline{pr}.(B); i.(B) + \overline{pr}.(A).$

The relations of groups 1 and 2 may be termed balanced, and the relations of groups 3 and 4 compatible. Relations between nonhomologous terms belonging to nonhomologous deixes may be termed conflictual relations.

Two types of *conflicts between contrary terms* can be distinguished, according to whether we are dealing with the axis of injunctions or the axis of noninjunctions:

5. $pr.(A) + i.(B)$; $pr.(B) + i.(A)$ (strong conflicts).
6. $\overline{pr}.(A) + \overline{i}.(B)$; $\overline{pr}.(B) + \overline{i}.(B)$ (weak conflicts).

In addition, two types of *conflicts between contradictory terms* can be distinguished, according to whether we are dealing with schemata of interdictions or of prescriptions:

7. $pr.(A) + \overline{pr}.(B)$; $pr.(B) + \overline{pr}.(A)$.
8. $i.(A) + \overline{i}.(B)$; $i.(B) + \overline{i}.(A)$.

Let us take the case of socially permitted sexual relations; if we consider permitted marriage as invariant c_1 and $\overline{c}_2$ as subject to substitutions of individual values, we obtain four types of possible marriages (see accompanying chart).

Formula of the Combination $c_1 + \overline{c}_2$	*Structure of the Combination*
$c_1 + p_1$ (desired)	balanced (1)
$c_1 + p_2$ (phobic)	conflictual (5)
$c_1 + \overline{p}_1$ (not desired)	conflictual (7)
$c_1 + \overline{p}_2$ (not phobic)	compatible (3)

Let us take another example. If we considered $\overline{c}_2$ as an invariant and c_1 as subject to variation (with economic substitutions), we obtain four types of possible sexual relations (see accompanying chart).

Formula of the Combination $\overline{c}_2 + c_1$	*Structure of the Combination*
$\overline{c}_2 + e_1$ (profitable)	compatible (3)
$\overline{c}_2 + e_2$ (harmful)	conflictual (8)
$\overline{c}_2 + \overline{e}_1$ (not profitable	conflictual (6)
$\overline{c}_2 + \overline{e}_2$ (not harmful)	balanced (2)

A generalized combinatory arrangement of the terms of the three systems would produce sixteen possible situations for the socially permissible sexual relations; we shall see, however, that all the combinations cannot be manifested in the same way.

This combinatory could, for example, furnish an organon adequate to describe interpersonal relations in narrative. Thus, if we are describing sexual relations in Balzac's novels, we notice that in general the situation of the protagonists is dissymetric. For example, the relations of Père Rigou with his female servant will be not prohibited, desired, and not harmful; those of the servant with Père Rigou are not permitted, feared, and not profitable; thus there is conflict, whatever the manifestation of the relations. The nonhomology of the semiotic situations may serve to define "the romantic unsatisfaction"; the perfect love is the manifestation of relations from groups 2 and 3.

The Individual and Society

Integrated Substructures and Correlated Substructures. Not only do the systems of economic values and of individual values regulate sexual relations, they also combine preferentially, the former with socialized sexual relations, the latter with nonsocialized relations.

These two substructures must be distinguished one from the other for they do not have the same relations to the social system.

The economic values are *integrated* into the overall social system (although economic self-interest does exist). For example, it would be difficult to imagine that incest could be profitable in a society where it is prohibited; certain theoretically possible combinations, such as those of group 5, will not be able to take place.

On the other hand, the system of individual values does not necessarily appear integrated into the social system, and relations from group 5 are possible. They may, for example, appear as transgressions. The individual system will be said to be *correlated* to the social system (moreover personality includes socialized instances).

The Human World. Given that schema 1 of the social system includes socialized relations, schema 1 of the individual system may be considered individualized, to the extent indeed that the individual is invested in his or her desires.

If we study the compatibilities between the two systems (relations between nonhomologous terms situated in homologous deixes) we obtain these correlations:

$$p_1 \simeq \bar{c}_2 \text{ (desires are not prohibited)}$$
$$c_1 \simeq \bar{p}_2 \text{ (social prescriptions are not feared)}$$
$$\bar{p}_1 \simeq c_2 \text{ (prohibited things are not desired)}$$
$$\bar{c}_1 \simeq p_2 \text{ (not-prescribed things are not feared)}.$$

In other words, the schema assumed by the social system defines negatively the schema assumed by the individual system. Schema 1 of the individual system and schema 2 of the social system overlap, the injunctions of the one being combined with the noninjunctions of the other; likewise for schema 2 of the individual system and schema 1 of the social system.

In this situation, the axes of the two systems are correlated in the following way: the complex axis of the social system with the neutral axis of the individual system; the neutral axis of the social system with the complex axis of the individual system.

The conjunction of the two cultural deixes (social and individual) defines human values; that of the two natural deixes defines the nonhuman world.

The conjunction of individual culture with social nature defines the *space of transgression*; that of social culture with individual nature defines the *space of alienation*.

> *Note*: It was pointed out, in a study of the Russian folktale, that transgression and alienation are correlative. That is, in the semantic universe described, the enjoyment of values is defined by the compatibility of social and individual systems, so that $c_1 \simeq \bar{p}_2$ and $\bar{c}_2 \simeq p_1$. But then, there cannot be transgression without alienation. If we have
>
>   a. $c_1 \simeq \bar{p}_1$, and $\bar{c}_2 \simeq p_2$,
>
> we must also have
>
>   b. $c_2 \simeq \bar{p}_2$, and $\bar{c}_1 \simeq p_1$.
>
> Conversely, if we have (b), we must also have (a).

Toward Manifestation

The Interaction of Semiotic Systems

The concept of *usage* was introduced by Hjelmslev to account for the closure of manifestation in comparison with the possibilities defined by structure.

The rare attempts to study usage have been carried out by means of uncertain calculation: It has been pointed out, for example, that such and such an Indian community of two hundred members cannot exhaust the possibilities of a matrimonial system that allows for millions of combinations. Yet that does not mean that within that system the marriages take place at random; it is probable that the historic situation determines the choice of some marriages and not of other equally possible ones. We shall attempt to define this *historicity*.

It must not be concluded from the preceding conjectures on sexual relations that the manifestation of a system is defined solely by the relations it permits. If this were so, the manifestation would be quite simply the product of rules of the type s_1 and $\bar{s}_2$. This is not very probable, for the deixis of the permitted is defined in relation to that of the unaccepted. That is undoubtedly why certain American linguists do not choose corpora (conforming hypothetically to the permitted relations in the system described), but create for their own use nongrammatical corpora that manifest the "hidden" rules of type s_2 and $\bar{s}_1$.[3]

One thing can guide us: Whether it is a question of words or of marriages, nothing permits us to assert that a semiotic manifestation is dependent on only one system at a time. And so far as it is dependent on several, its closure can be attributed to the interaction of the different systems that produce it. Take, for example, any not-prohibited sexual relation; it is possible, but it is not certain, that it will be manifested. It may not coincide with the permitted relations of the economic system in question, or with the system of individual values of each of the protagonists. In the case of a free combinatory arrangement, there is one chance in eight that the permitted relations of the three systems will coincide, and one in sixty-four that a term of the social model will be manifested in a balanced combination. We can see that many of the combinations we have foreseen cannot take place, for example, a sexual relation that is socially prohibited, economically harmful, and phobic to the individual.

By the term usage we propose to designate the interaction of semiotic structures that is responsible for manifestations as well as for nonmanifestations. Several types of interaction are foreseeable:

1. Absence of permission in the two systems concerned: We have the combinations (1.*b*), (2.*a*), and (4). It would seem that there can be no manifestation.
2. Permission in one system but interdiction in the other: We have the combinations (5), (6), (7), and (8). We cannot say whether the manifestation will take place.
3. Permission in the two systems: We have (1.*a*), (2.*b*), and (3). The manifestation may take place.

The inventory of combinations that can bring about the manifestation is further restricted if we accept the hypothesis that at least one prescription is needed for it to take place: There remain only (1.*a*) and (3).

Here is an example of usage: In the French phonologic system the variant (*R*) of the phoneme (*r*) is not prohibited in the working classes and not prescribed in "polite society." It is connoted by the content *rusticity*. It will be manifested or not according to social class; the interaction between the social axiological system and the phonological system is clear here.[4]

The functioning of usage must be specified. In our presentation of sexual relations, the different systems in question are in a hierarchical relationship: In relation to the manifestation, each content of the social system of values appears to be mediated by two relays or substructures, the economic system and the individual system. It remains to be seen what determines the hierarchy of the systems.

This problem is of interest: The hierarchy of the systems allows us to decide, in the case of conflictual combinations (5), (6), (7), and (8), whether there will be a manifestation. Will a marriage conforming to the social prescriptions but that is both phobic (or nondesired) and profitable take place? There are several examples in Balzac of "money matches"; this means that in the society he invents or describes, the system of economic values has supremacy over individual values. It even has supremacy over social sexual values (prostitution, etc.).[5]

We propose calling the structure that defines the hierarchy of the semiotic systems concerned *epistemy* (here, bourgeois or Balzacian epistemy, whichever one prefers). It orders the combinations that can appear, and thus not only the closure of the manifestation (negative definition of usage by nonmanifestations), but the nature of realized manifestations (positive definition of usage).

> *Note*: The term *choice* can be used to designate the processes that produce the realized manifestations and define usage positively; and *constraints* to designate the processes that cause the nonmanifestations and define usage negatively (the *constraints* determine *asemanticity*, or incompatibility of the interacting terms of the systems).

Epistemy accounts for the historicity of the manifestations; its social component appears as *common sense*, implicit or not, which is an axiological and dialectical system immanent in all the semiotic structures of the society under consideration.

The Status of Manifested Contents

We have just seen under what conditions a content can be manifested. We can now define a little more accurately the nature of semiotic manifestation, and the movement from the deep structures to the surface structures.

An author, a producer of any semiotic object, operates within an epistemy, which is the result of his individuality and the society in which he is inscribed. Within this society it is possible for him to make a limited number of choices, which have as an initial result the investment of organized contents, that is, contents endowed with valencies (possibilities of relations).

Without going so far as to prejudge the structure of semiotic grammar, we must specify how these contents appear in manifestation. We shall take only the simplest cases.

As each term of a semiotic structure is defined by relations of conjunction and disjunction, it can appear as the conjunctive or disjunctive mode.

1. The *disjunctive* mode: Each content of a semiotic structure may appear:
   a. disjoined from the other three terms; it is then isolated in the manifestation. For example, we have s_1 (vs. s_2, $\bar{s}_1$, $\bar{s}_2$); thus there is one manifestation possible for each of the four terms.
   b. disjoined from another term; it becomes part of a distinctive opposition. We have, for example, s_1 vs. s_2, s_1 vs. $\bar{s}_1$; s_1 vs. $\bar{s}_2$. The other possibilities of manifestation of the same structure are $\bar{s}_1$ vs. $\bar{s}_2$; $\bar{s}_1$ vs. s_2; $\bar{s}_2$ vs. s_2. Thus there are six possible manifestations.

2. The *conjunctive* mode: In the manifestation, six binary conjunctions that define what are called the complex terms can correspond to the six immanent manifestations of the constitutional structure. There would thus be two deictic complexes, two complexes of contraries, and two complexes of contradictories.

The neutral term, which is a simple term in Vigo Brøndal's description, in reality would be the complex $(\bar{s}_1 + \bar{s}_2)$.

It is uncertain whether what Brøndal calls a balanced complex term is the conjunctive manifestation of two contraries or of two contradictories; our limited experience in description has allowed us to identify two kinds of complexes, of the type (*white + black*), and (*white + nonwhite*).

We must also envisage the problem of *extension.* Brøndal defines, and one does come across, complex terms with positive or negative dominances; they are perhaps produced by the interaction of hierarchically unequal systems.

These exploratory reflections could be extended in two directions:

A study must be made of how the production of a semiotic object comes up against, with the superficial structures, a second level of constraints and choices: It is a question of discursive structures (narratives, for example). They account for the syntagmatic aspect of the manifestation. They impose the choice of certain operations, such as the establishment of roles (contents of the actants), and of "archifunctions" (contents of the functions).

A study must then be made of the relations between the form of deep structures and the rules of the semiotic grammar system employed; the deep structure could, for example, define the orientation of dialectic algorithms.

But first, it would be well to define the mode of existence of the contents at the level of surface structures, and, once their logical status has been described, to set up the computation of their combinations.

Chapter 4
Elements of a Narrative Grammar

Narrativity and Semiotic Theory

Historical Overview

The increasing interest shown over the years in narrativity should be placed alongside the hopes and goals of a general semiotics that is gradually defining itself.

In the first instance, a comparison of the results from various independent research activities — those of Vladimir Propp on folklore, Claude Lévi-Strauss on the structure of myth, Etienne Souriau on theater — has allowed us to confirm the existence of an autonomous field of study. New methodological refinements — those by which Claude Bremond interprets narration from the perspective of decisional logic, or by which Alain Dundes focuses on giving a narrative grammar form to the organization of story — have subsequently provided us with a diversity of theoretical approaches. Our own concern during this period has been to extend as much as possible the area of application of the analysis of narrative and to formalize to an ever greater extent the partial models produced in the course of this research. It has seemed important to us to emphasize above all the semiolinguistic nature of the categories used in setting up these models. This is seen as the guarantor of their universality and the way to integrate narrative structures into a generalized semiotic theory.

Narrativity and Its Manifestation

The methodological sophistication of narrative analysis and the possibilities for its application to areas other than folklore or mythology have led us to recognize considerable problems. The most generally accepted concepts in linguistics have been brought into question.

We first must admit that narrative structures can be found elsewhere than in manifestations of meaning effected through the natural languages. They can be found in cinematographic and oniric languages, in figurative painting, and so forth. This amounts to recognizing and accepting the need for a fundamental distinction between two levels of representation and analysis: an *apparent level* of narration, at which the diverse manifestations of narrative are subject to the specific requirements of the linguistic substances through which it is expressed, and an *immanent level*, which is a kind of common structural trunk where narrativity is located and organized at the stage preceding its manifestation. A shared semiotic level is therefore distinct from the linguistic level and logically precedes it, whatever the language chosen for the actual manifestation.

On the other hand, if narrative structures exist before they are manifested, for manifestation to occur it must use linguistic units whose dimensions are much greater than those of utterances—units that would constitute a *grande syntagmatique*, to cite the expression Christian Metz uses in his work on the semiotics of cinema. Therefore the *linguistic structures of narrative* correspond, at the level of manifestation, to *narrative structures*, and the analysis of narrative has discourse analysis as its corollary.

Narrativity and Semiotics

Thus it becomes apparent that on top of having to admit that signification is distinct from the modes of its manifestation, we have to recognize the existence of a common structural level where vast fields of signification are organized. This level must be integrated into any general semiotic theory precisely because such theories attempt to account for the articulation and manifestation of the semantic universe as a totality of meaning belonging to the cultural or personal order. At the same time, the general organization of such a theory is turned upside down. Formerly we could believe that the linguistic project consisted in putting into place a combinatory or generative mechanism that, starting with simple elements and original kernels, would account for the production of an unlimited number of utterances, with the latter in turn being transformed and combined in order to create successions of utterances in discourse. Now, on the contrary, we have to conceive of *ab quo* instances of generation of signification such that, starting with agglomerations of meaning that are as little articulated as possible, we can, as we descend through successive levels, obtain more and more refined significative articulations. This in turn allows us to attain simultaneously the two goals of meaning when it becomes manifested: to appear as *articulated meaning*, that is, as signification, and as *discourse on meaning*, that is, as a great paraphrase that in its own way develops all earlier articulations of meaning. In other words, *the gener-*

ation of meaning does not first take the form of the production of utterances and their combination in discourse; it is relayed, in the course of its trajectory, by narrative structures and it is these that produce meaningful discourse articulated in utterances.

Given this, one can see that the development of a theory of narrativity that would justify and legitimize the analysis of narrative as a methodologically self-sufficient area of research consists not only in the refinement and formalization of the narrative models obtained through increasingly numerous and varied descriptions, nor in a typology of these models that would subsume them all, but also, and above all, in the inclusion of narrative structures as an *autonomous instance* within the general economy of semiotics, considered to be the science of signification.

The Instances of a General Semiotics

To accomplish this, we must construct a semiotic theory in such a way that between the fundamental *ab quo* instances (where the semantic substance receives its first articulations and constitutes itself as a signifying form) and the final *ad quem* instances (where signification manifests itself through multiple languages) a vast area will be set aside in which to place a *mediating instance* that would include autonomous semiotic structures (narrative structures included)—loci where there would be developed complementary articulations of content and a sort of grammar that would be both general and fundamental and that would regulate the setting up of articulated discourses. Thus the structural project that concerns this mediation instance is twofold: On the one hand we must propose models for the articulation of contents, such as they can be conceived of at this level of the trajectory of meaning; on the other hand we have to set in place those formal models by which we will be able to manipulate those contents and arrange them in such a way that they will be able to control the production and segmentation of the discourses and organize, under certain conditions, the manifestation of narrativity. In other words, semiotic theory will not be satisfactory unless it reserves a place at its center for a *fundamental semantics and grammar.*

Toward a Fundamental Semantics

The project of a fundamental semantics, a semantics that differs from the semantics of linguistic manifestation, is absolutely dependent on a theory of meaning. It is therefore directly linked to the process that makes explicit the conditions under which meaning can be grasped, and it is also directly linked to the *elementary structure of signification* that can be deduced from it and that ultimately shows itself to be an axiomatics. This elementary structure, described and analyzed in chapter 3, must be conceived of as being the logical development of a binary semic category, of the type *white* vs. *black*, whose terms are in a relation of contrariety and that can also, each one, project a new term that would be its contradictory. The contradictory terms can, in turn, enter into a presupposition vis-à-vis the contrary term set off above it (see accompanying diagram).

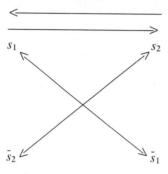

————→ indicates presupposition and ←————→ indicates contradiction.

What follows is the working assumption that this elementary structure of signification furnishes us with an appropriate semiotic model by which to account for the first articulations of meaning within a *semantic microuniverse*.

At this point it is important to make the following clear concerning our concept of the semantic universe. Earlier (in our *Sémantique structurale*), we had proposed that it be considered the totality of the "semantic substance" being used to signify and which does so through the network of articulations governing it, meaning thus being apprehended only if it has been articulated. We thought that these articulations of meaning could be explained as being the result of a combinatory arrangement that is brought about by using a limited inventory of semic categories. Now we can go one step further and suggest a more refined representation of this tissue of articulations. In fact, our new concept is that *each constitutive category of the combinatory* arrangement — which as we have seen can, at any moment, develop into an elementary structure — may be transformed *into a constitutive semiotic model* and, subordinating to itself other categories from the same inventory that serve as its subarticulations, thus subsume a vast field of signification and encompass a semantic microuniverse. The fundamental inventory of the semic categories necessary for the articulation of the semantic universe in its totality is, consequently, also the virtual inventory of all possible microuniverses, and each culture, each personality, can, through privileged articulations, favor one microuniverse at the expense of another (wine culture in France, use of spring water in Turkey).

Given these considerations, the constitutive model is none other than the elementary structure of signification used, as form, in the articulation of the semantic substance of a microuniverse. The isotopy between the terms of the elementary structure ensures and is, in a way, the foundation of the microuniverse seen as a unit of meaning, and it allows us, within our axiomatizing activity, to view the constitutive model as a canonical form, as a point of departure for a fundamental semantics.

It is not our purpose here to examine the conditions of such a semantics. We simply wish to identify the two levels – semantic and grammatical – of the present study. Thus it would perhaps be preferable to note this distinction between the two levels by using a terminological disjunction. We would thus speak of *content values* when dealing with semic units that have been selected from within a micro-universe by using articulations of the constitutive model, and we would reserve the expression *structural term* for the formal units of the semiotic model alone.

Toward a Deep Grammar

If, however, the elementary structure thus serves as a model for the articulation of contents that are semantic substances, if it can make meaning signify, it is still no less a semiotic form that can be considered independently of any investment. It is this "semiotic principle" that according to Louis Hjelmslev establishes and organizes all language, in the most general sense of the term. This is why, although as a constitutive model it is the basis for the organization of contents, the elementary structure is at the same time a formal model that, thanks to its constitutive categories, manipulates the organized contents without becoming identified with them. We have already noted elsewhere that the categories necessary for the formalization of the elementary structure of signification are the same epistemological categories used in the construction of any semiotic theory. It is with these "language universals," constituting a semiotic model – and this is the original instance of any manipulation of meaning – that we can undertake to develop the first premises of a deep grammar.

Elements of a Deep Grammar

The Taxonomic Nucleus

At the present time it is difficult to develop an axiomatics on which narrative structures would rest; for this we would need to have at our disposal a fully developed semiotic theory. Thus we can only sketch out, while referring to the global concept of such a semiotics, the main articulatory instances and predictable operational sequences, using a narrative grammar that is still being worked out.

All grammars, in a more or less explicit way, have two components: a morphology and a syntax. The morphology has a taxonomic nature and its terms are interdefining. The syntax consists of a set of operational rules or ways of manipulating the terms provided by the morphology.

To illustrate what such a taxonomic model might be we refer to the structural analysis of the Oedipus myth done by Lévi-Strauss in 1955. This analysis resulted in the construction of a simple achronic model, from which, according to the author, all Oedipus myths, including the Freudian one, can be generated. This model, which is the result of a paradigmatic reading of mythic discourse, can be defined—we have examined it on other occasions—as the setting in correlation of pairs made up of contradictory terms.

It is easy to see that such a model is quite comparable to the constitutive model we have already mentioned and that it can be interpreted using the same relational categories. Thus, if we call *schema* a structure that includes two terms in a relation of contradiction ($s_1 \longleftrightarrow \bar{s}_1$, or $s_1 \longleftrightarrow \bar{s}_2$), and *correlation* the relation between two schemata whose terms, taken individually, are in a relation of contrariety with the corresponding terms of the other schema (see "Toward a Fundamental Semantics," this chapter), we can then say that the taxonomic model is a *structure made up of four terms* mutually interdefined by a network of precise relations that can be described as being *the correlation between two schemata*.

According to Lévi-Strauss, as we have seen, such a model accounts for the achronic apprehension of the signification of all the stories that could possibly be generated by a given semantic microuniverse. It is a formal model: All it does is articulate invested contents. Furthermore it is not dependent on its mode of manifestation: The discourse that manifests it might be a mythical story, but it could also be the didactic discourse of Freud; it could just as easily be present, in a diffuse way, in endless anthropological or psychoanalytic discourses.

In other words, it is starting from this primary taxonomic instance that systems of values or *axiologies* can, in the static mode, be articulated and manifested. The same can be said for the creative processes of recurrent values or *ideologies*. Although it is able to generate nonnarrative discursive forms, the taxonomic instance is also the necessary basis for any dynamic process that generates *narrative syntax*.

The Narrativization of Taxonomy

We can see that the taxonomic model, because of the stability of the relations that define its structural terms, can be considered a primary nucleus of an elementary morphology. Nevertheless, an examination of the conditions under which meaning is apprehended shows clearly that if signification, to the extent that one seeks to find it in an object, appears as an articulation of stable fundamental relations, it can also be represented dynamically, if one considers it as an apprehension or production of meaning by a subject. Taking into account this dynamic aspect, one can establish a network of equivalences between the fundamental constitutive relations of the taxonomic model and the projections of these same relations, or *operations*, this time having to do with the already established terms of this very same elementary morphology, operations of which the regulating mechanisms would constitute syntax. Thus, contradiction, as a relation, enables us to establish binary schemata at the taxonomic level. As a contradictory operation it will, at the syntactic level, negate one of the terms of the schema and at the same time affirm its contradictory term. Such an operation, when carried out on terms already invested with value, results in the transformation of contents by negating those that are posited and installing in their place newly asserted contents.

> *Note*: We have seen that the so-called achronic apprehension of myth is an unstable instance, that its "dogmatic" structure is capable, at any moment, of turning into a story. Studies carried out on certain minor genres (proverbs, Wellerisms, headline accounts, etc.) that seem at first to be purely axiological manifestations have, on the contrary, shown that they are very unstable and have a pronounced tendency toward narrativization.

The Orientation of Syntactic Operations

The representation of syntax as a series of operations carried out on the defined terms of a taxonomic structure allows us to identify more easily a new property: *Syntactic operations are oriented.*

Thus, within the framework of any given taxonomic schema, there will be two syntactic operations, and two possible transformations of content:

either $s_1 \implies \bar{s}_1$
or $\bar{s}_1 \implies s_1$.

Since, on the other hand, the taxonomic model is made up of two schemata, the question of the logical priority of the syntactic operations has to be raised: The oriented operations can begin

either with the first schema: $s_1 \implies \bar{s}_1$ or $\bar{s}_1 \implies s_1$
or with the second schema: $s_2 \implies \bar{s}_2$ or $\bar{s}_2 \implies s_2$,

which, as we can see, is enough to give rise to a first combinatory arrangement of syntactic operations.

Finally, our knowledge of the relational properties of the elementary structure — which are also those of the syntactic operations — reveals the following: The contradiction operation that, for example, by negating the term s_1 at the same time posits the term $\bar{s}_1$, must be followed by a new presupposition operation that gives rise to, and joins to the term $\bar{s}_1$, the new term s_2. Thus, syntactic operations are not only oriented, but also organized in logical series.

The Characteristics of a Deep Grammar

The characteristics we have just identified, and that can serve as the foundation for the development of a deep grammar, can be summed up as follows:

> 1. Narrative grammar is made up of an *elementary morphology* provided by the taxonomic model and of a *fundamental syntax* responsible for operations carried out on the taxonomic terms that have been interdefined at an earlier stage.

2. Narrative syntax consists of operations carried out on terms that can be invested with content values; the syntax thus transforms and manipulates these terms by negating or affirming them, or, and it amounts to the same thing, *disjoining* and *conjoining* them.
3. Syntactic operations, since they are within the established taxonomic framework, are *oriented*, and thus predictable and calculable.
4. These operations are also *ordered in series* and constitute processes that are segmentable into *operational syntactic units*.

Although incomplete, these minimal criteria for a deep grammar allow us to attempt a solution to the problems in constructing a surface narrative grammar.

Elements of a Surface Narrative Grammar

The Problem of Levels of Grammar

Once we have a deep grammar, it should be possible to identify levels of grammar that are even "deeper" and that, by making the categories we use more specific or by transcribing them in a more complex way, would get progressively closer to grammar as it is manifested in natural languages. Thus, by way of simplification, one can say that deep grammar, which is of a conceptual nature, in order to be able to produce stories that are manifested in a *figurative* way (where human or personified actors would accomplish tasks, undergo tests, reach goals), must first, at an intermediate semiotic level, receive an *anthropomorphic*, but not figurative, representation. It is this anthropomorphic level to which we will give the name *surface narrative grammar*, making it clear that the qualifier *surface*, being in no way pejorative (the French is *superficielle*), indicates only that we are dealing with a semiotic level, one whose grammatical definitions and rules can, with the help of one last transcoding, move directly into discourse and linguistic utterances.

The term *grammatical level* begs definition. If we say that a grammar can be constructed at two different levels, that means that it is possible to construct two different metalanguages that can account for one and the same linguistic phenomenon present at a third level, in our case that of manifestation. We can also say that these two metalanguages are *equivalents*, because they are isotopic but not isomorphic, indicating that a given segment of a metalanguage can be transcoded into an isotopic segment of another language without the constitutive elements of the two segments being at all formally identical.

Because of their *anthropomorphic nature*, the constitutive elements of such a surface grammar can be distinguished from the *logical nature* of the categories of the deep grammar.

Narrative Utterances

Anthropomorphic Doing. If, therefore, one of the basic concepts of *deep* grammar is the *syntactic* operation, at the *surface* level it will correspond to syntactic *doing*.

Establishing the equivalence between the operation and the doing introduces the anthropomorphic dimension into the grammar. This can be interpreted in different ways.

1. A logical operation is conceived of as an autonomous metalinguistic process that allows us to put the subject of the operation between parentheses (or to use "some" operator or other), whereas a doing, be it practical or mythical, implies, as an activity, a *human subject* (or at least anthropomorphized: "The pencil writes"). In other words, doing is an operation that is specified by having joined to it the classeme *human*.

2. When we speak of doing, it is clear that we are not thinking of "real" doing at the level of the semiotics of the natural world, but of a *linguistic doing* (whatever the language, natural or not, in which it is manifested). That is, we are dealing with a doing that has been transcoded into a message. Whether we have an *enacted doing* or a *spoken doing* with respect to the semiotic reference system, its status as a metasemiotic doing (because it is described) makes a message-object of it, one that is located within the process of communication and that thus implies a sender and a receiver.

Doing is thus an operation that is doubly anthropomorphic: As an activity it presupposes a subject; as a message, it is objectified and implies the axis of transmission between sender and receiver.

The Basic Narrative Utterance. Conversion (the movement from one grammatical level to another) can thus be defined as being the equivalence between operation and doing. By this the concept of doing takes on the form of a *basic narrative utterance*

$$NU = F(A),$$

in which doing, as a process of actualization, is called a function (F) and in which the subject of the doing, being a potentiality of the process, is designated *actant* (A). One can say that any operation of the deep grammar can be converted into a narrative utterance whose minimal canonical form is $F(A)$. Nonetheless it remains understood that narrative utterances are syntactic utterances; that is, they are independent of the content with which any given doing can be invested. It is also understood that the constitutive elements of the F and A utterances are isotopes: Any semantic restrictions of F will have necessary repercussions on A, and vice versa. To give an example, the actant is the isotope of its function in the same way as the name of an agent is the isotope of its verb (e.g., fisherman—to fish).

Modal Utterances and Descriptive Utterances. Thus, a typology of narrative utterances—and at the same time of actants—can be constructed by progressively introducing specific semantic restrictions. If, for example, a certain class of functions is specified by having the classeme *wanting* attached to it, the actants, which are isotopes of these functions, will constitute a restrictive class that can be called *subject-actants.* Indeed, *wanting* is an anthropomorphic classeme (but not necessarily figurative; cf. "this rule requires that . . .") that sets up an actant as subject, that is, as a possible operator of the doing. Now, together with descriptive utterances (*DU*), we can constitute a new type of narrative utterance: *modal utterances (MU).*

Indeed, from the linguistic point of view, *wanting* is a modal predicate that regulates descriptive utterances. For example:

1. John wants Peter to leave.
2. Peter wants to leave.

These linguistics utterances, once they have been transcribed into semantic utterances, appear as follows:

1. *F*: wanting/*S*: John; *O(F*: departure; *A*: Peter)/.
2. *F*: wanting/*S*: Peter; *O(F*: departure; *A*: Peter)/.

We can see that, linguistically, the introduction of the classeme *wanting* is something more than just the overdetermination of the predicate. We can see that it requires us to construct two distinct utterances, the first of which is a modal utterance and the second a descriptive utterance that, being hypotactic to the first, serves as its *object-actant.* If for the moment we ignore the fact that, in the first example, the semantic subjects of the two utterances are different and, in the second case, identical, we can interpret the modal utterance as being the *desire for realization* of a program that is present in the form of a descriptive utterance and that is at the same time, because it is the object, part of the modal utterance.

We can now formally specify modal utterances as:

MU = F: wanting/S; O/.

These are enunciations of specified virtual programs within the framework of object-actants, it being understood that the object-actant of the modal utterance can at any moment be converted into any descriptive utterance whatsoever.

If we now introduce a supplementary restriction that postulates that the semantic subject of the descriptive utterance must be the same as that of the modal utterance, we can to a certain extent say that syntactic doing consists of the transformation of a *virtual* program into an *actualized* program.

Since we have not changed our concept of the descriptive utterance as program, the transformation can be interpreted as a substitution of the modal utterance containing the "wanting" function with a *modal utterance of existence* that, as we know, is an implied presupposition of any descriptive utterance.

Attributive Utterances. To say that the object of desire, present as an object-actant, is in fact a program-utterance, requires clarification. Other examples will allow us to introduce new characteristics of these descriptive utterances:

3. Peter wants an apple.
4. Peter wants to be good.

These linguistic utterances can be semantically represented as:

3. *F*: wanting/*S*: Peter; *O*(*F*: acquisition; *A*: Peter; *O*: apple)/.
4. *F*: wanting/*S*: Peter; *O*(*F*: acquisition; *A*: Peter; *O*: goodness)/.

As we can see, the semantic explication allows us to establish, alongside the utterances already mentioned and whose functions are of the *order of doing*, the existence of two other types of descriptive utterances characterized by functions that are sometimes of the *order of having*, and at other times of the order of *doing*. As subclasses of descriptive utterances, we can designate them as attributive utterances (*AU*). At the level of semantic description, what distinguishes these two types of utterances is not so much the specifics of their functions—since in both cases we have a relation of attribution between the semantic subject and object—but rather the external or internal nature of the attributable objects. To the extent that, if for the purposes of interpretation we see as one the functions of both modal and descriptive utterances, we can say that the desire to possess institutes the object of a virtual possession as a *value*, we can see that the *apple* is an external value vis-à-vis the subject of the desire, whereas *goodness* is a value that is internal to the subject. In syntactic terms this difference is expressed through the fact that the relation between the subject and object of the attributable utterance is, in the first case, *hypotactic* and, in the second, *hyponymic*.

In summary, we can say the following:

First, introducing the modality of *wanting* into the surface grammar allows us to construct modal utterances that have two actants: the *subject* and the *object*. The axis of desire that joins them in turn allows us to interpret them semantically as a virtual *performatory subject* and an object *that has been assigned value*.

Second, if the modality of wanting valorizes the object, this object, being an actant of the modal utterance, can be converted into either an utterance that is *descriptive of doing* (examples 1 and 2)—and doing as such will be thereby valorized—or into *attributive* utterances (examples 3 and 4), with the actualization of wanting then being expressed by the possession of the object-values indicated in the attributive utterances.

Finally, the distinction between two types—*hypotactic* and *hyponymic*—of attribution of object-values must be retained: It provides us with a formal criterion with which to distinguish between two value orders—objective and subjective—which are of primary importance in our understanding of narrative structure.

Modal Utterances as a Function of Attributive Utterances. We must now complete our list of narrative utterances with

    5. Peter wants to know (something).
    6. Peter wants to be able (to do something).

We can immediately see, without any semantic transcription, that what is unique to this type of utterance is that a modal utterance can have as its object not a basic description utterance, but rather another modal utterance that functions as a descriptive utterance and that can thus be valorized.

Several observations can be made in this regard:

    1. At the present state of our knowledge it appears that only the knowing and being-able modalities should be taken into consideration when we construct our surface grammar.
    2. Among the properties of these modalities we will retain:
        a. the possibility of forming canonical modal utterances: $MU(k$ or $b-a) = F$: knowing or being-able/S; $O(F$: doing; $O)/$.
        b. the possibility of being objects of modal utterances of wanting: $MU(w) = F$: wanting/S; $O(F$: knowing or being-able; A; $O)/$.
        c. the possibility of being objects of attributive utterances: $AU = F$: attribution/S; O: a knowing or being-able/.

Narrative Units

Performance and Its Polemic Nature. To be able to set in place the elementary units of the surface grammar that are the equivalent of those of the deep grammar and thus move to the construction of greater units, we have to emphasize the polemic nature that the relation of contradiction takes on at this surface level. The axis of contradiction, which we have called a schema, is, as we know, the locus of negation and assertion of contradictory terms. If we agree that the anthropomorphic representation of contradiction is polemic, the syntagmatic series (which corresponds to the transformation of content values resulting, at the level of deep grammar, from the operations of negation and assertion) must appear here as a series of narrative utterances whose semantic restrictions will assume the function of conferring on it the characteristics of confrontation and struggle. This syntagmatic series postulates:

    1. The existence of *two subjects* S_1 and S_2 (or of a subject and an anti-subject), which correspond to two contradictory *doings*, with the relation of contradiction being, as we know, an unoriented relation;
    2. The semantic restriction of the syntactic doing through establishing

equivalence between the operation of *negation* and the function of *domination*, the result of polemic antagonism;

3. Recognition of the principle of *orientation* that is valid for both levels of grammar: To such and such an orientation of logical operation there corresponds such and such an arbitrary choice of negating subject and of domination of one of the subjects by the other;

4. Admission that the dialectal procedure according to which the negation of one term is *at the same time* the assertion of its contradictory terms is represented, at the surface syntax level, by two independent narrative utterances, of which the first, with its domination function, corresponds to the negating instance and the second, with its attributive function, corresponds to the asserting instance.

We can now represent as follows the syntagmatic series called *performance*:

$NU_1 = F$: confrontation $(S_1 \Leftarrow \rightarrow S_2)$.

Note: This narrative utterance, which anthropomorphically expresses the relation between the two terms of contradiction, is in reality a syncretism of two modal utterances, one for each subject.

$NU_2 = F$: domination $(S_1 \longrightarrow S_2)$.

Note: The utterance corresponds to the triggering of the oriented negating operation in which S_1 negates S_2, or vice versa; as we have seen negation consists of the transformation of the virtual into an actualized or, what amounts to the same thing, in the substitution of the modal utterance of wanting by the modal utterance of existence or being, and of the desire to dominate by domination.

$NU_3 = F$: attribution $(S_1 \Longleftarrow O)$.

Note: The last utterance corresponds to the asserting instance: The latter is anthropomorphically expressed by the attribution of an object-value.

The Constitutive Elements of Performance. In this outline of surface grammar, we have, by taking as an example only one syntagm, emphasized the establishment of term-by-term correspondences between the two levels of grammar. We have also highlighted the antropomorphic categories that become substituted for logical terms and operations. This results in our constructing one particular narrative unit, performance: Given that it constitutes the operational schema for the transformation of contents, it is likely *the most characteristic unit of narrative syntax*.

Performance so defined is a syntactic unit, a formal schema capable of receiving the most diverse contents. On the one hand, the two subjects of performance are interchangeable—either one can be dominant or dominated; likewise, the class of object is subject to variation according to the particular mode of the syntactic attribution.

From the point of view of its syntactic status, performance takes the form of a series of narrative utterances that are constructed according to the canonical formula: The narrative utterance is a relation between actants. This relation, which is called a function, is able to receive semantic specifications that, because of the isotopy of the utterance, are transmitted to the actants and indeed go so far as to determine their number.

If functions and actants are the constitutive *elements* of this narrative grammar, if *narrative utterances* are the elementary syntactic forms, then *narrative units* (of which *performance* is the example here) are syntagmatic series of narrative utterances.

The Constitutive Relations of Performance. The problem of the relation between utterances that come together to form narrative units must now be addressed. We have seen that performance, as a narrative unit, corresponds to the taxonomic schema and that therefore the utterances that make it up are equivalent to the logical operations located within the schema. We have also seen that the constitutive logical operations of the schema are oriented.

It must be noted that there corresponds to this *orientation* (which is a rule of the deep grammar) a relation of implication at the level of the surface grammar, with this important difference: If the orientation follows the same order as the utterances

$$NU_1 \longrightarrow NU_2 \longrightarrow NU_3,$$

the implication is oriented in the opposite way:

$$NU_3 \supset NU_2 \supset NU_1.$$

This conversion, which allows us to define the narrative unit as a series of implications between utterances, has a certain practical importance when we come to analyzing narrative at the level of manifestation because, here, it gives rise to rules governing ellipsis and catalysis: The narrative utterances logically implied within the framework of a given performance can undergo ellipsis at the level of manifestation; the presence of the last link in the chain of implications (NU_3) is enough to permit, given the intention to reconstruct the narrative unit, a catalysis that will reestablish it in its integral form.

The Modalization of Performances. If we go back and reflect on the properties of modal utterances, we will be able to establish a distinction between two possible types of performances. It will be remembered that modal utterances, when they have wanting as a function, set up the subject as a virtuality of doing, whereas two other modal utterances, characterized by the modalities of knowing and being-able, determine eventual doing in one of two ways: as a doing that is the result of knowing or one that is based solely on being-able.

These two different modalizations of doing are subsequently recognized in performances. Thus we will distinguish performances modalized by *knowing-how-to-do* (P_k) – according to whether or not the performing subject acts, at the level of manifestation, through ruse and trickery – from performances that are accomplished through *being-able-to-do* (P_{b-a}), in which the performing subject uses only his own energy and strength, be it real or magical.

Performance Series

A Syntax of Communication. Up to now, we have considered the final narrative utterance of performance (NU_3) – which is, at the surface level, the equivalent of logical assertion at the level of deep grammar – to be an attributive utterance (*AU*). One might wonder, however, if such a formulation is satisfactory.

Such an attribution – or acquisition of an object by the subject – seems very much to be a reflexive doing: The performing subject attributes to himself, seeing himself as the subject of the descriptive utterance, an object-value. If this is so, reflexive attribution is nothing more than a special case of a much more general attribution structure, one that is well known in linguistics as the *communication schema* or, even more generally, as the *structure of exchange*. It is, as we know, represented in its canonical form with three actants – sender, object of communication, and receiver:

$$TU = F: \text{transfer } (S \longrightarrow O \longrightarrow R)$$

The possibility of using a very general schema is the first advantage afforded by this new formulation. Furthermore, this formulation allows us to clearly distinguish between two different syntactic levels: (1) the level at which the syntactic operator of assertion is located, this same operator, at the level of the surface grammar becomes the performing subject of attribution (it is in fact a metasubject and the first cause of the transfers that are brought about); and (2) the level at which the transfers themselves take place. The terms *sender* and *receiver* serve only to camouflage the distinction.

The second level – which is the descriptive and not the operational level – can now be given an anthropomorphized topological representation: The actants are no longer conceived of as operators but instead as the loci where object-values can be located, loci to which they can be assigned or from which they can be withdrawn. Transfer in this case can be interpreted *at the same time* as being a privation (at the surface level) or a disjunction (at the deep level) and an attribution (at the surface level) or conjunction (at the deep level).

Such an interpretation, one that replaces attributive utterances with *translative utterances* (*TU*), seems to offer a more exact representation of performance. The consequence of a given instance of performance (NU_3) is no longer just the simple acquisition of value; it is instead a transfer: If the object-value is *attributed* to the dominant subject, it is because the dominated subject is at the same time deprived of it; the two logical operations are thus contained in just one utterance.

The Topological Syntax of Objective Values. Such a topological representation of the way in which object-values circulate amounts to the identification of the deixes of transfer with the terms of the taxonomic model, with the latter being considered as morphological units able to receive content investment. Earlier we saw that the investment of content values took place according to two correlated schemata. Now we might say that at the anthropomorphic level the schemata correspond to *isotopic spaces* (i.e., the loci within which performances unfold) and that each space is made up of two deixes that are *conjoined* (because they correspond to the same axis of contradiction), but *not conformed*: They are equivalent, at the deep level, to the contradictory terms:

From another point of view, the hypotactic axes $\bar{d}_2 \longrightarrow d_1$ and $\bar{d}_1 \longrightarrow d_2$ constitute *heterotopic spaces* whose deixes are *disjoined*, because they do not belong to the same schemata, but *conformed*, since they are linked by the relation of presupposition.

Now, the circulation of values, being seen as a series of transfers of object-values, can follow the two trajectories:

$$1.\ F(d_1 \longrightarrow O \longrightarrow \bar{d}_1) \longrightarrow F(\bar{d}_1 \longrightarrow O \longrightarrow d_2),$$

which in the case of Propp's Russian folktales can be interpreted as follows: Society (d_1) experiences a lack, the traitor ($\bar{d}_1$) kidnaps the king's daughter (O) and takes her elsewhere in order to hide her (d_2).

$$2.\ F(d_2 \longrightarrow O \longrightarrow \bar{d}_2) \longrightarrow F(\bar{d}_2 \longrightarrow O \longrightarrow d_1),$$

which will mean: The hero ($\bar{d}_2$) finds the daughter of the king (O) somewhere (d_2) and returns her to her parents (d_1).

The Russian folktale thus shows a *circular transmission of values* by successively using two performing subjects and by valorizing one of the conformed spaces (that of the hero) at the expense of the other (that of the traitor). However, we can see that we are not dealing with just a simple dual story. Origin myths usually consider the lack of such and such an object of value to be an original situation and the acquisition of values is accomplished according to just one trajectory (2). In any case this is perfectly understandable: What constitutes an acquisition of a value for deixis d_1 is necessarily and simultaneously a depriving of a value for deixis d_2, and vice versa. According to this point of view, the same trajectory for value transfer can receive two different interpretations: The story is at the same time a story of victory and defeat. What determines the choice between these interpretations has to do not with narrative syntax but rather with the axiological articulation of content values. Of the two *conformed spaces*, the investment of one is initially given as being *euphoric* and that of the other as being *dysphoric*.

If for the moment we deal only with objective values, one can say that the topological syntax of transfers, because it follows the processes of the apprehension of meaning as they were described in terms of logical operations at the level of deep grammar, organizes narration as a process that creates values. It is thus this topological syntax that is responsible for giving meaning to the story and it is the story's mainspring. Thus from the formal point of view, since translative utterances are the final utterances of performances and logically imply them, the syntactic trajectories that are expressed as transfers are in fact *syntagmatic series of performances*, that is, syntactic units of a higher order.

Syntactic Operators. Such a topological syntax is purely descriptive: We have emphasized that by not assigning any operational identity to the actants of translative utterances. In order to avoid any misunderstanding, we have called these actant deixes and not senders and receivers. This is because a *syntax of operators* must be constructed independently of a *syntax of operations*: A metasemiotic level must be established in order to justify value transfers.

Syntactic operators will be conceived of at that level as being subjects who possess a virtuality of the particular doing that will make them able to accomplish the eventual transfer operation. This virtuality is no more than a modality: knowing or being-able. As we have seen, we can formulate this virtuality in two different ways: either as a modal utterance that represents knowing-how-to-do or being-able-to-do on the part of the subject, or as an attributive utterance that signals the acquisition, on the part of the subject, of a modal value.

If the subjects become transformed into operators as the result of the attribution of a modal value (an attribution we have just replaced with the more satisfactory function of transfer), then the setting up of the operators can be effected according to the same model as that for the topological syntax of transfers, with one proviso: Here the loci of transfers are no longer deixes but rather subject-actants. The operator thus established and provided with a being-able-to-do or knowing-how-to-do is not able to accomplish the performance for which it has just been created.

Two series of performances can now be identified: performances intended to bring about the acquisition and transmission of modal values, and performances characterized by the acquisition and transfer of objective values. The first set up subjects as operators, the second ones then effect the operations; the first create virtualities, the second ones actualize them.

Thus, alongside the topological trajectory we envisage for the transfer of objective values and which, as we have seen, establishes an initial syntagmatic series of performances, a second trajectory of the same type can now be envisaged for the transfer of modal values.

We cannot devote more space here to the question of the origin of the first operator-actant who sets the syntactic trajectory in motion; that would lead us to a close examination of the particular narrative unit of the *contract* that establishes the subject of desire by attributing to it the modality of wanting. This, in turn, is likely an actualization of a "causing-to-want" on the part of an original sender. Suffice it to note for now that it is the subject's wanting that makes him able to accomplish the first performance, a performance that is marked by the attribution of the modal value of knowing or being-able.

An initial hierarchy of modal values can now be set up; it orients the syntactic trajectory as follows:

$$wanting \longrightarrow knowing \longrightarrow being\text{-}able \Longrightarrow doing$$

and it serves as the organizing principle for the syntagmatic series of performances. Certain implications of such an orientation are immediately obvious:

1. Only the acquisition of the modal value of being-able makes the subject operator able to accomplish the performance that attributes to him the objective value.

2. This means that the acquisition of the modal value of knowing has as a consequence the attribution of being-able-to-do (whose mediation is necessary if we are to move to the actualization of the doing).

3. On the other hand, the mediation of knowing does not seem necessary for the acquisition of being-able-to-do. This last observation allows us to distinguish between two kinds of subjects: the "knowing" subjects whose ability to accomplish performances comes from an initially learned knowing-how-to-do, and those who are "able" by nature.

> *Note*: The acquisition of a modal value by the subject (or anti-subject) that, for example, is manifested by the acquisition of a magical agent or of a message-object of the order of knowing, establishes the subject as *helper* (or as *opponent*) who can now proceed to the next performance.

Such a syntagmatic series, which is established outside the formal framework of the translative utterances (that is, without considering the actants that are implicated) is enough to allow us to clarify the nature of the relations between two different types of performances—one that is *oriented* (since the performance that establishes the syntactic operator is followed by the performance that affects the syntactic operation) and one in which, at the same time, the objective performance *implies* the modal performance.

The Topological Syntax of Modal Values. Given the polemic nature of narrativity, two syntactic operators are necessary in order to establish a narrative syntax: This has led us to envisage two subjects (S_1 and S_2) for constructing the performance. Consequently it is the axis of exchange between two subjects that constitutes the locus for the transfers of modal values. The attribution to S_1 of a given modal value presupposes that S_2 is at the same time deprived of that value.

Two trajectories for the transfer of modal values are thus envisaged, according to whether we are dealing with a "knowing" or "able" subject, that is, according to the priority assigned to the acquisition of one or the other of the two modalities in question.

In the first case, the syntagmatic series will be oriented as follows:

$$TU_1(S_1 \longrightarrow O: \text{knowing} \longrightarrow S_2) \longrightarrow TU_2(S_1 \longrightarrow O: \text{being-able} \longrightarrow S_2).$$

It can be interpreted as being the acquisition, by S_2, of a being-able, thanks to a knowing obtained earlier. At the same time it can be seen as the loss, by S_1, of being-able, and this because of having lost knowing.

In the second case, the orientation is reversed:

$$TU_1(S_2 \longrightarrow O: \text{being-able} \longrightarrow S_1) \longrightarrow TU_2(S_2 \longrightarrow O: \text{knowing} \longrightarrow S_1).$$

The sequence can be interpreted as being the acquisition, by S_1, of a knowing, and this would be thanks to a recognized being-able. Conversely, it could be seen as being the loss, by S_2, of any knowing that would follow the loss of being-able.

One of the two series suffices, by combining with the series of transfers of objective values, to constitute the completed story. If, however, for each of the trajectories we have chosen two different subjects (S_1 and S_2) to be the receivers of modal values — this choice is obviously arbitrary — it is in order at the same time to account for the unique organization of the *mirrored story* as it is found, for example, in the Russian folktale studied by Propp. Indeed, there we first see the subject S_2, axiologically identified as *traitor*, acquiring modal values at the expense of S_1:

$$S_2 = O_1: \text{knowing} \longrightarrow O_2: \text{being-able}$$

and then giving way to the subject S_1, called the *hero*, who progressively deprives him of the earlier acquired values, by appropriating them for himself:

$$S_1 = O_1: \text{being-able} \longrightarrow O_2: \text{knowing}.$$

The General Form of the Narrative Grammar. We have just given a broad outline of a surface narrative syntax, or rather, of just that part of the syntax that is relevant to the very body of the story. What is still lacking, and we can only briefly mention it here, is the identification and examination of the syntactic units framing the story and which correspond to the initial and final sequences of the manifested story.

Here we would have to account for syntactic units that would correspond to what, at the deep grammar level, are the hypotactic relations of the taxonomic model, that is, to the relations that can be established in this model between the terms s_1 and $\bar{s}_2$ and between s_2 and $\bar{s}_1$. The triggering of narration would be represented here as being the establishment of a *conjunctive* contractual relation between sender and receiver-subject, followed by a spatial *disjunction* between these two actants. The completion of the story would be marked, on the contrary, by a spatial conjunction and one last transfer of values, this time setting up a new contract through a new distribution of values, both objective and modal.

Although it remains incomplete, our attempt at least gives an idea of what a syntactic organization of narrativity might be. We have identified two kinds of *oriented syntagmatic series* that organize the transfer of modal and objective values within the framework of a topological syntax. The object-values are located within the framework of final narrative utterances that represent the consequences of the performances and that logically imply those consequences. These syntagmatic series are in reality orderings of performances that, as syntactic units, are recurrent and formally identical. We have also identified another principle of syntagmatic organization: Performances are distributed in such a way that the first, characterized by the attribution of a modal value that establishes the *subject-operator*, must be followed by a second that actualizes the *operation.*

As to the typical syntactic unit that performance is, we have seen that it can be conceived of as a series of three narrative utterances connected by implication. In examining narrative utterances we have been able to sketch out a brief typology. By introducing further semantic determinations of their functions and by varying both the number and the specifics of their actants, we have been able to identify three principal types of narrative utterances: descriptive, modal, and translative. Every utterance, at the level of surface narrative grammar, represents either a relation or an operation of the deep grammar.

Once such a narrative grammar has been completed it will at the same time be of a deductive and analytic nature. It will trace a group of trajectories that are followed in the manifestation of meaning: Starting with the elementary operations of the deep grammar (which follow the process of the actualization of signification) and continuing with the combinations of the syntagmatic series of the surface grammar (which are nothing more than the anthropomorphic representations of these operations), the contents, through the effect of the performances, become invested within the narrative utterance. These are organized in linear sequences of canonical utterances that are connected, like the links of a single chain, by a series of logical implications. Once we are able to identify such series of narrative utterances, and if we also enlist the help of a rhetoric, a stylistics, and a linguistic grammar, we will be able to conceive of the linguistic manifestation of narrativized signification.

Chapter 5
A Problem of Narrative Semiotics: Objects of Value

The Semiotic Status of Value

Cultural Values

To choose the world of tales of the fantastic as a reference corpus is to guarantee the universality of the narrative forms therein to be found. So it is, for example, with a particular class of figurative actors traditionally known by the term *magical objects*: Once they have been placed at the disposal of the hero or antihero, they help them in various ways, and can even be substituted for them, in their quest for values. These objects, which usually, but not necessarily, go in threes, will at different times manifest themselves as

A purse that fills itself
A hat or helmet that can carry one over great distances
A horn or a whistle that summons soldiers.

After particular study of type 563 in the classifications of Antti Aarne and Stith Thompson,[1] Georges Dumézil arrived at the conclusion that these talismans, as he calls them, are readily classifiable within the already tested model for the functional tripartition of Indo-European ideology. From this point of view magical objects are no more than figurative and lower-order forms of the principal spheres of divine sovereignty, or, and it amounts to the same thing, the essential attributes of human competence. It is these attributes that institute, justify, and enable human doing in the mode of the imaginary.

Without for now going into a detailed examination of the different tasks performed by magical objects, and also without questioning at this point whether it is legitimate to go beyond the Indo-European domain and generalize about the totality of the characteristics of narrative on the basis of results obtained in Aarne and Thompson's study, we can still note the obvious fact of one distinction that allows us to divide these objects into two classes, according to whether they provide *goods* or *services*. If by services we mean the *powers* of the objects, powers by which the hero comes into possession of the qualities he will need to accomplish great deeds (the gift of immediate departure and unlimited travel furnished by a magic carpet, the gift of invisibility and omniscience one acquires by putting on a given hat or helmet, or the ability to subdue one's enemies by giving instructions to a magical staff), then one can readily view the objects belonging to this class as modal helpers whose spheres of competence correspond to the first two functions of sovereignty. In turn magical objects that provide goods appear, and maybe even more sharply so, as being "lower-order" representatives of the Dumézilian function that identifies mediators between a mythical sender and the man for whom the goods are intended: The magical object—a calabash, for example—is not worth possessing in and of itself. It is, rather, a provider of goods. It is by constantly replenishing its contents that it offers food in abundance.

It is unfruitful and impossible to proceed with a classification of magical objects that provide goods; such a classification belongs to semantic analysis and the results would take the form of a typology that includes a certain number of constants that correspond to human basic needs and as many variables that account for relative sociocultural differences. At the level of ethnic literature we can identify *consumable goods* (= abundant food) and *goods that can be hoarded* (= wealth, gold). Other oppositions appear after a more careful examination. They include a distribution of helpers according to modes of production:

> *Gathered* fruit vs. *cultivated* fruit[2]

or according to the tools used in production:

> *hunters'* knives vs. *farmers' hoes*.[3]

The replacement of draft animals[4] for these magical objects in the role of providers does not change anything in this relatively simple and stable inventory of desirable values. Only by extending the corpus to include ever more complex stories can we draw up the, if not exhaustive at least representative, inventory of elementary values (love, health, beauty, fecundity) that Indo-Europeans placed under the protection of the third-function divinities.

Object and Value

When we speak of objects of lack or of desire such as, for example, food or gold, and when our reference is limited to stories from folklore, there is a tendency to confuse the notions of *object* and *value*; the figurative form of the object guarantees its reality and at this level value becomes identified with the desired object. Even at this level things are not in fact that simple. When, for example, someone in our society today acquires an automobile, it is perhaps not so much the car as an object that he wants to acquire, but a rapid means of transportation, the modern substitute for the magic carpet of old. Often what he is buying is also some prestige or a feeling of power. In such cases the object is no more than a pretext, a locus of value investment, an elsewhere mediating the relationship between the subject and himself.

The problem thus posed is not just a psychological one. The lexicographer concerned with giving appropriate definitions for the lexemes of his dictionary is also implicated. This problem is the first thing facing any semantic analysis because it makes exhaustive description almost impossible. It is obvious, for example, that the definition of the lexeme *automobile* would, to be exhaustive, have to include not only (1) a *configurative* component, which breaks the object down into its constitutive parts and then recomposes it as form, and (2) a *taxic* component, which through its differential characteristics accounts for its status as object among other manufactured objects, but also (3) its *functional* component, which is both practical and mythical (prestige, power, escape, etc.).

The lexeme that is a linguistic object thus appears as a set of virtualities, a set whose internal organization—if there is one—is not obvious, virtualities of which the eventual realizations are specified thanks only to syntactic trajectories established outside discursive manifestation.

Underlining the indefinable nature of the lexeme reminds us of our earlier preoccupations[5] when, in inquiring into the conditions in which signification appears, we were led to postulate:

1. That no object is knowable in and of itself. Only by its determinations can it be known;
2. That its determinations could be apprehended only as differences etched against the object, and that this differential nature gives to these determinations the status of linguistic value;
3. That the object, while remaining unknowable as such, was nonetheless presupposed as a sort of support, by the existence of values.

If we use a metaphor from logic, we might say that the object is comparable to a concept of which only its comprehension can be manipulated, since that comprehension is made up only of differential values. The object thus appears to be a locus of fixation, a locus of circumstantial clustering of the value determinations.

To speak of objects as such does not make any sense, and even a taxonomic treatment of a class of objects—such as the organization of the field of chairs made popular by Pottier—operates only with semic categories, that is, with values alone. There is always a distance between the cluster of semes that metalinguistically organizes the representation of an *armchair* and the final lexeme *armchair*.

Only when syntax is brought into play can we account for the meeting of the object and the values invested in it. Taking syntax for what it is (that is, an imaginary representation, which is also the only way to conceive of the apprehension of meaning and the manipulation of significations), we can understand that the object is a syntactical concept, an end term of our relation with the world. It is at the same time one of the terms of the elementary utterance that is a semiotic simulacrum representing, in the form of a drama, this relation to the world. Nevertheless, as we have seen, the apprehension of meaning meets, in its process, only values determining the object, not the object itself. Given this, the lexeme, which emerges as a *trompe-l'oeil* where the object is supposed to be, is readable only in terms of some of its values.

It is in syntagmatic unfolding that syntax joins semantics. The syntactic object, which is no more than the subject's intended project, can be recognized only through one or more of the semantic values that manifest it. Recognizing a value allows one to presuppose the object in terms of the syntactic locus of its manifestation. The enunciation that produces an utterance brings out the value that manifests and determines the object, and this is done independently of the mode of lexicalization of the value itself.

Subject and Value

Up to now we have used the term *value* only as it is used in linguistics, that is, as an arbitrarily designated term covering an inexpressible semantic structure and which can be defined only in negative terms, as an exclusionary field in relation to what it is not and as a field that is nonetheless fixed as a syntactic locus called object. Nevertheless, this definition of value, which makes it operational in semiotics, is not far removed from its axiological interpretation. This is so even for no other reason than that value, fixed in this location called object and there to manifest that object, is in a relation with the subject. Indeed, to the extent that the elementary utterance can be defined as an oriented relation that engenders two end terms—the subject and the object—the value invested in the object in question in a way semanticizes the whole utterance, and thereby becomes a value of the subject that meets it upon seeking the object. The subject is, therefore, semantically determined through its relation with the value. For this reason, in a later final step it will be enough to assign to the subject a *wanting-to-be* in order for the *value of the subject*, in the semiotic sense, to be transformed into a *value for the subject*, in the axiological sense of the term.

A practical problem is thus temporarily resolved: In a given semantic universe that is filled with the innumerable potential objects that lexemes are, the only lexemes that will count and that will be taken into consideration are those that can be inscribed on the syntactic axis

subject ——> object

because only the underlying syntactic network is able to select lexemes in order to extract values from them. This it accomplishes by at the same time transforming the verbal manifestation into a discoursive organization of meaning.

Objective Values and Subjective Values

These refinements made to the status of *value* — something that is readable only when it has been inscribed in the syntactic structure — further require a rapid examination of the relationships one can conceive of between semiotic syntax and its different manifestations in the natural languages.

Let us return to the search for a point of departure, to the usual source of our inspiration — folklore. We have seen that the search for and the acquisition of wealth are favorite and almost universal themes in folklore. *Wealth* can be present in various ways in different stories and is initially present in figurative form as, for example,

1. John has a pot full of gold pieces.

The analysis of such a semiotic "fact" allows us to interpret the status of the object at three different levels:

The syntactic level: actor: figurative object *pot full of gold pieces.*

However, figurativity is only one among many modes of manifestation, and the possession of wealth can be rendered in a natural language such as French by a linguistic utterance of the type:

2. John has a great fortune,

in which we recognize the first two levels identical to those of example 1, but:

mode of manifestation: actor: nonfigurative object *great fortune.*

A third mode of manifestation appears with linguistic utterances of the type:

3. John is rich,

in which we readily recognize the presence of the value *wealth*, which, as we have said, necessarily presupposes that of the syntactic object, but whose *attributive* mode of manifestation poses a problem.

On several occasions[6] we have sought to account for this twofold linguistic manifestation of a single narrative fact by appealing to the opposition between the verbs *to have* (and its parasynonyms) and *to be* as used to express the same logical function by which utterances describing a state undergo constitutive *conjunction*. While considering them as realizing one and the same function, we tried to discover a source of differentiation that might permit us to distinguish *objective values* (produced with the aid of utterances using *to have*) from *subjective values* (produced by utterances using *to be*). This distinction would then have allowed us to speak of *exteriorization* and *interiorization* of values. Without being false, such an interpretation is too close to the languages of manifestation (the distribution of the roles of *having* and *being* can differ from one language to another; other linguistic means of manifestation, possessives, for example, can bring our postulated dichotomy into doubt). Also, the foregoing interpretation does not account for what is proper to any discursive manifestation, independently of the language used: the actorial form of the manifestation of actants.

Indeed, if in examples 1 and 2, two manifested actors, John and "pot full of gold pieces"/"great fortune," corresponded in each case to the two actants (subject and object), in the case of example 3 the same two actants are manifested within the same actor, John. In other words, a single semiotic utterance of the type

$$S \cap O$$

can be postulated as subsuming a great variety of linguistic manifestations of the same relation of conjunction between subject and object, with the proviso that we will later have to set up a structural typology of manifestation and even a typology of the rules governing the engendering of utterances. This typology could correspond to the surface levels of grammar.

If we accept the principle of positional nonconcomitance for *semiotic actants* and *discoursive actors* (which must not, in turn, be confused with phrastic linguistic actants) and also the principle of the distance separating the two, this will guarantee the autonomy of narrative syntax and institute it as an organizing instance that regulates discursive manifestation. In the case now at hand, the *syncretism of the actants*, if we can, from the point of view of the actorial structure, so describe the presence of two or more actants in one single discursive actor, might be interpreted within the general framework of reflexivity.

Thus, talking about the same John, we can say not only that he is rich, but also that

4. John is always torturing himself.

A surface analysis of this linguistic utterance reveals that within an actor named *John*, which is also considered a locus in which syntactic events take place, *John*, in his role as subject actant, tortures the same *John* seen as object actant. We can see that the status of what we call the *reflexive utterance* can readily be interpreted by inscribing a syntactic utterance within its syncretically located actor, and it is of little importance whether the utterance is a *doing utterance* (in the case of torture) or an *utterance describing a state* (in which wealth can become a taxic and axiological qualification governing one type of predictable kinds of behavior).

If this is correct, we can see that it is the type of relation maintained between the actantial structure and the actorial structure that determines as borderline cases, the *reflexive organization* of individual universes and, at other times, the *transitive organization* of cultural universes. We can also see that one and the same syntax is able to account for both *psychosemiotic* narrativization ("the inner life") and *sociosemiotic* narrativization (mythologies and ideologies). The most frequent form of narrativity is, of course, a mixed one, at the same time both psycho- and sociosemiotic (corresponding to the set of interindividual practices).

The Narrative Status of Values

The Narrativization of Values

Whether it be we ourselves who, being immersed in the semantic universe, find ourselves surrounded by an infinity of semiotic objects able to reveal themselves as values, or whether it be our discourses that, following the procedure of actantial disengagement, we populate with subjects who possess or who seek values, the elementary syntactic schema guides the subject and selects, in all cases, the values that occupy the position of object. They thus, given this underlying relation, call the subjects and objects into a *semiotic existence*. Only when a value is inscribed into an utterance that describes a state whose function establishes the junctive relation between the subject and the object can we consider this subject and this object as semiotically existing one for the other. Such as assertion, far from being a metaphysical flight of fancy, on the contrary serves an eminently practical end: By defining semiotic existence as a structural relation, it excludes from our considerations the ontological problematics of subject and object, and by formulating this relation as constitutive of a canonical utterance describing a state, it gives us a formal framework and identifying criteria for semiotic facts that are relevant to any analysis.

The semiotic status of values being thus defined, we can conceive of narrativization as being their syntagmatic emplacement, as a discursive organization that manipulates the constitutive elements of the canonical utterance

1. Either by effecting substitutions of subjects
2. Or by substituting object-values one for the other
3. Or by going on to transformations of functions.

The object of our study being the search for the elementary forms of narrativity, we must first envisage the simplest cases: Thus, considering the subject and object of the utterance describing a state as constants, we will first examine only transformations of the constitutive function of the utterance.

One can define this function as a junction that, as a semic category, is articulated in two contradictory terms: *conjunction* and *disjunction*. This gives rise to two types of *utterance describing a state*:

Conjunctive utterances = $S \cap O$,
Disjunctive utterances = $S \cup O$,

it being understood that the movement from one utterance to the other can occur only at the instigation of a metasubject operator whose formal status can be made clear only within the framework of an *utterance of doing* of the type:

$$F \text{ transformation } (S_1 \longrightarrow O_1)$$

in which S_1 is the subject bringing about the transformation and O_1 is the utterance describing a state that is the end point of the transformation.

Now one can understand our provisional definition of narrativity as consisting of one or more transformations that result in junctions, that is, either conjunctions or disjunctions between subjects and objects.

Applying these definitions to the syntagmatization of values, we will apply the term *realization* to the transformation that establishes conjunction between subject and object:

$$Realization = F \text{ transformation } < S_1 \longrightarrow O_1 \ (S \cap O)>.$$

Now we can use the term *realized value* to describe the value invested in the object at the time (= in the syntactic position) when that object comes into conjunction with the subject.

The relations of conjunction and disjunction being contradictory, any transformation of a state of conjunction can produce only disjunction between subject and object. Disjunction, being the denial of conjunction and no more, does not abolish all relations between the two actants: In other words, the loss of all relation between subject and object would result in abolishing semiotic existence and would relegate objects to their original semantic chaos. Denial thus maintains subject and object in their status as semiotic *beings*, while at the same time conferring on them a mode of existence that differs from the conjunctive state. We would say that all disjunction does is to virtualize the relation between subject and object by maintaining it as a possibility for conjunction.

Now we can use the term *virtualization* to describe the transformation that brings about disjunction between subject and object and consider as a *virtual value* any value invested in the object that is disjoined from the subject:

$$Virtualization = F \text{ transformation } < S_1 \longrightarrow O_1 \ (S \cup O)>.$$

If then we consider only transformations of constitutive functions of utterances describing a state, then narrativity, in its most simplified form, appears as a syntagmatic string of virtualizations and realizations. Without forgetting the arbitrary nature of the terms we have just chosen, we must keep in mind that they apply to definite syntactic forms. This allows us to use a seemingly metaphorical terminology and speak of a subject that, in order to be *realized*, must first be established as a *virtual subject*[7] possessing values whose realization will cancel out their status as *virtual* values, etc. This should be possible without our being accused of being unscientific in our terminology.

Origin and Destination of Values

To consider story as being a string of virtualizations and realizations of values, of course, poses the problem of their origin and destination. Where do they come from when they appear for the first time as virtual values, subsequently to be conjoined with subjects? Where do they go once they have become irrevocably disjoined from the subjects that once possessed them?

Finding and *losing* at first sight appear to be extreme forms of gratuitous conjunction and disjunction. To find an object is to apprehend it as a value coming from nowhere and to establish the first relation between it and the subject. To lose an object, through accident, destruction, or neglect, is not only to become disjoined from it, but also to cancel any relation with it, while at the same time destroying the subject in terms of its semiotic existence.

Nonetheless when we seek examples that might illustrate these extreme examples of appearances and disappearances of values, we come up against embarrassing ambiguities. Maître Hauchecorne finds a bit of string in the famous Maupassant story. But society quickly makes a suspect of him. According to society's logic, *finding* quite naturally presupposes *losing*, a losing that postulates some other subject of disjunction. This amounts to negating the possibility of *ex nihilo* appearance of values. The reader in turn, because he *knows* that it is just a bit of string "without value," cannot stop himself from invoking "fate" that placed it in Maître Hauchecorne's path. The reader thus postulates the existence of some other and earlier subject, in the form of a nonfigurative sender. When the calabash that furnishes abundant food to a once-starving African family breaks itself, is it definitely lost? The loss is explained in terms of there having been a transgression against a taboo and appears as a disjunction brought about by some other implicit subject who has taken on the role of law keeper. It is as if, within a given axiological universe, values circulate in a closed space and that instance of *finding* and *losing* in reality covers the absolute conjunctions and disjunctions by which that *immanent universe* communicates with a *transcendent universe*, source and depository of values that are outside the circuit.

When Paolo Fabbri,[8] in his analysis of *Pinocchio*, found the problem of the *hidden treasure*, he proposed a sociological interpretation of it. Tuscan agricultural society, as is probably the case for all autarkic societies, sees riches as being available in limited quantities, so that a closed universe of values corresponds to any given closed community. In it, the circulation of wealth is a closed circuit, and the syntactic trajectories of values are such that for every instance of acquisition on the part of one member of the society there corresponds necessarily a loss on the part of another. The myth of the quest for hidden treasure, on the contrary, introduces values that are no longer of this closed universe, and this is so according to a twofold point of view:

First, to goods considered to be the result of work are opposed found treasures, unmerited, illegitimate, and desirable at the same time. In relation to positive values, these riches appear as anti-values or *negative values* having to do with an axiological anti-universe. What proves this is that values, once realized, and in the case where certain rules of behavior have not been observed when the treasure was taken into possession, are able to be changed into what they really are, into horse dung, for example, or into birch bark (Lithuanian folklore).

Second, this treasure is often kept and sometimes given by a supernatural being who does not belong to the society of the subject of the quest. Be he keeper or giver of the treasure, this character plays the role of mediator between the universe of transcendent values and the immanent universe into which the new values are introduced for circulation.

This brief examination, at the level of ethnic literature, allows us to distinguish between different kinds of manipulation of values.

The first, and simplest, case has to do with the circulation of constant values (or equivalent ones) between equal subjects in an isotopic and closed universe.

The second case poses the problem of the introduction and removal of these immanent values to and from the given universe, and it presupposes the existence of a universe of *transcendent values* that encompasses and encloses the first in such a way that subjects who possess the *immanent values* appear as receivers vis-à-vis the subject-senders of the transcendent universe.

Opposed to these two first cases, which call into question the quality and number of subjects engaged in the manipulation of values, is the whole problem of the transformation of values themselves, that is, of the mode of organization of values in polarized microuniverses that allow one to determine the relations existing between *positive values* and *negative values* and to predict their narrativization in the form of posited and inverted values.

Taking these problems one at a time, we will now examine the first case.

Communication Involving Only One Object

The Complex Junction Utterance

We will now try to conceive of and analyze only those relations that exist between subjects and objects within the framework of a closed axiological universe in which values, which are accepted by all and never negated, circulate in a uniform way by going from one subject to the other. We will take Fabbri's Tuscan model (for his work on *Pinocchio*) or the similar axiological universe of the Mediterranean play *Mors tua, vita mea* analyzed by A. Cirese.[9] The narrativization of such a universe, since it is obliged to give the form of a syntagmatic string to the play of conjunctions and disjunctions of values, will always, for each operation, set in place two subjects that are oriented toward only one object, and will thus manifest one of the perhaps most primitive forms of story. These have been described, for example, by Heda Jason. In them, two characters, who are each in turn a rogue and a dupe, successively take possession of an object of value that can thus go indefinitely from one to the other.

Here we have two subjects who are simultaneously present and share the same desire for one and the same object. Such a situation can be considered typical of elementary narrativity because it satisfies the hypothesis we formulated earlier and according to which there are no values that are absolutely lost or found. To the extent that senders, as the transcendent source of values, are not made explicit in a given story, the subject S_1, who is disjoined from the object, can be considered a virtual subject only if that object is already in conjunction with the subject S_2. In other words a subject will attribute a value to an object only if that object already belongs to someone else.

We can see that a narrative state of this type can be described using two utterances that describe states

$$(S_1 \cup O) \;\rule[0.4ex]{1.2em}{0.4pt}\rule[-0.6ex]{0.4pt}{1.4ex}\; (S_2 \cap O),$$

which are linked by a relation of reciprocal presupposition. If S_1 is disjoined from O, then S_2 is conjoined with O in such a way that any change in the status of one of the utterances will have predictable and necessary repercussions on the status of the other one that is bound up with it. If, following a transformation, S_1 were to become conjoined with O, then S_2 would become disjoined from it.

There is even more. Solidarity, the term we will use to indicate the reciprocal presupposition between the two utterances, is paradigmatically a relation between two known relations, that is, conjunction and disjunction, the relation by which we define contrariety between two terms of the semic category[10] (contrariety, which in the case of binary categories—as is the case here—is identified with contradiction, which consequently is no more than a given instance of the first one). When we remember that we defined the elementary utterance through and by a relation that projects the actants as its end terms, and we called it function, then we can see that solidarity can in turn be considered as a function located between two functives (that is, between functions considered as terms, according to Hjelmslev's terminology). We can now use the term *junction* to designate a category whose semic terms are conjunction and disjunction. *Junction* will thus define the function that, when it is established, results in the concomitant appearance of two utterances in a relation of solidarity:

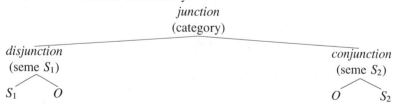

junction
(category)

disjunction
(seme S_1)

S_1 O

conjunction
(seme S_2)

O S_2

The two terms of the semic category of junction constitute the semic invest-ment of the constitutive functions of two utterances of state. The category itself, designated as junction, appears as a metafunction that subsumes the two utter-ances. The existence of an object O that is common to both utterances also autho-rizes us to modify slightly our notation by giving to this sort of metautterance the form of a *complex utterance with three actants*:

Junction utterance $= (S_1 \cup O \cap S_2)$.

Syntagmatic Junctions and Paradigmatic Junctions

This new definition of junction requires us to introduce some further refine-ments. It will be remembered that we initially used the term junction in order to be able to designate with one term the two types of constitutive functions of utter-ances of state. We were thereby considering the two relations from a typological point of view, *s* terms in a system, independent of their realization in the discour-sive process. In effect, the semic category of junction subsumes its two contradic-tory terms of conjunction and disjunction. The junction utterance we have just formulated represents, on the contrary, a *complex narrative state* that, at a given point in the unfolding discourse, brings into play two subjects in the presence of one object of value.

We propose to use the term *paradigmatic junction* to designate the logically necessary concomitance of two utterances of conjunction and disjunction, affect-ing two distinct subjects. Nevertheless, since narrativity can be considered as a string of narrative states, a conjunction utterance presupposing a disjunction ut-terance concerning one and the same subject (and conversely), we can reserve the term *syntagmatic junction* for a series of two junctive utterances (conjunction and disjunction, or conversely) having the same subject and linked by a relation of simple presupposition. The workings of a simple story thus appear character-ized by a double stringing:

	syntagmatic junction
paradigmatic junction	$(S_1 \cup O) \longrightarrow (S_1 \cap O) \longrightarrow$
	$(S_2 \cap O) \longrightarrow (S_2 \cup O) \longrightarrow$

As we see, such a simple narrativization brings not just one program into exis-tence, but rather *two narrative programs* whose solidarity is guaranteed by the concomitance of functions, in a relation of contradiction, and which define the two subjects while keeping the concomitant but inverse program implicit.

Such an interpretation, although it is still limited in its field of application, can serve as a point of departure for a structural formulation of what is sometimes called *perspective*. Be that as it may, story, because it centers on just one object (or on a series of multiple values that are isotopic and syntagmatically distributed), manifests its twofold syntagmatic and paradigmatic nature as it simultaneously plays on the two types of discontinuity.

Transfers of Objects and Communication between Subjects

The description of the syntagmatic unfolding of narrative states should not lead us to forget the existence of a transforming doing that assures the passage of one state to another and, above all, the existence of the subject of the producing-doing belonging to utterances of state. As we have seen, this third subject is metataxic in relation to the subjects of utterance of state. It alone allows us to account for the dynamics of story, that is, its syntactic organization. Thus, while temporarily setting aside the problems of enunciation and its subject (which, in its role as narrator situated outside discourse, has various subjects at its disposal for its story-utterance), and by considering only the transforming subject assigned and installed in the narrative discourse, we can attribute to each junction utterance a doing-utterance that produces and regulates it.

At first sight, two possibilities are then open to us:

1. *Either* the transforming subject that we have designated as S_3 becomes identified with S_1, a virtual subject, in disjunction vis-à-vis the object of value;
2. *Or* S_3 becomes identified with S_2, a realized subject, in conjunction with the object of value.

Note: We can see that *verbal communication* is, from this perspective, no more than a specific instance of communication. Communication can use all manner of means and can be broken down into a *causing-to-know*, that is, a doing that effects the transfer of an object of knowing.

A topological representation of narrativity that accounts for the transfer of objects is not contradictory vis-à-vis its interpretation as a syntagmatic organization of acts of communication.

Narrative Transformations

Let us now examine the two cases we have already identified in which we have syncretism of the subject of doing and the subjects of a state. Given that (1) *the* subject of transformation can be identified either with the subject S_1 or the subject S_2, and (2) *each* of these two subjects can, prior to the transformation, be either a virtual subject (in disjunction from O) or a real subject (in conjunction with O), four types of transformation can be noted:

1. If

      S_3 transformation = virtual S_1,

    then

      F transformation $<(S_3 = S_1) \longrightarrow (S_1 \cap O)>$.

The transformation can be called a *reflexive realization*. On the figurative level it will appear as an *appropriation* (of the object).

2. If

      S_3 transformation = real S_2,

    then

      F transformation $<(S_3 = S_2) \longrightarrow (S_1 \cap O)>$.

The transformation is a *transitive realization*. On the figurative level it consists of an *attribution* (of the object).

These two transformations are *conjunctive transformations* giving rise to two modes—reflexive and transitive—of the *realization of the subject*.

3. If

      S_3 transformation = real S_1,

    then

      F transformation $<(S_3 = S_1) \longrightarrow (S_1 \cup O)>$.

The transformation will be called *reflexive virtualization*. On the figurative level it can be called *renunciation* (of the object).

4. If

      S_3 transformation = virtual S_2,

    then

      F transformation $<(S_3 = S_2) \longrightarrow (S_1 \cup O)>$.

The transformation appears as a *transitive virtualization* and can be called, on the figurative level, *dispossession* (of the object).

The last two transformations are *disjunctive transformations* giving rise to two types—reflexive and transitive—of *virtualization of the subject*.

The Syntagmatic Point of View. From the preceding we can see that for just one object there exist two modes—reflexive and transitive—of *realization* to which, on the figurative level, two modes of acquisition of objects of value correspond. In *appropriation* the subject seeks to acquire the objects by its own devices. In *attribution* the objects are conferred on the subject by another subject.

Parallel to this there are two modes — reflexive and transitive — of *virtualization* to which, on the figurative level, two modes of deprivation of values correspond. In *renunciation* the subject separates itself from the values. In *dispossession* it is deprived of them by another subject.

It might be useful, for the furtherance of this terminology, to present it schematically in the accompanying diagram.

transformations

conjunctive transformation = *realization* (acquisition)

reflexive (appropriation)

transitive (attribution)

disjunctive transformation = *virtualization* (deprivation)

reflexive (renunciation)

transitive (dispossession)

These four types of transformation can be involved in the case of just one subject (S_1 or S_2) in relation with just one object O and, in becoming part of its narrative program, constitute its elementary syntagmatic structure.

The Paradigmatic Point of View. Given that narrativization, in the case under study, consists in the concomitant unfolding of two narrative programs in a relation of solidarity simultaneously implicating two subjects, we can see that for each instance of acquisition on the part of one of the subjects there will be, in the parallel program, an instance of deprivation vis-à-vis the other subject. This means that there will be concomitance between

appropriation and *dispossession*
attribution and *renunciation*.

If we use the term *test* to designate the transformation that gives rise to a concomitant appropriation and dispossession, and the term *gift* to designate the transformation that produces a solidary attribution and renunciation, we will obtain the two principal figures by which, at the surface, the communication of values manifests itself. A simple table can illustrate these paradigmatic relations of story:

	acquisition	*deprivation*
test	appropriation	dispossession
gift	attribution	renunciation

The solidarity between *renunciation* and *attribution* we have just postulated is, however, brought into question by an important exception, into which we will have to inquire. There is the problem of the unique status of the sender that, in situations as yet to be determined, can effect attributions without at the same time requiring the sender to renounce values he continues to possess.

Communication with Two Objects

The Reciprocal Gift

Test and *gift* can, according to the narrative program envisaged, appear as either two modes of realization of the subject or as two modes of its virtualization.

The virtualization of the subject, when it is manifested in the form of a dispossession corresponding to the Proppian "lack," includes a positive aspect: It constitutes one of the necessary conditions for the evolution of the virtual subject into a subject of wanting. *Renunciation*, on the contrary, being a general virtualization, does not bring about an increase in the subject's potentialities. The two "situations of lack," although comparable, are not identical, because the *syntagmatic positions* of the subjects in the narration are not identical. In the first case the doing can follow the virtualization of the subject; in the second, it precedes it.

It is in this last context that, as might be expected, a unit often called a *countergift* appears. It can be formulated in terms identical to those for *gift* except that the operator-subject of the countergift will be syncretic with the subject of the opposed narrative program. If the object of the two transfer operations remains the same (as in the case, for example, of the king's daughter whom the hero returns to her father in order to later receive her in marriage), the countergift takes the form of a reestablishment of the *status quo ante*. Following the renunciation on the part of S_1, the transformation of the state

$$(S_1 \cap O \cup S_2) \implies (S_1 \cup O \cap S_2)$$

is canceled out by the transforming doing of S_2:

$$(S_1 \cup O \cap S_2) \implies (S_1 \cap O \cup S_2).$$

A syntagmatic series composed of two renunciations implicating two reciprocal attributions of the same object, or, in other words, of two transformations the
second of which cancels out the effects of the first and reestablishes the initial
equilibrium, can be designated as a *reciprocal gift*. Whatever its narrative significance, it constitutes, on the formal level, only the general framework of bipolar communication, although this does not mean that it can be identified with the
structure of *exchange*.

Virtual Exchange

Putting the structure of exchange in place, contrary to the situations we have
been examining, requires two objects of value O_1 and O_2: the object one of the
subjects renounces (O_1) and another object (O_2) that the same subject covets and
that will be attributed to it. The converse occurs when it is the second subject that
is involved. Each of the two subjects taken separately is thus, preceding the triggering of the transformation, both a real and a virtual subject. The transformation
that we figuratively call *exchange* will, from this perspective, constitute a new
realization and a new virtualization of the subjects.

Nonetheless the fact that each of the subjects S_1 and S_2 is simultaneously in
relation with two objects O_1 and O_2 requires us to consider the narrative programs
of the two subjects separately and to formulate first the *narrative state* that sums
up the situation each is in, in the form of an *utterance with three actants*:

$$(O_1 \cap S \cup O_2).$$

We can see that the complex utterance thus produced is—just as the junction
utterance analyzed above, $(S_1 \cap O \cup S_2)$—a reduction of two elementary utterances into a single complex one. The reduction is possible thanks either to our
being able to identify two objects belonging to two utterances or two subjects that
are separate from each other. In effect, since the subject is defined by its relation
to the object, and by that alone, the presence of two objects O_1 and O_2 obliges
us initially to postulate the existence of a distinct subject for each of the objects.
It is only later that identification of the two subjects in actorial syncretism allows
us to reduce the two elementary utterances to one complex one. This allows us
subsequently to distinguish between the two kinds of junction utterances that have
a comparable structure: *utterances junctive of subjects* and *utterances junctive of
objects*.

Exchange can now be described as a twofold transformation of two utterances
junctive of objects, a transformation brought about concomitantly, and simultaneously, by two subjects. If the first transformation, brought about by the subject
of doing associated with S_1, can be written as

$$(O_1 \cap S_1 \cup O_2) \implies (O_1 \cup S_1 \cap O_2),$$

the second transformation, which is effected by the subject of doing associated with S_2, is in a relation of solidarity with the first one and is characterized by the simple inversion of the functions of conjunction and disjunction:

$$(O_1 \cup S_2 \cap O_2) \implies (O_1 \cap S_2 \cup O_2).$$

Exchange, as a unit of communication of values, can de defined as F transformation $<S_1 \longrightarrow (O_1 \cup S_1 \cap O_2)>$ ⟂ F transformation $<S_2 \longrightarrow (O_1 \cap S_2 \cup O_2)>$ given that, in the first transformation the S transformation $= S_1$, and in the second the S transformation $= S_2$.

It is as though, as a result of the two concomitant transformations in a relation of solidarity, the two subjects concerned found themselves once again realized and virtual—as if, having each acquired an object of exchange, they remained nonetheless "attracted" by the object they have just renounced. We prefer to say that in this case the exchange as such has not been completely realized, that it is subject to reversal. We would thus designate it as a *virtual exchange*.

Realized Exchange

Exchange can be considered as realized only if the relation of disjunction that links each of the subjects to the renounced object ceases to be a realization virtuality, in other words, if with every canceled relation, the value associated with S_1 ceases to be a value for S_2, and conversely. The formula for *realized exchange* would thus be written as

$$F \text{ transformation } <S_1 \longrightarrow (S_1 \cap O_2)> \text{ ⟂ } F \text{ transformation } <S_2 \longrightarrow (O_1 \cap S_2)>.$$

This formula can be considered correct only if it can account for the cancellation or at least the suspension of the virtual relations binding the subjects to the abandoned values.

The interpretation we wish to propose consists in allowing for a possible *equivalence* between realized and virtual values and, at the same time, their substitutability. One might say, for example, that exchange is definitely realized (that is, without second thoughts about recuperating renounced values) if

$$O_1 \simeq O_2 ,$$

or, in other words, if O_1 and O_2 are considered substitutable occurrences of the class of objects O.

We can see that, in this case, the structure of realized exchange is relatively speaking like that of the reciprocal gift, although the objects inscribed in the utterances that account for the gift and for the countergift are considered *identical*, whereas they are considered to be only *equivalent* in the constitutive utterances of exchange.

However, establishing equivalence between the values of exchange presupposes a *knowing* that is prior to the "value" of the values, and balanced exchange requires reciprocal trust. In other words, it requires a *fiduciary contract*, whether implicit or explicit, between the partners in the exchange. Thus, exchange, considered as one of the forms of the communication of values, indeed has its own definite structure, and its interpretation depends essentially on the form of the contract that precedes and encloses it, a form that will admit all kinds of manipulation of the categories of *being* and *seeming*.

It will not be surprising to note that simple stories from folklore, which are based almost exclusively on the structure of exchange,[11] seem to be founded on the ignorance or naiveté, whether real or faked, of one of the subjects (or of both of the subjects, intermittently and with no psychological justification). Also the syntagmatic strings we find in stories from folklore show crescendos or decrescendos of those values that result from one's possessing a needle or acquiring a bull, or vice versa. Introduced as a semiautonomous narrative sequence within a wider story, exchange finds its equilibrium broken by the modalities of a given contract by which the knowing it implies often appears as a case of trickery in which only the deceiving subject is realized, by becoming conjoined with the object of value and offering only a non-value object to the duped subject. Such an exchange, insofar as its consequences are concerned—and they are all that is taken into consideration when the narrative schema of transfer is set up—is scarcely distinguishable from appropriation that results from a test. The formulation of the transformations brought about, in order to account for the nonreciprocity, would have to use the concept of *suspension* for that transformation effected only in the mode of seeming by the deceiving subject. A stylistic interplay of *conversions* takes place that consists of the manifestation of certain surface narrative structures in the place of others the narrative syntax leads us to expect. Only if the exchange is inscribed within a much wider syntagmatic context can the narration be freed of ambiguity.

Participative Communication

When we tried to account for the transfer of objects and for the subjects' communication in an axilogical universe reduced to its simplest expression, in a universe of values that already exist and indeed are recognized as values, we were obliged to close that universe up with the help of the senders that guarantee the circulation of values within an enclosed space and which mediate between this *immanent universe* and the *transcendent universe* whose presence they manifest in their form as actants in a syntax of anthropomorphic inspiration. We have already seen the extent to which mythical thought—and probably in a very general way all of our imaginary activity—was reluctant to recognize the *ex nihilo* status of ambient values and preferred to substitute an axiological elsewhere for that status, thus postulating the possibility for some communication between these two universes. Here we want to give a representation, albeit summary, of this particular kind of communication. Given that senders, in their role as possessors of transcendent values, can be considered as *subjects that are at the same time both real and transcendent*, it is possible to conceive of their communication with receivers functioning in their own right in the immanent universe, that is, in their role as *immanent and virtual subjects*. This is at least valid for their original, first state. It is as subjects that they can be included in communication, and it is as subjects that their status can be described in terms of canonical utterances.

The difficulty in describing this transubstantiation of transcendent values into immanent values, using the structure of communication, is first caused by the fact that the very definition of communication (understood as a transformation bringing about, in a solidary way, the disjunction of the object from one of the subjects and its conjunction with the second subject) is not always applicable to the relations between sender and receiver. The existence of a relation of unilateral presupposition between the presupposed sender-term and the presupposing receiver-term makes communication between them asymmetrical. Thus, the paradigmatic status of the sender in relation to the receiver is defined by hyperonymic relation whereas the status of the receiver in relation to the sender is characterized by hyponymic relation. This means the asymmetry can be accentuated only when the actants are placed syntagmatically, being considered as subjects that are interested in only one object. Let us take the case of the sender that, as a transforming subject, ensures that a *gift* is given to the receiver: If the transformation results in the *attribution* of a value to the receiver, that attribution will not thereby be in a relation of solidarity, as we might have expected, with a renunciation on the part of the sender. In other words, instead of bringing about, as we would expect

$$(\text{sender} \cap O \cup \text{receiver}) \Longrightarrow (\text{sender} \cup O \cap \text{receiver}),$$

the transformation results in

$$(\text{sender} \cap O \cup \text{receiver}) \Longrightarrow (\text{sender} \cap O \cap \text{receiver}).$$

The object of value, while still attributed to the receiver, remains in conjunction with the sender.

There are many examples of this unexpected phenomenon. For instance, in verbal communication, once the *knowing* of the sender is transferred to the receiver, it remains a shared knowing. The sender is not deprived of it. Even when the queen of England has one by one delegated all of her *powers* to duly constituted bodies, she remains the supreme sovereign. You might say this is a nice fiction, but without it you cannot found the concept of sovereignty.

Transfers of this kind are not limited to modalities. In the Gospels, the multiplying of the loaves can only be explained in terms of the inexhaustible nature of the sender's possessions. The Lithuanian divinities called *Kaukai* do not directly furnish riches to those in their care. They just render their goods inexhaustible so that their consummation does not diminish their quantity.

Given such universally shared concepts, semanticists are not called on to inquire into the reality of the queen's powers or the capabilities of the *Kaukai*. They must limit themselves to proposing suitable descriptions of them. We would say that here we have a specific type of communication and propose to call it *participative communication*. The term reminds us of the unique structural relations between sender and receiver that we interpret within the general framework of the *pars pro tota* formula.

However that might be, at this stage of our development of the elementary structures of narrativity, it is difficult to go any further in our examination of participative communication without fundamentally integrating our concept of the actantial structure. Above all, we must also describe the structure of verbal communication and, in a general way, that of the semiotic transmission and manipulation of knowing, which alone constitutes an autonomous level of narrativity. Further, what little we have said in that regard should be considered as an *aidemémoire*, a black box whose place has been reserved but whose contents are yet to be explored.

It has been our intention in this chapter to present *cultural values* — it matters little whether they participate in social semantic universes or whether they are integrated into individual universes. We wish to distinguish them from *modal* values, which, although they are of a semantic nature, are used in the construction of grammar. The possibilities for linguistic, sociological, and axiological definitions of value have been explored with the sole purpose of demonstrating their complementary and noncontradictory character, a necessary condition for the pertinence of our semiotic enterprise. The universe of values, which is, in the strictest sense of the term, semantic, has thus been placed within the framework of those elementary syntactic structures that assure their being grasped and account for their narrativization.

Conclusion

Narrativity, considered as the irruption of the discontinuous into the discoursive permanence of a life, a story, an individual, a culture, disarticulates that discoursive permanence into discrete states between which it sets transformations. This allows us to describe it, in the first instance, in the form of utterances of doing that affect utterances of state. These latter are the guarantors of the semiotic existence of subjects that are in a relation of junction with objects invested with values. The evenemential syntax we are trying to develop here is, whether we like it or not, of an anthropomorphic inspiration. It is, after all, a projection of the fundamental relations mankind has with the world — or, and it does not matter, the converse.

In our search for simple situations and elementary syntactic structures, our point of departure has been a simple syntactic configuration representing two subjects attracted by the same object of value. The examination of this configuration has allowed us to identify several simple narrative states that we can formalize in syntagmatic or paradigmatic junction utterances and also show how each subject is able to deploy its own narrative program. According to our topological interpretation, the various displacements of objects are alone enough to account for the organization of story, with the subjects being no more than the loci of their transfer. To fill in this interpretation, we have sought to show that communication between two subjects, being regulated by transformation operators, also constitutes a satisfactory explicative dimension because it allows us to establish an initial typology of elementary transformations that, at a more superficial level, are manifested as acts of communication.

Building on this typology, we have been able to push our analysis in two different directions, the first being toward the syntactic representation of the structure of exchange, which requires us to introduce, alongside the two subjects, two distinct objects of value. The equivalence of the values invested in these objects (which we have been led to postulate) identifies the presupposed existence of an earlier fiduciary contract, stopping our investigation there. On the other hand, our analysis has been directed toward inquiry into that unique status of communication between sender and receiver that is, curiously enough, characterized by an attribution of the object but without a concomitant renunciation. As was the case for the first direction in which our analysis took us, the consequences of the discovery of this form of participative communication cannot yet be fully developed for lack of a sufficiently advanced conceptual apparatus. The last simple form of narrative that might account for the transformation of positive values into negative ones, or the converse, cannot even be sketched. To examine it would require us to postulate the existence of an anti-subject and of an anti-sender. This we might intuitively consider obvious, but, in fact, their existence – within the framework of what we want to be a scientific enterprise (if only because of the internal coherence necessary for the interdefinition of the concepts we use) – is not self-evident.

It is obvious that an examination of axiological investment, and of its narrativization, constitutes only one relatively unimportant chapter in narrative semiotics. Cultural values, although they occupy a privileged place in stories from mythology and folklore, are accorded very little importance in so-called literature. However, the narrative organization of values continues to be the foundation of narrativity because its "effacement" is no less significant than its presence.

Chapter 6
Actants, Actors, and Figures

Narrative Structures

Actants and Actors

The linguistic reinterpretation we have proposed for *dramatis personae* and which is based on the Proppian description of the Russian tale of the fantastic, in the first instance seeks to establish a distinction between *actants*, having to do with narrative syntax, and *actors*, which are recognizable in the particular discourses in which they are manifested. This distinction, which we continue to consider relevant—if only because it has allowed us to separate neatly the two autonomous levels on which analysis of narrativity should be centered—of course has raised several problems from the beginning. Of itself this demonstrates the complexity of the problematics of narrativity. For example, we know that the relation between *actor* and *actant*, far from being a simple relation of inclusion of a given occurrence into a class, is instead twofold (see accompanying diagram).

We have learned that if an actant (A_1) can be manifested in discourse by several actors (a_1, a_2, a_3), the converse is equally possible, just one actor (a_1) being able to constitute a syncretism of several actants (A_1, A_2, A_3).

Subsequent research has enabled us to understand better the actantial organization of the "characters of a story," even to envisage the possibility of an independent narrative grammar of discursive manifestations. On the other hand, actorial organization is not significantly included in that research, a weakness easily explained by the fact that we lack a coherent discourse theory.

Taking advantage of the fact that research into narrativity, to a certain extent, seems to be marking time, we think it would be useful to initiate some terminological and didactic refinements, this with a twofold purpose. First, we hope to draw up an inventory of what, in this area, might highlight the ever-increasing number of problems we urgently must solve. These are especially due to the fact that interest has shifted from oral to written literature. It is also hoped that we can demonstrate what directions further research should take.

The Actantial Structure

More and more the actantial structure appears able to account for the organization of the human imaginary, which is just as much a projection of collective as of individual universes.

Syntagmatic Disjunctions. If we consider story to be a global utterance, produced and communicated by a narrating subject, that same global utterance can be decomposed into a series of concatenated *narrative utterances* (= Propp's "functions"). By attributing the status of *function* to the predicate-verb of the utterance, with function being used in the logical sense of formal relation, we can define the utterance as a relation between the actants that constitute it. We can encounter two kinds of narrative utterances (see accompanying diagram).

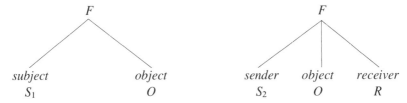

Or, with a notation system borrowed from logic:

$$F(S_1 \longrightarrow O)\ F(S_2 \longrightarrow O \longrightarrow R_2).$$

Whether we interpret these syntactic structures (1) on the social level, the relation of a person to work that produces value-objects, thus putting them into circulation within the framework of a structure of exchange, or (2) on the level of the individual, the relation of a person with the object of his or her desire and the inscription of that object within the structures of interhuman communication, the disjunctions brought about by these elementary schemata seem sufficiently general to provide us with the bases for an initial articulation of the imaginary. Whether they are verbalizations of "real" structures that precede the linguistic doing, or projections of the human spirit as it organizes a meaningful world, is not important: They are formal *positions* that allow for the generation and articulation of meaning.

Paradigmatic Disjunctions. The concept of structure, a postulate that is implicit to all of our study, presupposes the existence of a paradigmatic relational network that is inferable to the actants as they appear in narrative utterances. It is as if the subject (sender or receiver of the narration), to become able to produce or read narrative messages, first must have access to an elementary structure that articulates signification into isotopic sets for which the semiotic square

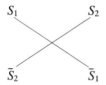

can serve as a model. In any case, it distinguishes the *positive deixis* $(S_1 + \bar{S}_2)$ from the *negative deixis* $(S_2 + \bar{S}_1)$. This at least produces a doubling of the actantial structure in which each actant can be referred to one of the two deixes, thus giving rise to the following distinctions:

> *positive subject* vs. *negative subject* (or anti-subject)
> *positive object* vs. *negative object*
> *positive sender* vs. *negative sender* (or anti-sender)
> *positive receiver* vs. *negative receiver* (or anti-receiver).

Although it remains understood that the terms *positive* and *negative* are pure designations implying no value judgment, confusion will still abound in certain cases. For example, this is the case for ethnic literature, which is often characterized by a rigid moralization in which the *positive* vs. *negative* opposition is invested with *good* vs. *evil* contents, thus giving rise to the pairs of *hero* vs. *traitor*, *helper* vs. *opponent*, etc.

Such a moralizing investment is, however, neither necessary nor sufficiently general. It can easily be replaced by an *aestheticizing* investment, or it can be distributed not simply according to the two opposed deixes, but instead according to the numerous terms of the semiotic square. Here the "characters" cease to be exclusively "good" or "bad." It will be enough to maintain the very principle of the paradigmatic disjunction of actants by explaining their dichotomization in terms of their *conformity* or *noncomformity* to the deixes in question. This requires us then to envisage the possibility of defining a particular class of stories in terms of specific *valorizing* investments.

> *Note*: According to this perspective, the paradigmatic disjunction of actants can be generalized and is applicable to even minimal stories with only one actant. This is so to the extent that this one actant, in its doing, meets some obstacle or other, and that obstacle will be interpreted as the metonymic representation of the anti-actant associated with the nonconforming deixis for the manifested activity of the actant.

Actantial Roles

Alongside structural disjunctions (which account for the dramatization of narration) and syntactic disjunctions (which, as projections of a virtual human doing, make it possible for that doing to be represented), other categories come into play and make the actantial structure more diverse. However, as opposed to the disjunctions we have just referred to and that decompose the space of the imaginary into as many distinct loci (which, when projected or apprehended, remain in a certain equilibrium with each other), new categories overdetermine the actants when it comes to their syntagmatic progression.

Competences and Performances. We introduced the concept of *performance* into the terminology of narrative in place of such vague terms as *test* or *difficult task* that the hero is supposed to accomplish, and we introduced it also in order to be able to give a simple definition of the subject (or of the anti-subject) in terms of its status as the *subject of a doing* — this doing being reduced to a canonical series of narrative utterances. Performance, however, requires reference to *competence*. At the narrative level, we propose to define *competence* as the *wanting and/or being-able and/or knowing-how-to-do of the subject* that presupposes performative doing. It has become almost banal to say that, for any semiotic system, the production of an act of *parole* presupposes the existence of a *langue* and that the performance of the signifying subject presupposes his competence in signifying. If every manifested utterance implies the faculty of forming utterances on the part of the subject of the enunciation, that faculty, in a general way, remains implicit. On the contrary, narration, to the extent indeed that it is an imaginary projection of "real" situations, does not fail to make explicit these presupposeds by successively manifesting both the competences and the performances of the subject. It does even more. If, for example, the competence of the speaking subject can be conceived of as a syncretism of the modalities of wanting + being-able + knowing-how-to-say, then narration, while manifesting these diverse competences as being the competences of a semiotic doing, can at the same time disjoin them, either by attributing the modalities of knowing-how-to-do or of being-able-to-do to different actants, or by bringing it about that these different modalities are separately and successively acquired by just one actant in the course of just one narrative program.

This is what we have been leading up to: If the *competent subject* is different from the *performing subject*, this does not mean that they constitute two different subjects. They are just two instances of the same actant. According to *motivating logic (post hoc, ergo propter hoc)*, the subject must first acquire a certain competence before it can become a performer. According to the *logic of presupposition*, the performing doing of the subject implies an existing competence for that doing.

We will just say that the subject actant can assume, in a given narrative program, a certain number of *actantial roles*. These roles are defined both by the *position* of the actant in the logical linking of the narration (its syntactic definition) and by its *modal investment* (its morphological definition), thus making grammatical regulation of narrativity possible.

It should be possible to have a terminology for actantial roles that will allow us to distinguish clearly between the *actants* themselves and the *actantial roles* they are called on to assume in the unfolding of the story. Thus, we could distinguish the *virtual subject* from the *subject of wanting* (or instituted subject), and we could distinguish the latter from the *hero by virtue of power* (Ogre, Roland) or from the *hero by virtue of knowing* (Tom Thumb, Renard the Fox).

Veridiction. A strategy using actantial roles that are acquired or exchanged throughout the story is not limited to the interplay of competence and performances. We must not forget that, even just within the framework of the folktale, the subject's *competence* (= *qualification*) can be acquired only with the help of a *simulated* performance. When we say that this performance is simulated we imply that it is accomplished so that it will *appear true*, although it *is not so* in reality.

The problem of veridiction goes well beyond the framework of the actantial structure. For the moment, by introducing the category of *being* and *seeming* into the framework we have sketched out, we are trying to show how that category, while complicating the workings of narrative, considerably increases the number of actantial roles possible. By proposing a semiotic interpretation of the category of *truth* vs. *falsehood* according to the articulations of the square

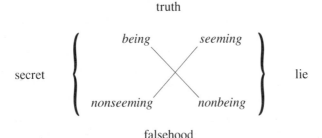

we are seeking not only to free this modal category from its relationships with the nonsemiotic referent, but also and above all to suggest that veridiction constitutes an independent narrative isotopy that can posit its own referential level and typologize the deviations from that level, thus instituting the "intrinsic truth of the story."

The overdetermination of actants according to this category of *being* and *seeming* accounts for the extraordinary game of disguises (*jeu de masques*), which includes confrontations between heroes who might be hidden, unrecognized, or recognized and disguised traitors who are unmasked and punished and which constitutes one of the main axes of the narrative imaginary. However, what we will underline from all this for now is the possibility for new diversifications of narrative programs. Thus—again staying within the framework of the folktale—the instituted subject (endowed with the modality of wanting), immediately gives rise to a subject and an anti-subject, each of which can acquire competences according to *being-able* or *knowing* (or both successively), thus raising the possibility of at least four (or eight) *actantial roles*. This legitimizes a typology of competent subjects (heroes or traitors), which in turn allows us to identify different narrative trajectories. The overdetermination of these various competent subjects by the modalities of *truth* vs. *falsehood* and of *secret* vs. *lie* multiplies by as much the number of actantial roles, diversifies the subjects' syntactic trajectories, and also—and this is important—allows us to calculate (using additions, subtractions, and overdeterminations of the modalities defining the roles) the narrative transformations produced within the framework of a given program.

In other words, starting with elementary actantial structures, the introduction of the concept of actantial role allows us to envisage with greater confidence the construction of a narrative syntax.

The Actorial Structure

If it is to be present in narrative discourse, the actantial structure needs to be mediated by a typology of actantial roles that alone, defined by their respective modalities and syntagmatic positions, can cover and give life to the totality of discourse. Only then can a new process be engaged that will bring about the discursive manifestation of narrativity. This process will end up superimposing two structures, actantial and actorial, and will give rise to interlockings of actants and actors.

Thus, without first trying to define precisely the structural status of *actor*, and while relying completely on the naive concept of it as a "character" who in some way remains constant throughout a given narrative discourse, we might hope that the use of the concept of *actantial role* will shed some light on the simple observation that actants and actors are not identical (one actant can be manifested by several actors and, conversely, one actor can at the same time represent several actants). This observation, if one were content with it alone, would constitute nothing less than an admission of defeat for a theory that seeks to offer answers. Some examples will enable us more easily to situate this problem that arises from the fact that actants and actors are not identical.

1. An examination of the object actant allowed us to identify two kinds of objects: those that are invested with "objective values" and those that possess "subjective values." Although our terminology is not perfect, the distinction is most certainly based on a structural criterion, that of their mode of attribution. This, in the first case, is accomplished according to *having* and, in the second, according to *being*. Another criterion must, however, be added to this one, that of their actorial manifestation in discourse. Whereas those objects invested with "objective values" are present in discourse in the form of individualized and independent actors (food or children in Tom Thumb), objects having subjective value are manifested by actors who are conjointly and simultaneously subjects and objects (Tom Thumb, as actor, is at the same time a hero-subject and an object of consumption for the giant, and ultimately a provider for his whole family). Thus, actantial roles can be distributed among actors in a conjoined or disjoined way.

> *Note*: Likewise objective values can be doubled or trebled in the same story (food and children) and be represented by distinct *subactors* who nonetheless maintain between themselves relations of syntactic interdependence (the absence of food bringing about the loss of children).

2. Actantial roles that define the competence of the subject can be manifested either by the same actor as the subject itself, or by actors disjoined from it. In this latter case the individualized actor, given his ancillary status, and according to whether he is ranged with the positive or negative deixis, will be called *helper* or *opponent*.

3. The receiver can be its own sender (e.g., the Cornelian hero who "owes it to himself"). The actor then, although he is just a single actor, has to subsume both actantial roles.

4. The subject and the anti-subject can be brought together in one entity and thus, as just one actor, carry out an "interior battle" to the end (Faust).

These examples seem sufficiently important for us to be able to say that every actant, every actantial role, can be invested in a disjoined and autonomous actor, and that conversely, all disjunctions brought about at the level of the actantial structure can, in some sense, be neutralized by being invested conjointly in ever more complex actors. If we polarize these observations we can theoretically conceive of two extreme types of possible actorial structures: (a) Actorial manifestation can have a maximal expansion characterized by there being an independent actor for every actant or actantial role (a mask, for example, is an actor having the modality of seeming as its actantial role). We would say that, in this case, the *actorial structure* is *objectivized*. (b) Actorial distribution can show a minimal expansion and be reduced to just one actor responsible for all of the necessary actants and actantial roles (giving rise to absolute interior dramatization). In this case, the *actorial structure* is *subjectivized*.

Between these two extremes we find actorial distributions with both objectivizing and subjectivizing tendencies, and we suspect that they represent the majority of cases. Once the inventory of narrative programs has been established (problems of initiation and rites of passage grouped around qualifying tests, problems of recognition centered around glorifying tests, etc.) and once the number of actantial roles possible for each narrative trajectory has been tallied, the actorial distribution of these roles could be used as a typological criterion for the development of a general theory of genres.

Discoursive Structures

How to Identify Actors

As demonstrated, beginning with the elementary articulations of the imaginary and proposing the first structures—paradigmatic and syntagmatic—of its organization, we have gradually and deductively reached the point of being able to represent narrative discourse as being made up of a relatively complex network of actantial roles that are manifested in a conjoined or disjoined way by actors who can now be viewed as elements of discourse. It is impossible to deny the importance of these actanial models. This is so in the first instance for theoretical reasons: They constitute an attempt to account for instances and trajectories of meaning that generate discourse. But their importance is also pragmatic: They have to be considered as models of predictability, as hypotheses presented in the form of logical articulations that, once projected onto texts, can enhance their readability.

Despite all this, researchers, when faced with a sparse or bare text, will be troubled by not having objective procedures that would allow them to make the necessary choices and to recognize narratively relevant elements of discourse (in the present case, actors). The gap between what they believe they know about narrative structures and the reading techniques they possess is still too wide. The relative weakness of a *textual analysis* that claims to disallow and not use preexisting narratological expertise is just as significant as the difficulties deductive constructionism faces when it attempts to deal with discoursive manifestation.

Thus once again, while provisionally abandoning deductive procedures, we will try to take up the problem, starting with general considerations concerning linguistic manifestation.

Figures and Configurations

The weakness in the results of textual analysis, when it attempts to establish procedures by which to identify the actors in discourse and further attempts do so from among the innumerable syntactic actants of its utterances (and when it attempts at the same time to define those actors in both their permanent modes and in their mutations), is caused by the fact that such an analysis situates its investigations at the very superficial level of the syntax of signs. Now, since Hjelmslev we know that nothing useful can be done in linguistics if we do not go beyond that level and begin to explore, after separating the two levels of signifier and signified, those units that are both the smallest and at the deepest level of that signifier and signified taken separately. These Hjelmslev called *figures*.

The kind of narrative analysis we are dealing with here is in fact situated entirely at the level of the signified. For it, narrative forms are no more than particular organizations of the semiotic form of the content for which the theory of narration attempts to account. The discourse theory that, from every point of view, is seen as urgently needed, will thus be responsible for exploring discursive forms and the different modes of articulation for those discursive forms. This the theory must do before moving on to linguistic theory *stricto sensu*. At the present what seems to be most difficult is to establish this theoretical mediation between narrative forms and linguistic forms that have phrastic dimensions.

To begin, let us therefore come back to strictly semantic problems. In effect, if the concept of *actant* is of a syntactic nature, that of *actor*, at first sight at least, is not. The latter concept is, instead, of a semantic nature. An actor functions as an actant only when it is put into play by either narrative syntax or linguistic syntax. As far as its syntactic uses are concerned, the actor is in a situation comparable to that of a nominal lexeme that accepts every kind of manipulation at the hands of syntax.

The semantic examination of a lexeme (of the lexeme *head*, for example, as analyzed in *Structural Semantics*) shows us that it is endowed with a relatively stable kernel, that is, with a nuclear *figure* from which certain virtualities develop, certain sememic trajectories that permit its placing in context (i.e., its partial realization in discourse). Consequently the lexeme is a virtual semic organization that, with rare exceptions (when it is monosememic), is never realized as such in manifested discourse. Any discourse, once it has posited its own semantic isotopy, is nothing more than a very partial exploitation of the considerable virtualities the lexematic thesaurus makes available to it. As a given instance of discourse unfolds, it leaves on its way a string of rejected figures of the world that nonetheless continue to live out their virtual existence, always ready to be reactivated.

Research on "lexical fields" has successfully demonstrated this potential that lexematic figures have. Whether they are described within the framework of a dictionary (as is the case for the lexeme *oeil* analyzed by Patrick Charaudeau) or taken from a homogeneous text (as with *coeur* in the works of Jean Eudes, studied by Clément Legaré), we immediately see that these figures are not objects that are closed in on themselves. Instead they are constantly extending their sememic trajectories as they meet and appropriate other related figures. They therefore give rise to figurative constellations that have their own organization. Thus, to take a familiar example, the figure *sun* organizes around itself a figural field that includes *rays, light, heat, air, transparency, opacity, clouds*, etc.

Such an observation leads us to say that if *lexematic figures* manifest themselves, theoretically, within the framework of utterances, they easily transcend this framework and build a relational figurative network that can be strung out over entire sequences, thus constituting the *discoursive configurations* of those sequences.

Discoursive theory, to the extent that it does not want to be an appendix to phrastic linguistics, should not underestimate the importance of this phenomenon. The configurations in question are none other than the figures of discourse (in the Hjelmslevian sense of the term). They are distinct both from narrative forms and from phrastic forms and can thus, at least in part, constitute the basis of the specificity of discourse as a form of organization of meaning.

The recognition and attribution of a specific structural status to discoursive configurations allow us to regroup under the same rubric a certain number of problems that might, at first sight, seem disparate.

We know, for example, that narrative analysis of folktales leaves the problem of *motifs* hanging. Motifs are mobile sequences that can be substituted for each other to fill the same narrative functions. They also can assume different functions and appear as autonomous variants or as independent stories. The distinction between two levels of semiotic organization—narrative and figurative—theoretically allows us to remove this problem by, among other things, explaining the structural permanence of stories and intertextual migrations of motifs.

A better knowledge of discoursive configurations also allows us more precisely to situate the scientific enterprise represented by the work of Georges Dumézil. This comparative grammarian's tour de force is a new *comparative mythology*. Essentially this consists of a transfer to the level of the signified of the methodological procedures of the level of the significr. It also seeks to enlarge the dimensions of the units to be studied. That is, for the comparative study of phonemes taken from a corpus of realized morphemes, Dumézil substitutes a comparative study of discoursive configurations found within mythological discourses. The discoursive level of this research can thus be situated within the framework of the general economy of semiology.

In a different area, that of *thematic research*, many studies, going from Gaston Bachelard to Jean-Pierre Richard, are the products of a shared concern with exploring figurative trajectories that cut across discourses. At the most one might reproach Bachelard for his more or less implicit postulation of the universality of the configurations he seeks to describe. Whereas narrative structures can be considered as characteristic of the human imaginary in general, discoursive configurations—motifs and themes—while being capable of wide generalization and of translinguistic migrations, are subject to a relativizing filtering mechanism that appropriates and adapts them for given semio-cultural communities.

Here then is a group of figurative facts—and we have mentioned only the most characteristic—that we must bring together and refine in order to give them a homogeneous semiotic formulation. Further, and this is no less important, that formulation must conform to the requirements of narrative grammar.

Thematic Roles

The identification of two autonomous yet linked levels—narrative and discursive—accounts quite well for the ambiguous manner in which the subject of narration functions. The subject is asked simultaneously to pursue the two syntagmatic trajectories imposed on him: both the narrative program determined by the distribution of actantial roles and the privileged pathway established by a discursive configuration in which a figure that is only barely posited proposes a relatively constricting figurative sequence.

Nonetheless these two kinds of trajectories, while being in some way parallel and predictable, are of different natures. The first is a deliberately chosen program within the framework of a narrative grammar. The second belongs to the order of a *discoursive dictionary*, an inventory of configurations constituted from closed collective and/or individual universes. In effect, just as a phrastic dictionary is a list of lexematic figures, each of which includes an enumeration of its contextual sememic possibilities, so can we conceive of a discoursive dictionary that would offer a stock of "themes" and "motifs." This stock would be constituted by and for the use of the participants in a given semantic universe (and its originality would be in its tracing out of possible but as yet unrealized neological trajectories).

We must not forget that configurations are none other than the "content forms" proper to discourse. The discoursive manifestation of narrativity is thus, according to this perspective, no more than an integration of its *semantic component* into the narrative objects generated by narrative grammar. This semantic component, it is true, is presented in its syntagmatic form and it is already developed as the form, and not the substance, of the content. The conjunction of these two instances—narrative and discoursive—brings about the investment of contents within the canonical grammatical forms of narration and allows for the production of meaningful narrative messages.

The fact that discourse appears as the elaborated form of content manifesting itself with the aid of syntagmatic configurations raises the problem of the structural organization of those configurations. Some examples, which are at first sight quite disparate, may perhaps allow us to catch sight of, if not a solution, at least the directions that should be taken by future research.

It is the concept of discoursive configuration that allows us to account for the manner in which a single culinary isotopy is maintained in the Bororo myth of the origin of fire, whose syntagmatic organization we analyzed elsewhere. This isotopy is maintained despite the isotopic variations that characterize each sequence. A single configuration occupies the length of the mythical discourse, but at various times is articulated—while at the same time segmenting *figurative sequences*—either according to actors who are food consumers or according to the object itself that is being consumed or, finally, according to the producers of the cooked and the raw (*fire* and *water*). Here we see the discursive configuration organizing itself according to the canonical utterance schema (sender —> object —> receiver). Each term in this schema is capable of producing an autonomous figurative trajectory. This contribution that configurations make to the syntagmatic organization of discourses partially clarifies one of the chapters of what is sometimes called *macrostylistics*.

But it is yet another property of these configurations—the polysemy of the figures that constitute them—that allows us to understand, by referring to other texts, how the choice of a plurisememic figure that virtually proposes several figurative trajectories can, on condition that the figurative terms that emerge as a result of the realization are not contradictory, give rise to the *pluri-isotopic organization of discourse*.

In other cases, by contrast, a slight hesitation in the choice of such and such a figure, and in the assigning to it of a determinate role, can give rise to distinct yet parallel figurative trajectories. The realization of these figurative trajectories thus introduces the problem of *variants*. According to whether the figure given the responsibility of representing the sacred is that of the priest, the sacristan, or the beadle, the figurative unfolding of the whole sequence will be affected by the choice. The modes of action and the loci for the sequence will always have to be in conformity with the initially chosen figure, and they will be different, and consistently so, according to the different choices made for that figure. If we polarize these two phenomena we can say that, in the case of pluri-isotopy, a single original figure gives rise to significations that are superimposed within a single discourse. In the case of plurivariance, figurative diversification, kept in check by the implicit presence of only one role, nonetheless cannot prevent comparable, if not identical, significations from taking place in several manifested discourses.

The importance of this last example is above all that a single *thematic role* appears in different figurations. The problem raised within the framework of the theory of narrativity and, more particularly, vis-à-vis its actantial component, is how to establish whether this analysis can identify discrete nominal elements capable of being aligned and identified one on one with our actantial roles. This problem could be solved if ultimately we were to reduce configurations to discoursive roles.

In our unrelated examples of this line of thought—*eye, heart, sun, fire,* sacristan—it seems in every way that *nominal figures* (nominal because they are endowed with a "universal" seme that allows us to consider them as *objects* and not *processes*) are concentrations of virtualities that permit us to foresee not only their phrastic sememic realizations but also the possible clusterings of their figurative predicates, of the possible figurative objects they might seek to possess if placed in the position of subjects or of the possible subjects that manipulate them as objects. The projection of their virtualities onto any given discoursive isotopy, while allowing for their diffuse manifestation throughout the length of the discourse (or even in just one segment), imposes a certain discipline on them by allowing for the realization of only certain figurative trajectories to the exclusion of others, which are denied realization. All things being equal, within the framework of discourse, discoursive configuration corresponds to thematic roles in the same way as lexemes correspond to sememes within the framework of the utterance.

This observation is enlightening but not sufficient: Configuration encompasses all figures—nominal and verbal, as well as circumstantial ones such as space and time. That is, configuration encompasses all the figures it can associate with itself. The thematic role, for instance, is no more than a nominal figure. If it can be said that the thematic role, to a certain extent and within the limits imposed on it by discoursive isotopy, subsumes all of the nonnominal figures of its configuration, it is because of another of its structural properties. In addition to *theme*, it is also a *role*, and at the linguistic level we can find its structural equivalent in the *name of the agent* that is both a *name* (= a nominal figure) and an agent (= a parasyntactic role). The lexeme *fisherman*, for example, is a very condensed surface construction. It designates someone who possesses a competence limited to a certain doing that is capable of expansion and that, when made explicit, can cover a long discoursive sequence. At the same time, it maintains its semantic character, at least at this level. In both the linguistic and narrative grammars it can occupy several different actantial positions.

A *thematic role* is defined in terms of a twofold reduction. The first is the reduction of the *discoursive configuration* to a single *figurative trajectory*, realized or realizable within discourse. The second is the reduction of that trajectory to a competent agent that virtually subsumes it. When a given figure that we meet in discourse is, under conditions we will have to clarify, invested with a thematic role, it can, for the purposes of our argument, be described and analyzed as either an overall configuration or as a figurative trajectory enclosed within the discoursive universe.

The figure of *fisherman* being manifested in discourse as a thematic role (we are thinking of Guy de Maupassant's *Deux Amis*) is a good example that perhaps will allow us to go beyond the limits that, at first sight, separate dictionary figures (established by usage and theoretically codifiable) from figures that are in the course of being created (for example, characters in a novel). The *fisherman* of course represents all the possibilities of his doing, everything that can be expected of him by way of activity. Placing him into a discoursive isotopy makes a thematic role of him, one that can be used by story. A character in a novel, supposing that it is introduced by the attribution of a name conferred on it, is progressively created by consecutive figurative notations extending throughout the length of the text, and it does not exist as a complete figure until the last page, thanks to the cumulative memorizing of the reader. To this memorization, which is a psychological phenomenon, we can substitute the analytic description of the text (= the *reading* of it in the sense of a semiotic doing), which allows us to identify the discoursive configurations that constitute it and then reduce these to the thematic roles of the text. From the point of view of production of the text, we are still obliged to reverse the procedures and grant logical priority to the thematic roles. These latter appropriate figures and develop them into figurative trajectories that implicitly include all of the virtual configurations of the manifested discourse.

Now it should be easy to take a last step and say that the selection of *thematic roles*, whose logical priority over configurations has just been asserted, can be done only with the help of the terminals to which the setting in place of the narrative structures ultimately leads, that is, *actantial roles*. It is when actantial roles bring thematic roles under their control that we have the mediating instance that allows for the movement from narrative structures to discoursive structures.

> *Note*: It is obvious that the introduction of the concept of *thematic role* will not fail to raise new and considerable difficulties, as every discipline—psychology, psychosociology, sociology—proposes its repertoire of roles. The distinction we proposed elsewhere between "semiotic form" and "scientific form" might be used here to distinguish between the two types of "roles." The work of Claude Bremond in this area is important for us.

Conclusions

Our reexamination of these deductive processes allows us provisionally to refine our concept of the narrativization of discourse. Narrative grammar generates narrative objects (= "stories"), conceived of as narrative trajectories chosen with a view to their manifestation. These trajectories are defined by a given particular distribution of actantial roles endowed with modalities and determined by their respective positions within the framework of the narrative program. The narrative object, in possession of its grammatical structure, is invested with a specific content, thanks to its manifestation in discourse. This semantic investment is accomplished by a selection, carried out by the actantial roles, of thematic roles. These thematic roles, in turn, in order to realize their virtualities, call into play the lexematic level of language and are manifested in the form of figures that are extended into discoursive configurations.

Discourse, considered at the surface level, thus appears as a syntagmatic deployment sprinkled with polysemic figures that possess multiple virtualities and that are often combined in uninterrupted or diffuse discoursive configurations. Only some of these figures, those that can occupy actantial roles, become thematic roles. At this point they take on the name of *actors*. An actor is thus a meeting point and locus of conjunction for narrative structures and discoursive structures, for the grammatical and the semantic components. This is because the actor is at the same time responsible for at least one actantial role and at least one thematic role, both of which make clear what his competence is and set the limits for his doing and being. At the same time the actor is the locus for the investment of these roles and for their transformation. This is because semiotic doing, functioning within the framework of narrative objects, consists essentially of the play of acquisitions and losses, substitutions and exchanges of values, whether modal or ideological. The actorial structure thus appears as a topological structure. Although being implicated with both narrative and discoursive structures, it is no more than the locus of their manifestations. It does not belong exclusively to one or the other.

Chapter 7
Toward a Theory of Modalities

Simple Modal Structures

The Act

If we take as our starting point the provisory definition of modalization as "the modification of a predicate by a subject," we could consider that the *act* — and, in particular, *the language act* — providing the instance of the modalizing subject is sufficiently determined, is where modalities appear.

Every act is the product of a reality devoid of linguistic manifestation. Thus the language act can be apprehended solely in and by its results, that is, as an *utterance*, whereas the *enunciation* producing it simply has the status of logical presupposition. The act in general can be formulated linguistically in only two different ways: either when it is described, in an approximate and variable way, within the framework of uttered discourse, or when it becomes the object of a logicosemantic reconstruction employing presuppositions taken from the analysis of utterance, within the framework of a semiotic metalanguage. In both cases the only rigorous way to speak of this is by means of a canonical representation.

The naive and most neutral definition of the act we can give is that of "making to be." From this we can easily identify a hypotactic structure having two predicates:

doing vs. *being*.

Elementary Utterances

To construct a linguistic simulacrum of the act requires that we define the *predicate* beforehand. The latter in turn must refer back to a specific concept of the structure of the *elementary utterance*. This is a fundamental choice since it decides on the form that linguistic theory as a whole will take.

We shall postulate that the predicate represents the nucleus, that is, the constituent relation of the utterance, a relation whose end terms are actants. If we leave aside the semanticism invested in the predicate and bracket it off in order to treat it separately later on, we can identify the predicate with the logical *function* and give the utterance the following canonical form:

$F(A_1, A_2, \ldots)$.

We shall also postulate that the function can be invested with minimum semantic characteristics. This enables us to set up the distinction between two predicate-functions, *doing* and *being*, and thus to posit the existence of two possible forms of elementary utterances: *utterances of doing* and *utterances of state*.

To give a more abstract representation of these two utterances we can then designate the predicate *doing* by the function called /*transformation*/ and the predicate *being* by the function /*junction*/.

> *Note*: The terms *doing* and *being* can be used insofar as they do not entail awkward polysemic consequences.

Transformation. From the paradigmatic viewpoint, *transformation* can be considered as a *semantic category* (even though its minimal investment makes it appear as a universal of language), and projected on the semiotic square:

where /$\overline{negation}$/ = /*assertion*/.

This gives rise to the internal definition of *contradiction*: S_1 and S_2 are contradictories if $\overline{S}_2 = S_1$ and $\overline{S}_1 = S_2$; contradiction thus appears as a particular case of *oppositeness*.

From a syntactic point of view, that is, from the point of view of the operations carried out on the square that form the series:

/$\overline{negation}$/ ≠ /*assertion*/.

This example, using the French words for yes and no,

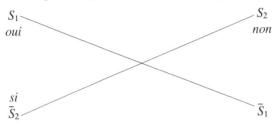

shows that *si* is not a simple assertion but a lexeme laden with "memory," which presupposes an anterior utterance of negation.[1]

We took this tangent for several reasons. We wished to justify the projection of binary categories (contradictories) onto the square. We also wished to show a difference in treatment between *logic* (which is phrastic in nature and functions only by means of substitutions) and *discoursive semiotics* (whose utterances have, in addition, a *positional* signification).

Junction. Taken as a semantic axis, *junction* in turn can be developed into the categories:

Note: Here also, the position of the object of value on the syntactic trajectory enables us to distinguish, for example, between /*disjunction*/, which characterizes the object we never possessed, and /*conjunction*/, the state of the object we have relinquished.

Performance and Competence

We can say that *junction* is the relation that determines the "state" of the subject with regard to any sort of object of value. Only the determinations, and not an "essence" of the subject, permit us to know something about the subject and, particularly, to consider it as an "existent." To simplify matters, if we consider junction as a binary category, we can then say that the subject may be described by means of two different utterances of state:

either $S_1 \cap O_1$

or $S_1 \cup O_1$,

whereas *transformation* (assertion or negation) accounts for what happens when going from one state to the other. Since it constitutes utterances of doing, transformation no longer has any value or other, but instead has an utterance of state as a syntactic object. Thus every transformation produces a junction, and every utterance of doing governs an utterance of state. The following schema represents the canonical organization of the preceding one:

$$S_2 \longrightarrow O_2(S_1 \cap O_1),$$

where

$\longrightarrow$ indicates transformation

$\cap$ indicates junction.

We call *performance* this hypotactic organization of two elementary utterances (which in natural language corresponds to the expression *causing-to-be*).

As we can see *performance* does not yet exhaust the naive definition of the *act*, for the act is not a "causing-to-be," but "that *which* causes to be." The "that which . . ." in a certain manner composes "the being of the doing" and can be formulated as a new utterance of state, hierarchically superior, accounting for the logically presupposed virtual existence of the instance producing doing. This "being of the doing," which we shall return to later, can hence be called *competence*, and the *act* itself can be defined as a hypotactic structure combining competence and performance, performance presupposing competence but not vice versa.

Since all modification of a predicate by another predicate has been defined as its modalization, both performance and competence must be considered as being *modal structures*.

> *Note*: Thus any predicate that governs another predicate becomes a *modal predicate* because of its syntactic position. And the latter, while maintaining its status of canonical utterance (that is, of forming either an utterance of doing, or an utterance of state), can in turn take on new semantic over-determinations even in spite of the identity of lexicalizations in natural languages.

Transitive Modalities

We have obtained the definitions of performance and competence by exploiting two modal organizations:

doing modalizing *being*
being modalizing *doing*.

Yet we can now see that there still exist two other possible combinations:

being modalizing *being*
doing modalizing *doing*.

The modal structures that we now propose to examine require the presence of two distinct modalizing instances; the modalizing subject must necessarily be different from the subject whose predicate is modalized. We can say that here we are dealing with *transitive modalizations*.

Veridictory Modalities. A modal utterance of state having S_1 as subject can modify any other utterance produced and introduced by the subject S_2.

When we are dealing with *language acts*, such a schema presupposes the existence of the two instances of enunciator and enunciatee, the latter supposedly the modalizing subject that sanctions the utterance produced by the enunciator. This distinction, which is necessary on the theoretical level because it permits us to determine the mode of generation of the modalities, can disappear when we are considering only the practical functioning of discourse: The actor, "speaking subject," is intermittently the enunciator-actant and the enunciatee-actant of its own utterances.

The modal predicate can be treated as a category and analyzed into:

the category is articulated into two *schemata*:

    The schema /s $\Longleftrightarrow$ s̄/, called *manifestation*;
    The schema /b $\Longleftrightarrow$ b̄/, called *immanence*.

It has two *axes*:

    The axis of contraries, called *truth*;
    The axis of subcontraries, called *falsehood*.

There are two *deixes*:

    The positive deixis /b + s̄/, called *secret*;
    The negative deixis /b̄ + s/, called *lie*.

A certain number of remarks must be made regarding this presentation of the modality of *being*.

1. It must be understood that the terms used are semiotic terms that have no relation whatsoever with the ontological concepts to which they can be compared.

2. The terms *manifestation* vs. *immanence* are borrowed from Hjelmslev, but they can be compared profitably with the categories *surface* vs. *deep* in linguistics, *manifest* vs. *latent* in psychoanalysis, *phenomenal* vs. *noumenal* in philosophy, etc. Moreover natural languages separately modalize the locus of manifestation and the plane of immanence ("it *is* necessary"; "it *seems* possible"; etc.) The usefulness of this distinction seems undeniable when analyzing narrative discourses.

3. The category /*true*/ vs. /*false*/ is in fact situated within discourse itself and thus the veridictory judgment can do without any external referent.

4. The lexeme *being* used in natural language has at least three different meanings. We have attempted to rid it of ambiguities by substituting the appropriate denominations for it: (a) It corresponds to *junction*, the constituent relation of the utterance of state; (b) it is used to designate the modal category of *veridiction*; (c) it designates at the same time the *positive term* of the schema of immanence (generally noted by the symbol *b*).

Factitive Modalities. Every modal utterance having *doing* (causing) as predicate and S_1 as subject can modify any other utterance of doing whose subject is S_2.

The projection on to the semiotic square of this modalization of *doing* by *doing* (*causing*) can be presented as:

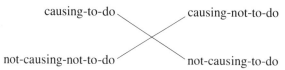

causing-to-do　　　　　causing-not-to-do

not-causing-not-to-do　　　not-causing-to-do

Such a presentation using the lexemes of natural language has its advantages and its inconveniences. It seems promising when exploring an unfamiliar domain; however, it considers modal and descriptive predicates simply as binary categories, and this can hinder the description of the modalizations' discursive paths (see "Transformation," this chapter). But since for the time being we are only positing the existence of an autonomous domain of modalization and not giving it a definitive canonical description, we can consider that the steps taken are justified. In the same way we believe that the more or less motivated designations of the modal positions (such as, for example, *order* and *prevent* for the axis of the contraries) are premature at this stage.

These modalities, traditionally called *factitive*,[2] at first glance seem to be some sort of delayed imperatives, although they are not necessarily, like the last examples, in a syncretic relation with the modality of /being-able/.

They should be both compared with and differentiated from the *transitive relation* established beween the subject and the object of the utterances of doing and which defines the description predicate. As for the *factitive relation*, it is established between the subject and the object that is already an utterance of doing, and from this very fact it does appear as the relation between two hierarchically distinct subjects, S_2, the modal subject, and S_1, the subject of doing. Thus,

causing a suit to-be-made	$\simeq$ doing so that S_1 makes a suit.
causing-to-know	$\simeq$ doing so that S_1 learns something.
causing-to-believe (persuading)	$\simeq$ doing so that S_1 passes a judgment of certainty on something.

We can see that the domain in which factitive modalization occurs, which is indeed difficult to circumscribe for the time being, covers totally or in part the concepts of communication, of representation, of delegation, etc. A deeper investigation would probably make this modal category appear as one of the universals that could account for a number of signifying human practices.

The Stringing of Simple Modal Structures.

Another common feature should be added to *transitivity* characterizing the factitive and veridictory modalities. They are no longer situated on the *pragmatic* plane that circumscribes it. Thus, factitive modalization appears as a cognitive doing that attempts to cause a somatic doing; in the same way veridiction is a cognitive operation that takes place as knowing on objects (of the world).

From this common ground we can obviously recognize what differentiates them on the syntagmatic plane. Whereas the veridictory modality modifies the predicate it governs *after the fact* ("downstream") – the utterance being modalized is supposed to have happened already – the factitive modality acts *before the fact* ("upstream") and serves as a sort of stimulant, which can activate the competence of another subject.

From the point of view of the *syntagmatic position* occupied in the representation of the series of human activities, the factitive modal utterance appears as a "causing-to-be," that is, a *cognitive* performance by the subject S_2. As such, this utterance is naturally capable of developing into an expanding cognitive program (thus, "causing-to-believe" is articulated as a program of *persuasive doing*). But at the same time, the *object* aspired after by this cognitive performance is the virtualization of the subject S_1's implicitly recognized *pragmatic competence*.

In its own right the veridictory modalization can be interpreted as a *cognitive competence* by S_2 ruling on the *pragmatic performance* of S_1.

> *Note*: It is obvious that the cognitive competence legitimizing "knowing-how-to-do" in turns allows for a particular performance (an interpretative doing) ending up in the cognitive act of judgment. This is another problem that must be treated separately.

This first investigation suggests the possibility of a syntagmatic representation of the four modal structures (see the accompanying diagram).

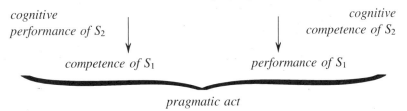

cognitive performance of S_2

cognitive competence of S_2

competence of S_1

performance of S_1

pragmatic act

We can see that it is as though the act of some subject or other were enfolded within the modalizing instances of a second subject situated on the cognitive dimension. From a syntagmatic point of view, the two enfolding modal structures presuppose and are not presupposed. To take place, the performance of S_2 presupposes the competence of S_1, and in turn the competence of S_2 presupposes the existence of the performance of S_1. The act of S_1, although sufficient unto itself, under certain conditions can be inserted in the transitive cognitive trajectory.

We should note here to what degree the syntagmatic organization of the act resembles that of narrative discourse or, rather, that of the canonical narrative program. The latter, which has two components, competence and performance, generally refers back to the pole of the sender, who is first of all responsible for requisitioning the subject and then sanctioning it afterward.

Overmodalizations

Competence and Its Overmodalizations

The establishment of the preceding syntagmatic framework for modalities should help us in setting up areas of future research and in outlining the epistemological domains rendering the conception and the construction of a theory of modalities possible. For example, we can see that a *theory of performance*, including both factitive doing and transitive doing, could be developed in two directions: a *theory of manipulation* and a *theory of action*. We would also hope that an analogous theory of competence that would integrate as much as possible the converging research of logicians and semioticians could also finally be worked out.

Indeed, whether we are dealing with the "being-of-the-doing" (the pragmatic competence of the subject about to act) or the "being-of-the-being" (the cognitive competence empowering it to bear judgments on the object-utterances of the world), the "being" of the "state" we are speaking about in both cases is intuitively apprehended as a *potential instance* where the set of preconditions of being and doing are found. Moreover, to use a term borrowed from Gustave Guillaume, this instance appears as a locus of "tension" stretching between zero point and the point where doing or being is actualized. Because of this very fact, this tense state takes on finer articulations in the form of *modal overdeterminations* like so many markers along the way.

Provisional Inventory

We can now propose a provisional inventory of these overmodalizations of competence that is in no way restrictive since it rests only on a limited experience of the analysis of narrative discourses and on the descriptions of a few European languages (German, English, French). It lists four modalities:

/wanting/
/having-to/
/being-able-to/
/knowing/.

These modalities can modulate the potential state called competence and so govern utterances of doing and utterances of state by modifying their predicates in a certain way.

The proposed inventory is provisional in two ways: It is not organized as a taxonomy, nor is it closed. Thus whereas the semiotician will have a tendency spontaneously to interpret *having-to* as the sender's wanting, for the logician *wanting* can appear as a self-intended having-to. The conclusion we can hope to draw from all of this is the possibility, after a semic and syntactic analysis, of establishing an interdefined and self-sufficient modal system.

Categorization and Denomination

By considering each of the modalities of the inventory as a form of modification of the "being-of-the-doing," it is possible to categorize them and project them on the semiotic square by setting the modal predicate and the predicate *doing* in a binary relation (see "Factitive Modalities," this chapter):

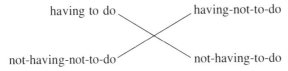

The modal category thus obtained can then be named by terms such as:

Thanks to the *naming* procedure we discover, with slight modification, the set of *deontic modalities* used in certain modal logics.

From a linguistic point of view, all naming is arbitrary, although it can be more or less semantically motivated at the moment of its lexicalization. In order to become operative at the metalinguistic plane that it helps to found, it must contain a structural definition integrating concepts belonging to the same level within a coherent whole.

Now, in our case the procedure of naming consists in what one could call nominalization, that is, in the conversion of a verbal formulation into a nominal formulation that transforms the *modal predicate* into a *modal value*. In addition, what is converted and nominalized is what we already called a modal structure corresponding to a hypotactic organization of a modal utterance and a descriptive utterance, and not simply to the modal predicate, so that, for example:

/prescription/ ≃ /having-to-do/.

Consequently, the *modal values* used in logic, from the viewpoint of semiotics, must be considered as *names* having *syntactic definitions* that happen to be the corresponding modal structures.

The Modalizations of the Subject and the Object

By using the same procedure we can categorize the modal structure of /having-to-be/ by endowing at the same time the taxic positions so obtained with the corresponding names:

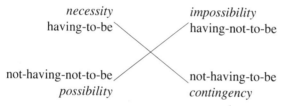

We can readily recognize the *alethic modalities* in the modal values so named.

A comparison between the deontic and the alethic modalities is suggestive. Whereas their denominations tend to separate them and make them appear as distinct modalizations, their syntactic definitions bring them together. Since in both cases the modal predicates are identical, only the nature of the modalized utterances (utterances of doing and utterances of state) distinguishes them from each other.

In addition, insofar as semiotics is attempting to work out a taxonomy and a typology of modalities, it must avoid using names too hastily; because they are semantically motivated, these denominations risk being tainted with a cultural relativism that is difficult to detect. At this stage, we should be content with modal definitions that can be categorized using a very simple notational system:

m = modal utterance
d = utterance of doing
s = utterance of state.

This system can be transcribed as follows:

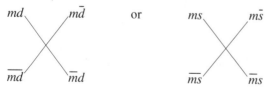

By successively investing the four predicates we have retained of the modal utterance (wanting, having-to, being-able, and knowing), we can obtain *eight modal categories* articulating the instance of competence. In addition, we can foresee the same number of *possible logics*. Along with a *deontic logic* based on the modal set stemming from /having-to-do/, it is possible to foresee a *volitional logic* or *bulistics* based on /wanting/, and so forth.

Yet the distinction between modalizations of doing and being must be maintained. We shall say that in the first case, modalization bears on the predicate considered in its relation with the subject, and in the second case, in its relation with the object. Two types of logic — *subjective logic*, describing and governing the modalizations of the subjects, and *objective logic*, dealing with the modes of existence of utterance objects — can be distinguished.

The Syntagmatic Approach. The procedure of categorization we have promoted here lets us perceive the possibility of *modal taxonomy*. However, it will be possible to set it up only if we can progressively establish a set of interdefinitions covering all of the modal categories and articulating their semic nuclei. In spite of some rather interesting attempts to set up these interdefinitions simply based on intuition, we still have not succeeded in doing so. Thus although we can imagine the distribution of modal spaces from which specific modal logics can be constructed, it is difficult to imagine how they are all interlinked.

That being so, we can try a different approach; that is, from a purely semiotic perspective, we can ask ourselves if it is not possible to imagine and to define the conditions under which the envisaged modalities could be constituted into ordered syntagmatic series or, if this is not possible, into predictable syntactic trajectories. This would help, at least in part, to answer naive questions such as, What trajectory is taken, starting from the generating *ab quo* instance, from zero point, to get to the *ad quem* instance, to the realization of the act, to performance? How, moreover, starting from simple state utterances, that is, beginning with specific determinations attributable to specific subjects, do we end up with an assured and assumed knowledge of the world?

It is evident that satisfactory answers to such questions are not possible for the time being. Yet the quest for knowledge almost always begins with naive questions. To pose "competence" as a block, as a nonanalyzable concept, is useful as a first step, but it cannot be maintained to the very end. To treat modal logic as a repertory of models is a good thing, but from a semiotic point of view, to be able to treat it as series of steps marking the successive stages of a discourse in truth would be even better.

The Organization of Pragmatic Competence. If we consider only pragmatic competence, and consider it only as the potential instance presupposed by the act, then we could articulate as *levels* of existence: (1) each level characterized by a specific *mode of semiotic existence*, and (2) levels having a relation of oriented *presupposition* beginning with performance (which presupposes competence). We thus obtain the accompanying tabulation.

	Competence				*Performance*
virtualizing		*actualizing*			*realizing*
modalities		*modalities*			*modalities*
having-to		being-able			
wanting		knowing			causing-to-be

The outline we propose for a syntagmatic organization of the modalities can have only an operative status. It was suggested to us in part by a long philosophical tradition, but it is especially founded on the recognition of the canonical schemata of narration where two instances — that of the institution of the subject (marked by the apparition of the virtualizing modalities /having-to/ and/or /wanting/) and that of the qualification of the subject (the modalities of /being-able/ and/or of /knowing/ determining the modes of ulterior action) — are very clearly distinguished.

Nonetheless, curiously enough, this syntagmatic organization we would like to consider as being canonical, although it does seem justified *in abstracto*, as a simulacrum of the passage to the act does not correspond to what happens at the level of manifestation and, particularly, in discourses describing the acquisition of competence-activating performances. For example, the subject can be endowed with a *being-able* without necessarily possessing a *wanting*, which should have preceded it. This is a problem that catalysis, the explanation of the presuppositions, cannot resolve alone: It is as if the successive modalizations constituting the subject's pragmatic competence did not stem from a single original instance, but from several (from several senders, we would say in terms of narrative grammar). The interpretation that proposes to distinguish the *intrinsic modalities* (having-to and being-able), no matter how interesting, does not yet seem to bring a definitive solution to the preceding problem.[3]

We think therefore that for the moment, while still seeking a suitable method, it is timely to proceed by confronting modal structures and by attempting to homologate them in pairs to derive, if possible, criteria for their compatibility.

Modal Confrontations

Alethic Modalizations

To being with — and because this coupling we have chosen does seem interesting from a methodological point of view — we can parallel two modal objective categories whose modal structures (corresponding to the term S_2 of the semiotic square) have already been identified as /having-to-be/ and /being-able-to-be/.

The operation can be envisaged as a series of four homologations:

Homologation 1 (compatibilities): simple superimposition of two modal categories articulated as semiotic squares.

Homologation 2 (conformities): superimposition of two categories with *inversion* of the axes of the second modality.

Homologation 3 (contrarieties): superimposition with *inversion of the schemata* of the second modality.

Homologation 4 (contradictions): superimposition with *inversion of the deixes*.

The accompanying diagram represents the results of the homologations; it will be followed by several explanatory and interpretative notes.

CONFRONTATION OF /HAVING-TO-BE/ AND /BEING-ABLE-TO-BE/

I. *Compatibilities*

1. Complementarities (homologation 1)

necessity (S)	having-to-be	having-not-to-be	*impossibility* (S)
possibility (O)	being-able-to-be	being-able-not-to-be	*contingency* (O)
possibility (S)	not-having-not-to-be	not-having-to-be	*contingency* (S)
necessity (O)	not-being-able-not-to-be	not-being able-to-be	*impossibility* (O)

2. Conformities (homologation 2)

necessity (S)	having-to-be	having-not-to-be	*impossibility* (S)
necessity (O)	not-being-able-not-to-be	not-being-able-to-be	*impossibility* (O)
possibility (S)	not-having-not-to-be	not-having-to-be	*contingency* (S)
possibility (O)	being-able-to-be	being-able-not-to-be	*contingency* (O)

II. *Incompatibilities*

1. Contrarieties (homologation 3)

necessity (S)	having-to-be	having-not-to-be		*impossibility* (S)
impossibility (O)	not-being-able-to-be	not-being-able-not-to-be		*necessity* (O)
possibility (S)	not-having-not-to-be	not-having-to-be		*contingency* (S)
contingency (O)	being-able-not-to-be	being-able-to-be		*possibility* (O)

2. Contradictions (homologation 4)

necessity (S)	having-to-be	having-not-to-be		*impossibility* (S)
contingency (O)	being-able-not-to-be	being-able-to-be		*possibility* (O)
possibility (S)	not-having-not-to-be	not-having-to-be		*contingency* (S)
impossibility (O)	not-being-able-to-be	not-being-able-not-to-be		*necessity* (O)

Next to the syntactic *definitions* of the modal structures (which we expressed in natural language, but which we will find formulated in "Modalizations of the Subject and the Object," this chapter), we considered it advisable to add their *names*. These being arbitrary, it seemed promising to us—following our intuition—to use the same names for the two modal categories, so that, for example,

S_1 (*htb*) = S_2 (*batb*)
htb = having-to-be
batb = being-able-to-be,

although we should investigate this unexpected result later on.

The four homologations enable us to compare coupled tactic terms of which eight are compatible and the other eight are incompatible. The couplings with terms belonging to the same deixis are *compatible* and those with terms belonging to different deixes are *incompatible*.

In addition, we can distinguish two types of *compatibility*: *complementarity* and *conformity*. *Complementarity* characterizes two terms occupying the same tactic position and can be interpreted as the possibility of inscribing them in the same modal program (marking either progression or regression in the process of modalization). *Conformity* is the result of two different terms belonging to the same deixis and marks their concomitance in the same syntagmatic position of the modal program.

There are two sorts of *incompatibility* of the modal structures. The term *contrariety* will be used to designate the *confrontation* of two terms in a tactic position of contradiction, whereas *contradiction* will designate two confronted terms in a tactic position of contrariety. In both cases, incompatibility corresponds to the impossibility of their being inserted in the same modal program and transforms opposition into confrontation.

> *Note*: A problem occurs at the level of the axes of the subcontraries in the third homologation, once again raising the question of knowing if the subcontraries can always be defined in relation to contrariety.

The comparison of two modal categories in the second homologation produces a particular case of *conformity* that, if we remain at the level of intuitive denomination, conflates them. Here two interpretations are possible. From a paradigmatic point of view, /having-to-be/, named *necessity*, appears equivalent to the contradictory of the contrary of /being-able-to-be/, which is /not-being-able-not-to-be/ and which we also named *necessity*. In this case, the two modal structures, /having-to-be/ and /being-able-to-be/, must be considered as *contradictories*, and this observation can be considered as the starting point for the taxonomic organization of our temporary inventory of the modalities. However, from a syntagmatic point of view, we can ask ourselves if these rather hasty namings do not indeed hide differences situated at another level, that is, if, for example, the two "necessities" cannot be distinguished in the same way as "determinism in minds" and "determinism in things," or "constructed structures" and "immanent structures" are opposed. If this were the case, and we could distinguish *necessity* originating from the *subject* (the coherence of models and of metalanguage) from *necessity* originating from the *object* (resistances of the referent), the confrontation of these two modal categories within the modal program of epistemic competence could be identified as the domain where we could situate the problematics of *adequation* (as a possible definition of truth).

This confrontation model, obtained by means of successive homologations, seems useful to test other compatibilities and/or incompatibilities of the modal structures that can partake in the same programs of modalization of both the subject and the object.

Deontic and Bulistic Modalizations

Armed with this procedure of homologation, we can now return to pragmatic competence and attempt in the accompanying diagram a new comparison between the virtualizing modalities /having-to-do/ and /wanting-to-do/.

CONFRONTATION OF /HAVING-TO-DO/ AND /WANTING-TO-DO/

I. *Compatibilities*

1. Complementarities

active obedience { having-to-do / wanting-to-do ╲ ╱ having-not-to-do / wanting-not-to-do }

passive will { not-having-not-to-do / not-wanting-not-to-do ╱ ╲ not-having-to-do / not-wanting-to-do }

2. Conformities

passive obedience { having-to-do / not-wanting-not-to-do ╲ ╱ having-not-to-do / not-wanting-to-do }

active will { not-having-not-to-do / wanting-to-do ╱ ╲ not-having-to-do / wanting-not-to-do }

II. *Incompatibilities*

1. Contrarieties

passive resistance { having-to-do / not-wanting-to-do ╲ ╱ having-not-to-do / not-wanting-not-to-do }

active abulia { having-to-do / wanting-not-to-do ╱ ╲ not-having-to-do / wanting-to-do }

2. Contradictions

active resistance { having-to-do / wanting-not-to-do ╲ ╱ having-not-to-do / wanting-to-do }

passive abulia { not-having-not-to-do / not-wanting-to-do ╱ ╲ not-having-to-do / not-wanting-not-to-do }

The interpretation of this schema suggests a certain number of remarks.

The couplings carried out represent a set of *modal positions* of the pragmatic subject at the moment it fulfills the necessary conditions to conclude the *contract*, that is, at the moment when the sender, with the help of *factitive* modalization, has already transmitted the deontic content of the message. The subject, endowed with two distinct modalities, is in a position that can give rise to either *acceptance* (in the case of modal compatibility), or *refusal* (in the case of incompatibility) of the contract. Acceptance and refusal (assertion and negation) come under cognitive performance called *decision*.

The simple combinatorial obtained has eight positions of acceptance and eight others of refusal.

> *Note*: It is obvious that refusal must also be considered a form of contract: It does not stop the deployment of the program of modalization of the subject, but rather shifts it in another direction.

In spite of the very approximate nature of the names (and since here are named only the axes of the coupled modalities), we can get an idea of the distribution of the actantial roles of the *consenting subject*:

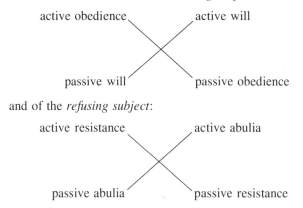

active obedience ╲   ╱ active will

passive will ╱   ╲ passive obedience

and of the *refusing subject*:

active resistance ╲   ╱ active abulia

passive abulia ╱   ╲ passive resistance

We can see that such a typology of subjects having to confront their duties and their will comes under both a *deontic semiotics* and a *bulistic semiotics*, but at the same time this typology can shed light on certain aspects of the *typology of cultures* and, more specifically, the description of an individual's "attitudes" in relation to society. For example, we see that European cultural contact valorizes the actantial roles active will and active resistance as "creators."

The modal confrontation prejudges neither the syntagmatic deployment of the modalizations nor their organization into series. Thus, according to the syntagmatic priority given to one or other of the modal structures, two types of contracts can be foreseen:

> *injunctive contract* = /having-to-do/ —> /wanting-to-do/
> *permissive contract* = /wanting-to-do/ —> /having-to-do/.

> *Note*: It should be pointed out, however, that the permissive contract is optional: It is not presupposed by the establishment of the volitive modalization.

Systems of Rules and Aptitudes of Subjects

We would like to propose a final model representing the functioning of social codes, that is, the more or less restrictive rules that are implicit or explicit, confronted with comparable sets corresponding to different articulations of the subject's competence to which this applies. In the accompanying diagram we shall confront the modalities of /having-to-do/ with /knowing-how-to-do/, but the juxtaposition of the former with /being-able-to-do/ would probably be as fruitful.

CONFRONTATION OF /HAVING-TO-DO/ AND /KNOWING-HOW-TO-DO/

I. *Compatibilities*

1. Complementarities

$$
\left\{
\begin{array}{cc}
\dfrac{\text{having-to-do}}{\text{knowing-how-to-do}} & \dfrac{\text{having-not-to-do}}{\text{knowing-how-not-to-do}}
\end{array}
\right\}
$$

$$
\left\{
\begin{array}{cc}
\dfrac{\text{not-having-not-to-do}}{\text{not-knowing-how-not-to-do}} & \dfrac{\text{not-having-to-do}}{\text{not-knowing-how-to-do}}
\end{array}
\right\}
$$

2. Conformities

$$
\left\{
\begin{array}{cc}
\dfrac{\text{having-to-do}}{\text{not-knowing-how-not-to-do}} & \dfrac{\text{having-not-to-do}}{\text{not-knowing-how-to-do}}
\end{array}
\right\}
$$

$$
\left\{
\begin{array}{cc}
\dfrac{\text{not-having-not-to-do}}{\text{knowing-how-to-do}} & \dfrac{\text{not-having-to-do}}{\text{knowing-how-not-to-do}}
\end{array}
\right\}
$$

II. *Incompatibilities*

1. Contrarieties

$$
\left\{
\begin{array}{cc}
\dfrac{\text{having-to-do}}{\text{not-knowing-how-to-do}} & \dfrac{\text{having-not-to-do}}{\text{not-knowing-how-not-to-do}}
\end{array}
\right\}
$$

$$
\left\{
\begin{array}{cc}
\dfrac{\text{not-having-not-to-do}}{\text{knowing-how-not-to-do}} & \dfrac{\text{not-having-to-do}}{\text{knowing-how-to-do}}
\end{array}
\right\}
$$

2. Contradictions

$$
\left\{
\begin{array}{cc}
\dfrac{\text{having-to-do}}{\text{knowing-how-not-to-do}} & \dfrac{\text{having-not-to-do}}{\text{knowing-how-to-do}}
\end{array}
\right\}
$$

$$
\left\{
\begin{array}{cc}
\dfrac{\text{not-having-not-to-do}}{\text{not-knowing-how-not-to-do}} & \dfrac{\text{not-having-to-do}}{\text{not-knowing-how-not-to-do}}
\end{array}
\right\}
$$

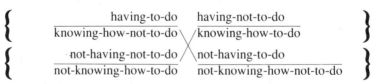

Note: Confronting these two types of modalities enables us to give a representation of the *application* of social codes of a normative nature such as laws of grammar, laws of jurisprudence, and laws of custom (codes of courtesy, propriety) for subjects endowed with /knowing-how-to-do/, that is, a sort of "syntagmatic intelligence" that can be typologized as a set of aptitudes and inaptitudes. Because of the diversity of the semantic isotopies on which such applications can be carried out, at this stage it would be prudent to seek an appropriate name for each coupling ("overreaction," according to the code of courtesy would correspond, for example, to "hypercorrections" in grammar).

Confrontation can be viewed in two different manners: At the level of competence it determines the possible modes of action and can give rise to the establishment of a typology of *social roles*; seen at the end of performances having taken place, it constitutes a grid within which sanction takes place (examinations and initiation rituals, the qualification and recognition of subjects, etc.), that is, a form of veridiction bearing on the competence of the subjects.

In Conclusion

The need we have felt for a long time, of introducing and explicating the modal component of a future discoursive grammar, forms the basis of this text and the reflections herein expressed. What began only as a desire to point out the existence of an area of investigation and an unexploited theoretical domain gave rise to more advanced developments, to certain temporary formulations, without in any way exploring the vast area of modal interventions, and here we are specifically thinking about the epistemic modalizations.

Chapter 8
On the Modalization of Being

Taxonomies and Axiologies

Any semanticism (*notion*, *field*, *concept*, *locus*, *territory*, etc.) can be articulated when it is grasped as a relation and posited as a semantic axis, as a *semantic category*, which in turn can be represented by means of the semiotic square.

A semantic category can be axiologized by projecting the *thymic category* with contrary terms named /*euphoria*/ vs. /*dysphoria*/ onto the square articulating it. This is a "primary" proprioceptive category by which we seek to formulate in a fairly basic way how living beings within a given milieu "perceive" their own bodies and react to their environment. A living being is considered here to be a "system of attractions and repulsions." The thymic category can thus be homologated, in a certain way, with the term /*animated*/ taken from the category /*animated*/ vs. /*inanimated*/ generally accepted in linguistics.

The square and the categories it represents taxonomically can then be said to be axiologized. The identified and interdefined terms constituting them can be called *axiological values* (they are no longer simply descriptive – or linguistic – in the Saussurian sense of "value"), and they will have the status of virtual values at this abstract level. We can therefore say that the application of "thymic" categories on the "descriptive" level transforms the taxonomies into axiologies.

> *Note*: Regrettable homonymies have been inadvertently introduced in the designation of the terms defining different modes of semiotic existence: /*virtuality*/-/*actuality*/-/*reality*/. On the one hand, to distinguish the different levels of depth of the *semiotic structures* in general, we say the deep

structures are *virtual*, the semio-narrative structures *actualized*, and the discoursive structures /*realizing*/. On the other hand, to designate the different phases of the modalization of the *subject of doing* (the acquisition of modal competence), modalities are divided into *virtualizing* (wanting− and having-to-do), *actualizing* (having−and knowing-how-to-do) and *realizing* (causing-to-be). Nonetheless, cases of confusion are relatively rare among the former.

Problems of Conversion

We would like to remind the reader that the term *conversion* designates the entire set of procedures that account for the passage (of the transcription) of a semiotic unit situated at the deep level to a unit belonging to the surface structure. This new unit is considered to be both *homotopic* and *heteromorphic* in relation to the previous one; that is, it is considered as encompassing the same topic content and as having more signifying, syntactic, and/or properly semantic articulations than the other.

The conversion of the axiologized values that we will focus on for the moment consists in maintaining their status of axiologized values, and their actualization brought about by the subject taking on the values or, what amounts to the same thing, by the establishment of a certain type of relation between values and subjects.

Because the axiological value is defined as having two elements at the deep level (a semic term overdetermined by a thymic term), two aspects of this procedure of conversion must be envisaged separately.

1. From the semantic point of view, values considered as being semic terms that may be selected within the semiotic square are said to be converted when they are invested in syntactic entities called *objects*, defined by the relation of junction they maintain with *subjects*. Values are thus represented as being inscribed in utterances of state.
2. The conversion of values considered from their thymic aspect raises a new problem of a very general nature.

Thymic Space and Modal Space

This type of conversion requires that we postulate a general hypothesis that can be formulated as follows: *Signifying space, which, at the level of deep structures, is articulated by means of the thymic category, should be considered as being homotopic and heteromorphic in relation to the totality of modal articulations governing the relations between subjects and objects at the level of the surface semiotic structures.* In other words (for it is necessary to explicate this epistemological postulate), *thymic space*, which, at the level of the abstract structures is supposed to represent the elementary manifestations of a living being in relation to its environment (cf. /*animated*/), at the surface, anthropomorphic, level of the generative trajectory corresponds to *modal space*, which, while covering the same topical space appears as a development, as an overarticulation of the former (and can be linked to the term /*human*/).

We can thus say that the conversion of values—in addition to the taking on of a semic term, selected within the semiotic square and inscribed in the object as value—also includes the selection of a thymic term, to be *invested in the relation linking subject and object*. The relation between subject and object defining the subject as existing semiotically is also endowed with a "surplus of meaning," and the being of the subject is modalized in a specific way.

Modalization thus appears as the result of a series of signifying subarticulations of the amorphous thymic mass. This mass is constituted first of all as a thymic category at the deep level, and, once again, it is differentiated into modal categories at the anthropomorphic level. The modal configurations obtained by these successive categorizations must be considered at the same time as being both *universal* and *constructed*. They are constructed because—in spite of intuitive evidence (which is always questionable) and the inductive analyses of their lexicalizations by natural languages (which are never convincing)—only the syntactic criteria of semio-narrative grammar can found both what discriminates between them and what interdefines them.

Therefore it is only from the hypothetico-deductive perspective that we can say that, at the more surface level, four modal categories correspond to the thymic category, and that a thymic term, such as /*euphoria*/, for example, can be converted, by taking into account the syntagmatic position of the syntactic structure within which it will be invested, into four distinct modal terms: /*wanting*/, /*having-to*/, *being-able-to*/, and /*knowing*/.

> *Note*: We should not be surprised, at the level of the anthropomorphic structures (the semio-narrative surface structures), to find taxonomic organizations that are starting points for syntactic constructions. It is there that not only the relations between subjects and objects, but also the actantial structures (the splitting of protoactants into actants, negactants, etc.), without even mentioning the modal categories that permit us to establish a typology of subjects and objects, should be defined.

Modal Competence and Modal Existence

1. Relations, from a structural point of view, are considered as primary compared with terms that are simply their end points, and the latter can be recognized as intersection points with other relations.

2. Relations, from a syntactic point of view, are the constituents of the elementary utterances (utterances of doing and utterances of state).

3. Finally, the modalizations of these utterances are concerned with the constituent relations of utterances (called *functions*),

Therefore, according to the nature of the relation they modify, initially we should distinguish two sorts of modalizations and, at the same time, two classes of modalities: the modalities of doing governing *intentional relations* and the modalities of state, *existential relations*.

> *Note*: We can see that the modalizations precede the syntactic operations the utterances are supposed to describe: In order to do, one has first of all to "be-able-to-do"; the operations of assertion and of negation presuppose wanting and being able to assert or to negate. In the same way the object of value is "wanted" independently of the operations of conjunction and disjunction, and prior to them.

On the other hand, the observation of the way semantic charges are invested and distributed within canonical utterances (for example, "The seamstress is working"; "the young lady is sewing"; "she is sewing") enables semioticians constructing their own metalanguage to formulate this supplementary "semantic charge" as depending on one or other of the utterance's constituent elements. In this way a modalization can be said to bear sometimes on the relation-function itself, sometimes on the subject or the object.

Consequently we will say that the modalities of doing are to be interpreted as modifications of the status of the *subject of the doing* and that the modalities affecting it constitute its *modal competence*. In the same way, the modalizations of being will be considered to be modifications of the status of the *object of value*. The modalities affecting the object (or rather the value invested therein) will be said to be constituents of the subject of state's *modal existence*.

> *Note*: It is obvious that these distinctions were not made simply to facilitate the metalinguistic formulation of the modalities and that they correspond equally well to the intuitive apprehension of modal phenomena and to experience gained from textual analysis. The subject of doing appears as an agent, as an active element accumulating all of the potential of doing, whereas the subject of state appears as a patient and passively receives all the stimuli of the world inscribed in the objects surrounding it.

Hence, it is possible to bring to light the differences separating *modal semiotics* from *modal logics*. Whereas semiotics will concentrate on determining and formulating the modal competence of *subjects* (of doing) and the modal existence of the *objects* of value (defining the subjects of state), logic considers that modalizations bear exclusively on propositions (that is, on the relations constituting them), and takes an interest in them only insofar as they modify propositional *re-*

lations. An example will permit us to see the consequences that can be drawn from this twofold process:

Having-to-do		Having-to-be	
logic	*semiotics*	*logic*	*semiotics*
"obligation"	"prescription"	"necessary"	"indispensable"

Whereas in alethic logic the relation between the subject and the object (or rather the predicate) is defined as "necessary," in semiotics /having-to-be/ is interpreted as bearing on the object of value and specifying it as being "indispensable" for the subject of state. Similarly in deontic logic, "obligation" can be interpreted as the relation between two subjects (or two actantial instances). In semiotics, "prescription" is a /having-to-do/ "felt" by the subject and also is part of the subject's modal competence, whereas the sender (the source of this "prescription") is in turn characterized by a factitive /doing/.

We can see that these two approaches, as different as they may be, are also both legitimate in themselves. They remain quite distinct as long as we are dealing with utterances of state, yet they risk being confused with each other during the modal treatment of the utterances of doing. At first glance, however, the semiotic processes would seem to be more "sophisticated."

Modal Structures and Their Designations

The modalities of doing were previously closely examined (see chapter 7), yet the modalizations of the states of doing have been somewhat neglected. Their treatment was partially confused with what takes place in logic, which only focuses on *disengaged*, "objectivized" utterances. The need to separate the problems related to modalities (situated at the narrative level) from those of disengagement (specific to the discursive level), as well as the appearance of a new problematics of passions, forced us to question certain formulations that were too inflexible and to define better the boundaries between adjacent disciplines. Our investigation of the very possibility of describing the "passions" actually seems to be pushing semiotic research in the direction of a sort of *psychosemiotics*, whereas it is hard to imagine that logicians would willingly venture into this domain.

It is simple to take the four modalities that can modify utterances of state and project them onto the semiotic square to constitute the four modal categories that can serve as a taxonomic network for modal syntax. It is the actual naming of terms that, even though we do know that by definition this is arbitrary, raises problems. Whether we want to or not, naming includes some interpretation. Well-"motivated" names facilitate the use of interpretation in natural languages, a use no metalanguage can escape. The solitary terminological production practiced by certain researchers rarely gives results. Although we would like to suggest certain names as examples, we would, however, much prefer if it were generally accepted that we should hand this task over to a "terminology committee" that could judge use through the practice of textual analysis.

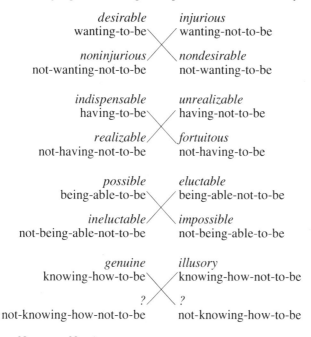

desirable	*injurious*
wanting-to-be	wanting-not-to-be
noninjurious	*nondesirable*
not-wanting-not-to-be	not-wanting-to-be

indispensable	*unrealizable*
having-to-be	having-not-to-be
realizable	*fortuitous*
not-having-not-to-be	not-having-to-be

possible	*eluctable*
being-able-to-be	being-able-not-to-be
ineluctable	*impossible*
not-being-able-not-to-be	not-being-able-to-be

genuine	*illusory*
knowing-how-to-be	knowing-how-not-to-be
?	?
not-knowing-how-not-to-be	not-knowing-how-to-be

Notes on Naming

1. As to modalization in respect to the object of value, we would, so to speak, naturally like to interpret /wanting-to-be/ as the "wished-for-being" of the object. Unfortunately French does not always lend itself to these "passive transformations": /having-to-be/ is not a "being-to-be-had," and so on.
2. Adjectives having the suffixes -*able* and -*ible*, by the very fact that they qualify "modalized" objects in relation to subjects, on the contrary seem well suited for terminological operations.
3. The names chosen must be different from those used in logic.

The interpretation of the modal structures that can take place because of naming lexicalizations, even though inadequate, nonetheless permits us in the main to derive the same setup of interrelations we encountered when examining the modalizations of doing.

Thus the *virtualizing* modalities of /wanting/ and /having-to-be/ seem more "subjective," closer to the subject, than the more "objective" *actualizing* modalities of /being-able/ and /knowing-how-to-be/, which determine more the status of the object of value.

In the same way, the distinction between the *endogenous* (/wanting/ and /being-able/) modalities and the *exogenous* ones (having-to/ and /knowing-how-to/), proposed by Michael Rengstorf[1] for the modalities of doing, seems operative here, since it distinguishes between people's desires and their needs, the possibilities of realizing them and the resistance proper to objects.

Modalized Values

Following this reexamination, we can see that what we were in the habit of calling *value*, beginning with *objects of value*, is in fact a modal structure:

$$V = me(s)$$

where s designates a semic entity, selected during conversion, and *me* a modal structure in which m designates one of the selected modalities and e, the existential relation modified by modalization.

> *Note*: It would perhaps be proper, when writing, to distinguish a lower-case v, used as a symbol for the axiological value, from an upper-case V, designating the value that has already been modalized.

When such a *modalized value* has been inscribed in the object, itself an actant of the utterance of state, it then undergoes the operations of junction (conjunction and disjunction) carried out by the subject of doing (situated syncretically within the same actor, or represented by an autonomous and distinct actor). Thus, for example, a /desirable/ object of value can be either conjoined with a subject of state or disjoined from it. From this perspective, we can say that a subject (of state) has a *modal existence* that can be perturbed at any moment and undergo transformations brought about either by itself as actor (subject of doing) or by other actors (subjects of doing) of the same scenario.

Temporary Conclusions

At this stage of our investigation it is too early to attempt to identify all the consequences of the clarification we have just carried out in establishing a sort of equilibrium between the modalizations of doing and the modalization of being, between modal competence and modal existence. Consequently the few remarks we would like to add here are intended only to highlight the importance of what is at play.

The fact that the modalizations of being can be concerned with any semic entities whatsoever (s) can signify two things: either that the invested value is a variable of the modal structure taken as invariant, or that this modal structure is to be considered as a permanent disposition independent of all semantic investment. Thus, for example, the lexeme *love* would designate the meaning effect of a modal structure as such, whereas *avarice* would have in addition the semantic investment *money* (without mentioning the other restrictions specifying it).

The fact that the invested semic entity seems "naturally" or "socially" endowed beforehand with a specific thymic connotation does not prevent its modalization from being either positive or negative. Thus, for example, the semic term /*life*/ can be modalized as /*desirable*/ or /*nondesirable*/, but the same thing can be said for its contrary /*death*/. The same phenomenon can be observed in the treatment of the category /*nature*/ vs. /*culture*/ or in the actualizing valorization of the elementary figurative axiology /*fire-water-air-earth*/ (on this point, see our *Maupassant*).[2] We can clearly see that the modal structure of the subject of state recategorizes the value systems it takes on.

Speaking about invested values as variable entities permits us to use the same label for descriptive values (the semantic values *stricto sensu*) and modal values. It is obvious that the modalizations of being can cover two classes of values, that modal values such as /*knowing*/ and /*being-able*/, for example, can be over-modalized in turn as /*desirable*/, /indispensable/, /*possible*/, or /*true*/.

In addition we can see that a given value invested in the object can be modally overdetermined either simultaneously, or successively, by several modalities at once. What we have said about modal confrontations with regard to the modalizations of doing also holds true here. In the first case—concomitance—we are dealing with the evaluation of modal compatibilities (an object of value can be considered by the subject as /*desirable*/ and /*impossible*/ at the same time); in the second case—succession—the modal subject's story—or at least the syntagmatic modal stereotypes therein—must be described. Yet, we should not forget that the story is already to be found on the discursive plane.

The last comment is related to the more or less everyday observation that a subject can have a modal relation not only with a single object value, but with several at the same time, and that the former's modal existence gives rise to value conflicts, to cognitive and fiduciary interrogations on the comparative value of values of unequal value. In addition, the subject comes under tensions of unequal importance and thus it is impossible to speak about neutral subjects, of indifferent states, of zero competence. It would seem that the subjects of state by definition are *worried subjects* and that subjects of doing are *wavering subjects*. Hence, if we want to speak of meaning in this modal turmoil, if we want to establish meaningful sequences of actions and passions for a subject, we are obliged to raise the problems of the dominating *modal isotopies* and their discoursivization.

Chapter 9
On Anger:
A Lexical Semantic Study

Introduction

Methodological Choices

Choosing the lexematic dimension when undertaking the examination of anger represents a choice of convenience. Lexemes are notorious for often appearing as condensations concealing, if one takes the trouble to analyze them, very complex discoursive and narrative structures. The existence within the discourse-statement of expansions that reproduce the same structures in a more or less loose and diffuse manner should not disturb us; quite the contrary. Since it is only a matter of a difference in dimension and not of nature, lexematic descriptions can constitute, in an economical way, models that can anticipate subsequent discoursive analyses.

However, as we can clearly see, these descriptions are situated within the context of French culture. The ways and means for going beyond this context by generalizing the models obtained constitute a separate problem.

Contrary to the taxonomic and classificatory approach taken by most philosophers of the classical period in working out a theory of the passions, our approach will be avowedly syntagmatic and even, quite often, syntactic. However, whereas the examination of a "simple" passion (for example, greed, which is recognized as one of the "object passions") has permitted us to postulate a phrastic model to account for it, with a "complex" passion such as anger we are dealing with a discoursive sequence constituted by an intertwining of states and of doing, which we must separate out in order to identify autonomous syntagmatic elements in it and must recompose into a *passional configuration* that we will take as its definition. It is the establishment of such a configuration for anger (French anger!) that guides this study.

Lexigraphic Approximation

If we take a dictionary definition for *anger* (for convenience's sake we will constantly refer to the *Petit Robert*)

"a violent *discontent* accompanied by aggressivenes;"

we see that it is possible to choose the lexeme *discontent* as the central point of the presumed sequence *anger*. There is no doubt that it is a passional state defined in turn as a "painful feeling."

This central lexeme permits us then to examine individually what is situated *afterward* and accompanies anger (that is, aggressiveness) and what is found *beforehand* and precedes it (namely, frustration). For *discontent* — and once again we have recourse to the dictionary — is the "painful feeling of *being frustrated* in one's hopes, one's rights."

In a first approximation we can say that *anger* appears to be a sequence that consists in the following succession:

frustration —> *discontent* —> *aggressiveness*.

Let us go one step further. If the subject (the one who is going to become angry) feels frustrated "in his hopes and rights," this state of frustration has been preceded by, or better, logically presupposes, a prior state of nonfrustration in which the subject, by contrast, has enjoyed hopes and rights.

Thus, prior to frustration we discover beforehand an "original state," a state of passion *ab quo* that we examine. The problem of its final state, as we will see, will be posed in quite different terms.

Expectation

The original state from which the passional story of anger seems to unfold is not neutral; it is the state of a strongly modalized subject.

Thus, if we were to look at definitions for the verb *to frustrate*, we would find two things:

1. *To frustrate* means "to deprive someone of goods, a privilege"; that is, to disjoin or maintain the disjunction of a person from an *object of value*.
2. But the definition continues: [to deprive someone of goods or a privilege] "to which he has *a right*" and that *he believed* he could count on."

This no longer indicates a relation subject with an object of value, but a *quasi-contractual* relation — which is, by this very fact, broken — *with another subject*.

To avoid, at this time, having to analyze the "rights" and "hopes" of the frustrated subject, let us return to the lexigraphic procedure, considering what the dictionary offers as a synonym for *to frustrate*, namely, *to disappoint*. Now, *to disappoint* is defined as "to fall short of (an expectation)," which gives us a definition broad enough to include both the "rights" and the "expectations" of the frustrated-disappointed subject; it also furnishes us with a common term — *expectation* — that favorably replaces the somewhat pretentious term *frustration*.

That given, using what the examined definitions give us, we can distinguish, following a more careful exploration, two kinds of expectation:

1. *A simple expectation*, placing the subject in relation to an object of value.
2. *A fiduciary expectation*, assuming, in addition, modal relations with another subject.

Simple Expectation

Putting aside for the moment the intersubjective fiduciary relation, we can say that initially simple expectation concerns first of all a modalization of the subject, which we can characterize as

/wanting-to-be-conjoined/.

This distinguishes the subject, for example, from the "greedy" subject definable in terms of a

/wanting-to-conjoin/,

a modal competence that is inscribed as such within the narrative program (*NP*) of doing. Thus, along with the *passions of action* represented by avarice, we encounter here a *passion of being acted upon*, that is, a passion in the classical, etymological sense of the word.

We ask ourselves if the distinction *to act* vs. *to be acted upon* is not capable of being placed in a homologous relationship with the long-established distinction between *the subject of doing* and *the subject of state*. Let us pause for a moment to understand the way in which they function. When we speak of the modalized *subject of doing*, the subject competent to engage in an action, we say that such a subject is *actualized*. Following the performance, when the doing has succeeded, we speak of a *realized subject*. However, this realized subject is the *subject of state* conjoined with its object, and not the subject of doing. But then we might well ask what "state" the subject of state is in at the moment of actualization of the subject of doing, that is, at the moment when it is not yet in conjunction with the object of value but desires this conjunction, not as the subject of doing but as the subject of state desirous that the conjunction be made by the subject of doing. In other words, the subject of state is first of all *actualized* — endowed modally with a /wanting-to-be-conjoined/ in order then to be *realized*, that is, conjoined with the object of value, a conjunction that guarantees its semiotic existence.

Note: Alongside a /wanting-to-be-conjoined/, we can easily fit a parallel position for the /having-to-be-conjoined/, which can be lexicalized as *fate*.

Thus, we already see emerging the first two positions of the subjects of state, characterized readily by oppositions situated:

1. At the semio-narrative level:

   /disjunction/ vs. /conjunction/
   /actualized/ vs. /realized/.

2. At the discoursive level:

   /tension/ vs. /relaxation/
   "expectation" vs. "satisfaction" (?).

As we can see, the stakes are not negligible. Parallel to the trajectory of the subject of doing, made up of the acquisition of competencies and the accomplishment of performances, we have to account for a comparable trajectory of the subject of state, presented as a succession of "feeling states" made up of highs and lows.

For its part, the passion of expectation may be formulated as follows:

$$S_1 \text{ wanting } S_2 \longrightarrow (S_1 \cap O_v),$$

whereby S_1 is the subject of state and S_2 the subject of doing.

Note: Although it is self-evident, let us explicitly note that the subject of doing may be either inscribed within the same actor as the subject of state or constituted as a separate actor.

Fiduciary Expectation

The time has now come to reverse direction and to reexamine the subject of state prior to frustration. We have seen, indeed, that the subject is characterized, according to the dictionary definitions that we sought to interpret in summary fashion, by a twofold relation maintained by the subject of state, on the one hand, with the object of value and, on the other, with the subject of doing. We have limited ourselves to saying that this last relation was intersubjective and modal in character. Let us try to zero in on this problem.

Actually the subject's expectation is not a simple wish; it is inscribed against a backdrop of confidence: The subject of state "thinks it can count" on the subject of doing to realize "its expectations" and/or its "rights." If the contractual nature of the relation that gives rise to the "rights" is obvious, the obligational nature of the fact of *expecting*, "considering (that which is desired) as having to be realized," also appears as soon as one scratches beneath the lexematic surface. Let us say straightforwardly that in the one case as in the other, we are led to record the presence of a deontic modality, a /having-to-do/, attributed to the subject of doing.

We cannot speak here of a true contract (which, as we know, engages both "contracting" parties) but rather of a contract of confidence, or a pseudocontract. We could perhaps consider it an *imaginary contract*, for at its conclusion—or rather its recognition—the subject of doing is in no way engaged; The subject's deontic modalization is the product of the "imagination" of the subject of state.

We are dealing here with a new dimension of semiotic activity that has until now drawn scant attention from analysts. It concerns the *construction of simulacra*, those imaginary objects the subject projects outside itself and that, even though they have in fact no intersubjective foundation, nevertheless effectively determine intersubjective behavior as such. Whether it is a matter of confidence in others or in oneself (when the subject of state and subject of doing are emerged), we are dealing with a fiduciary relation that is established between the subject and the simulacrum it has constructed, and not with an intersubjective relation.

> *Note*: Confidence may be more or less "grounded." It may be either "spontaneous" or based on repeated experience. This is a separately identified problem of construction of the simulacrum and not of its intersubjective use.

By giving—admittedly on a provisional basis—the name *belief* to this fiduciary relation between the subject and the simulacrum it has made for itself (but which it identifies with the "true" subject of doing), we can attempt a formulation of *fiduciary expectation* not only as a /wanting-to-be conjoined/, that is, as

$$S_1 \text{ wanting } S_2 \longrightarrow (S_1 \cap O_v),$$

but *at the same time* as faith in the conjunctive obligation of the subject of doing:

$$S_1 \text{ believing } S_2 \text{ having to } \longrightarrow (S_2 \cap O_v).$$

Realization

Satisfaction. The passional state of S_1—called *expectation*— is disrupted by the intervention of S_2. This subject of doing, whose passional status stems from a distinct problematics—that of generosity and of harmfulness, of deceit and of truth, etc.—exercises within the framework of its *NP* an attribution (and nonattribution) activity, an activity that, in turn, will have as an effect the realization or nonrealization of the subject of state.

The lexicalization of this doing and of this state in French leads to apparent confusion that can easily be freed from ambiguity. Indeed, the lexemes

> *satisfaction*, "the action of *contenting* (a need, a desire)," and
> *contenting*, "the action of *satisfying* needs,"

whose definitions are nicely circular, denote doing in its pure state without any other modalization by S_2. However, another sememe is discovered under this same lexematic covering. It no longer designates the action of S_2 as its result, which concerns S_1:

> *satisfaction*: "pleasure *resulting from the accomplishment* of what one expects, desires, or simply of a desirable thing."

To the result of the doing (the conjunction of the subject with its object of value) is therefore added a certain "pleasure" called *satisfaction*. Succeeding the expectation (designated by /tension/) that characterizes a /wanting-to-be/ is the realization of this "being," a /relaxation/ we will call /satisfaction/. At the same time we should not lose sight of the fact that satisfaction is only one of the possible results of expectation.

Patience. Recalling that the "passions" with which we are concerned at this moment are passions of the subject of state, that is, of the *patient*, the realization or nonrealization of which depends on a subject of doing or *agent*, we must stop for a moment for a closer examination of the notion of *patience*, if for no other reason than that it belongs to the same etymological and conceptual family as *passion*.

Patience, it is said, is the "state of mind of one who knows how to *wait* without losing his composure." *Patience* is linked intimately to expectation;[1] it characterizes expectation from beginning to end. We could say that patience, by filling in the space between the actualized object of state and the realized (or nonrealized) subject, is coextensive with expectation.

But with regard to its antonym *impatience*, right away it appears to be something other than expectation, a "state of mind of one who *knows* how to wait" and who is contrasted to the one who does not know how. However, "to know how to wait" is a surface lexematic manifestation; the modality corresponding to it is not a /knowing-how-to-do/ (which would consist, for example, in counting sheep while waiting to go to sleep) but a /being-able-to-be/.

The "state of mind" in which we recognize the presence of the modality /being-able-to-be/ is, in relation to expectation, an autonomous disposition. Whereas expectation is, as it were, an accidental passion, dependent on the *NP* within which the subject is implicated, *patience*, which focuses on the permanence of being in general, finds its application in taking hold of expectation, just as it could seek to persist under another name by taking possession of the durable state of satisfaction. What we have here is a phenomenon of overmodalization, of wanting by being able, a /being-able-to-want-to-be/.

Yet, for all that the question of the patience of the patient is posed: At what moment can we say that the patient "becomes impatient," that it "runs out of patience," that it is "at the end of its patience"?

This problem is that of the introduction of discontinuity into the midst of duration, of segmentation into slices of passional life that appears to us in its ordinariness to be an alternation of tensions and relaxations, of discomforts and moments of ease. Two cases in point—the one ordinary, the other exceptional—that can account for this intrusion come to mind: (1) that instance in which the patient subject is merged with the cognitive subject informed of the unfolding of the *NP* of the subject of doing and of the eventual timetable of this program; and (2) the instance in which tension, which characterizes patient expectation and is overdetermined by the category of intensity, becomes *excessive*, even intolerable, and brings about knowledge of the nonrealization of the *NP* of the doing subject.

In both instances it is *knowing*—prior in the first case, subsequent in the second—that produces a break in the passional flow.

Dissatisfaction and Disappointment. The malaise produced following this break, this modal shock between the ever-present /wanting-to-be-conjoined/ and the /knowledge-of-not-being-conjoined/ superimposed on it, we shall call /dissatisfaction/. We select this term from among the numerous parasynonyms such as "annoyance" or "displeasure" and in symmetry with the anticipated /satisfaction/. Whether dissatisfaction is the meaning effect created by this modal incompatibility or whether it provokes a more subtle "passional event," to clarify it we must return to more thoroughgoing analyses that focus on the discoursive sequences in their expanded form. For the moment it will be enough for us to indicate its place within the general situation of passional events.

One point remains to be noted, however, relative to the role of intensity. We get the impression that a direct relationship often exists between the intensity of the expectation ("wish," "want," "hope," "aspiration," "desire," "longing," etc.) and the corresponding degree of dissatisfaction due to its nonrealization.

Along with the visible dissatisfaction that follows on the nonattribution of the object of value is occasionally added another kind of unease, which is provoked by the behavior of the subject of doing and interpreted as nonconforming to the expectation. In the eyes of the fiduciary-expecting subject, this behavior, which was modalized by a /having-to-do/, does not take place, and the believing on the part of the subject of state is shown at once to be unjustified. The resulting disappointment is a crisis of confidence from a twofold point of view: not only because subject$_2$ has abused the trust placed in it, but also—and perhaps especially—because subject$_1$ may accuse itself for the misplaced trust. Both of these forms of dysphoria now brought together are prompted by "frustration" and, according to the dictionaries, constitute the "active discontent" that leads to the explosion of *anger*.

Discontent

The Passional Pivot

By approaching the examination of anger with the help of definitions provided by the dictionary, we have recognized in a first approximation three segments:

"frustration" —> "discontent" —> "aggressiveness,"

the suggestion of which is taken as constituting the passional syntagm "anger." *Discontent*—the position at which we have just arrived—thus appears to be a *passional pivot* that, by subsuming and assuming the structures that precede, permits the development of the structures that *follow*.

Let us explain. Dissatisfaction, as we have explained it, appears as the *terminal* feature of an *NP* put into discourse; as we have seen, it is the result of the nonconjunction of the subject with the object of value. But—and so much so that it risks being confused with it—this terminal state is situated very closely to an *inchoative* state that corresponds in discursive terms to a state of disjunction on the narrative level. In other words,

Nonconjunction is close to disjunction just as in certain cases *termination* can on the discoursive level be read as inchoativity and *dissatisfaction* on the passional level can be transformed into a *feeling of lack*.

> *Note*: These two "feelings" must not be confused with each other. We can imagine *dissatisfaction* without a sequel, diminishing progressively into resignation.

This feeling of lack has the distinct peculiarity of being able to give rise, under certain conditions, to the elaboration of an *NP* of *liquidation of the lack* by fully justifying the pivotal role we have just attributed to the "discontent" segment. Greater precision is called for, however. The distinction between two *expectations* (simple and fiduciary) and between two *discontents* (dissatisfaction and disappointment) should be maintained throughout, thereby permitting us to treat separately the *objectal lack* (lack of the object of value) and the *fiduciary lack* (or "crisis of confidence"). This twofold lack echoes the initial situation of the Proppian narrative: To the first lack (labeled as such and the result of the theft of the object of value) is added a second of a fiduciary sort (this is the "treason" of the children who violate the prohibition).

An Expanded Field

In order to see more clearly through a situating of the lexeme "anger" within an approximate but much wider semantic field, it suffices to suspend (that is, to put aside, when different definitions are being compared) the overdetermination of "discontent" by the *durative aspect* (long vs. short duration). As a consequence we obtain "parasynonyms" such as,

> *bitterness:* "a *lasting* feeling of sorrow, mixed with rancor, linked to a hu-
>   miliation, a disappointment, an injustice of fate";
>
> *rancor:* "bitterness that one *holds on to* after being disillusioned, after
>   an injustice, etc."

Here then are examples of "suspended" anger, of a dissatisfaction, and even a lasting disappointment, which are not developed, however, into a feeling of lack with programmatic consequences.

> *Note*: We will note in passing the physiological, gustative character—the
>   bitter and rancid aftertaste—of the semic kernel of these names.

On the other hand, a lack and even a rough sketch of the narrative program is to be found in other "parasynonymous" definitions such as,

> *resentment:* "remembering with animosity the hurts, the wrongs, that one
>   has suffered";
>
> *grudge:* "tenacious memory of an offense, a detriment, that one holds
>   on to *with hostility and desire for vengeance.*"

We can see that, far from taking us away from the definition of anger, on the contrary a widening of the semantic field brings us closer to a definition. The *animosity* and *hostility* that accompany this lasting discomfort (defined as a present "remembrance") share a family resemblance with "aggressiveness" which enters into the definition of anger. It is to be noted, moreover, that in *The Song of Roland, grudge* simply signifies "contained anger."

The family likeness we have recognized in this accompaniment by discontent could be designated *malevolence*, a "persistent feeling," as the dictionary defines animosity. In fact, it is as if, as a consequence of an unfulfilled expectation, the *benevolence* that characterized the trusting, intersubjective relation gave way to *malevolence*, which will regulate the new relations; it is as if *contractual relations* had been replaced by *polemical relations*. For animosity, the dictionary continues, is a "persistent feeling of malevolence that *prompts one to harm someone.*" Once again we encounter the passional organization of intersubjectivity where, in addition to generosity, we encounter harmfulness.

What appears to be at stake in the opposition *benevolence* vs. *malevolence* is the articulation—both positive and negative—of the subject's /wanting-to-do/ in its intersubjective relation. However, far from being an operation of volitive logic in which it would present itself as a simple inversion of signs, malevolence is interpreted, in the instance we are examining, as an original /wanting-to-do/ arising from a passional state (and not from a doing), and thus completing the inventory we have already begun to build of the conditions required by the sudden appearance of the *subject of doing*. We have clearly seen how disappointment can generate a feeling of fiduciary lack; on the basis of this feeling of lack, we now see how a wanting-to-do is developed, a modality that enters into the composition of the subject of doing's competence.

However, we must emphasize that such a description does not pretend to provide an account of any sort of causality or other; it is but an effort to provide an inventory of semio-narrative elements considered to be preliminary to the "miracle"—the emergence of the subject of doing.

The Other

The wanting-to-do that we have just recognized does not belong, moreover, to the modal competence of the subject. Without being accompanied by the actualizing modalities of being-able and knowing-how, without an *NP* within which the doing would be employed, this wanting is for the moment only a virtuality and an opening. At the very most, we can say that it has a meaning, that is, an actantial direction that proceeds from the entire semio-narrative arrangement preceding it; it is a negative wanting-to-do that bears on *another subject*, a subject responsible for the disappointment and the lack. We can even say that it is this directed character that will serve as the place where an *NP* is set up. More than that, this other subject, which is pointed to, is already presupposed; the other is the necessary condition for the appearance of the subject of doing.

By examining the actantial arrangement as it appears in the context of the general narrative schema, we can try to specify which semantic actant can occupy the position of this "other subject." Two conflicting possibilities clearly emerge:

1. The subject that has provoked the "feeling of malevolence" may be the actant *sender*; the wanting-to-do of the subject will then be integrated within the *NP* of revolt that contains the denial of the sender and the quest for a new axiology.
2. The subject that had inspired the malevolence may be the *anti-subject* actant; the wanting-to-do then will serve as a point of departure for an *NP of vengeance*.

The Offense

We have just seen that the *grudge*—this "contained anger" in the medieval sense—as disappointment is accompanied by "hostility" and by a "desire for vengeance." We were able to integrate hostility within the building of an inventory of the elements constitutive of anger by interpreting it as "malevolence." It now remains for us to examine a little more closely this "desire for vengeance."

Upon consulting the dictionary, we see that vengeance is defined as a "response to an offense"; based on at least a partial identification, *disappointment* and *offense* may therefore be brought closer together.

The verb *to offend*, "to wound someone's dignity (honor, self-respect)," is analyzed first of all as a structure made up of two actants: a subject of state, the offended party, which is "wounded" by the subject of doing, the offending party. The same actantial arrangement, as we have seen, enables us to explain disappointment. In both cases, the subject of state is in the position of being "victim"; the passional state that characterizes it is that of dissatisfaction, of more or less acute pain.

What distinguishes them, however, in the first place is that, in the case of offense, suffering comes from the action of the subject of doing, whereas in the case of disappointment, on the contrary, the inaction of the subject of doing is the cause. But once again by its mere presence, whether it be active or inactive, the subject of doing provokes a response that takes the form first of a feeling of malevolence and afterward of vengeance. This response may go even further and, by prompting the passage to action, be constituted into a suitable *NP*, bringing to the analyst's attention at the same time the problem of the new status of the responding subject.

The French verb *offenser* (*to offend*) contains a large parasynomy: *to offend* —> *to injure* —> *to upset* —> (*to anger*) —> *to annoy* —> *to goad* —> etc. Along with this transitive series is a corresponding passive series of terms: *to be offended* —> *to be injured* —> *to be upset* —> *to be goaded* —> *to be angered* —> etc.[2] They are defined as a more or less sharp *reaction* to what is considered an offense. Now the passive construction is interpreted in actantial terms as a syncretism, to copresence in the same actor of the subject of doing and the subject of state (cf. displacement: S_2 displaces S_1). As a consequence, the reaction we are dealing with here is "an internal matter" for the actor who "is injured," "is goaded," "is angered," etc., thereby provoking the feeling of injured self-respect, injured honor.

The mechanism of *offense* vs. *vengeance* is not therefore as simple as it would appear. In any event, it is not reducible to *action* vs. *reaction*, or to *question* vs. *response*. For it does not matter if the offense is an "injury"; the offender effectively "wounds" the offended party only if the latter injures himself by reproducing this "injury" on another level. For example, a slap is obviously the somatic manifestation of an offense. But in spite of the pain it can cause, it is certainly not the "injury" about which we speak. The supreme elegance in this area consists of barely giving a slap—but not going through with it fully—by grazing the face with a glove so as to leave behind the basic message it is supposed to transmit. What we have, in effect, is something quite different, namely, "moral injury," an "injury to one's honor."

Injured Honor

"Injured honor" is a curious rhetorical figure that links the somatic and the imaginary, the elementary and the sophisticated—or could this be two types of universals? We do not know in this case whether *injury* designates metaphorically the diminishment of the human person or whether *honor* is simply a metaphorical simulacrum for the living person.

We cannot expand our discussion here to cover the problem of honor, which we have already touched in speaking of the *challenge*.[3] We have seen that here lies one of the key concepts of moral life and that its use—for good or for ill—is nearly as widespread as that of Cartesian common sense. This simulacrum—for honor is very much the representation, the "image," of self that persons fashion for themselves as a function of their participation in social life—is a delicate kernel, at once protected and exposed. Indeed, this "feeling of meriting consideration and of protecting the right to one's proper esteem"—one of the definitions provided by the dictionary—rests on a positive evaluation of one's own image, that is, in the final analysis, a "self-confidence."

In reflecting on offense we discover the problematic already encountered with respect to disappointment. In the case of disappointment it was a matter of confidence in the other, the failure of which put into question once again *confidence in self*, taxing it with credulity. In the case of an offense, it is *self-confidence* that is shaken by the negation of confidence of others manifested by "injury." In both instances, we are dealing with a *fiduciary lack*, constituted by the gap noted between two simulacra.

The comparison remains equally valid when one envisages the reaction of the subject in which a lack has been caused; the partial synonymy—when, for example, *to be angry* signifies at the same time "to be offended" and "to get angry"[4]—confirms it. The violence of the reaction, in both cases of "defying," remains proportional to the pain provoked by the twofold injury. As for defending one's honor, this may be formulated at the level of modalization of the subject as the emergence of /being-able-to-do/.

Vengeance

A Passional Syntagm

Thus, the principal conditions for installing the subject of doing are brought together. As a consequence of the fiduciary lack and in the form of a wanting-to-do and being-able-to-do, the appearance of the essential components of the subject's competence enables us to envision its passage to action. Aggressiveness can give rise to aggression; the "desire for vengeance" can be transformed into vengeance.

Under these conditions it is appropriate to add, as we have seen, what can be called the directed character of competence, that is, the aim of the subject that already traces the trajectory on which the potential *NP* will be built. For even if the subject's program of action is still absent, we already know that it will be a "human," intersubjective *NP*; it will be concerned not with an object of value, properly speaking, but with another subject. We may even wonder to what extent the emergence of the aggressor subject of doing, armed with a /being-able-to-do/ that the dictionary—and certain psychologists—define as the affirmation of the self and/or the destruction of the other, does not already contain in "primitive" or "universal" form the decisive elements that go into determining this program.

However, we must underscore the point that the passional syntagm so constructed is far from being constituted as a causal succession. Indeed, the elements that go into making it up do not necessarily follow each other; quite the contrary. The syntagmatic unfolding of the sequence may be halted at any moment, giving rise at each stopping point to an extended passional state. Dissatisfaction thus fades into "resignation"; malevolence can persist as "hostility"; and desire for vengeance can remain in the state of a "grudge" without the passional arrangement necessarily leading to a doing.

We will also add that such passional states, as long as their iterative character is recognized and they be inserted as autonomous elements in the manner of motifs into the unfolding of different discourses, are ready to solidify into pathemic or psychological roles and then to be constituted for each cultural space into the connotative typologies suggested by Hjelmslev.

Regulation of the Passions

The passional syntagm we are concerned with could not be developed to its ultimate possible extent were we to omit the final missing piece—the narrative program—permitting the realization of condensed competence. By taking into account the comparability of the syntagmatic developments of disappointment and offense, and especially the possibility of the subsequent appearance of lack, we can use the definition of *vengeance* whose broad lines now seem subject to generalization.

Vengeance is defined either as "the need, the desire to avenge oneself"—which we have already examined—or as "an action" that can be regarded in two ways:

1. As "moral compensation for the offended party by the punishment of the offending party."
2. As "punishment of the offending party that morally compensates the offended party."

This is a somewhat awkward way of saying that the action in question concerns two subjects and seeks to reestablish the equilibrium between the two that was disrupted as a result of the offense (and, we should add, of the disappointment).

However, we can see right away that we are not dealing with a *simple liquidation of the lack*, which would situate the *NP* at the level of the circulation of objects of value, but with a *matter between subjects* in which the one must be "*morally* compensated" and the other "punished."

The *NP* of vengeance nevertheless remains a program of *compensation*, but this compensation is carried out at the level of the "passions"; the intersubjective equilibrium sought is a kind of passional equivalence. If a subject S_1 suffers, then it is proper to inflict "*pain*," that is, both punishment and grief, on the subject S_2 so as to cause it to suffer *as much*. As we can see, vengeance is first of all a *rebalancing of suffering* between antagonistic subjects.

Such an equilibrium in suffering is an intersubjective phenomenon, a social regulation of passions. The vengeance *NP* is not yet expended, due to this fact. In fact, the suffering of S_2 prompts S_1's pleasure—a satisfaction that normally accompanies any successful NP. To put it bluntly, S_1 delights in having caused its enemy to suffer. Vengeance is, as a consequence, no longer on the social plane but on the individual plane as a *reequilibrium of displeasures and pleasures*.

As an initial conclusion, we can say that to the extent that vengeance is located in the pragmatic dimension—and corresponds, when compared to the general narrative schema, to the *pragmatic sanction*—and by virtue of this fact admits of somatic and gestural activity, it is defined nevertheless by the passional effects of this activity and is understood then as a circulation of "passion" objects.

> *Note*: We see that such an interpretation of *vengeance* lends itself to a comparison with the *sadistic* syntagm whose constitutive elements are found in the following sequence:
>
> *suffering* —> *causing to suffer* —> *experiencing pleasure*.
>
> The balance between suffering and pleasure toward which vengeance is directed also explains the possibility of *substituting* somatic punishment with *redemption*: The deprivation of goods is supposed then to provoke displeasure; the acquisition of goods as "moral reparation" procures satisfactions deemed equivalent.

The Cognitive Sanction

What must have struck the reader on several occasions already is the parallelism between the development of the passional sequence studied here and the fundamental articulations of the general narrative schema. Such is the case for the lack and its liquidation, one of the principal mechanisms of every narrative. The moment we recognize that the objects of value that constitute the stakes for the narrative of vengeance are passion objects, the liquidation of the lack can only be the consequence of the *decisive test* composed of the pain inflicted and of the pleasure of the victorious hero.

However, this elementary narrative articulation is only the pragmatic part of vengeance. Attentive readers of Propp's work have often asked themselves about the raison d'être and the existence and profound significance of the *glorifying test* that seems to be a simple duplication of the principal test the narrative preserves. This test, however, possesses an otherwise important function in that it resolves the "crisis of confidence" that was instituted within the society by bringing about the recognition of the hero and the confusion of the traitor with the help of the *cognitive sanction*, that is, by reinstituting, in a categorical fashion, the language of truth.

By examining the terminal positions of the narrative schema, we consolidate (by making explicit) the initial positions, manifestations of a common paradigmatic organization projected on the narrative. The cognitive sanction (known as re-cognition) thus presupposes the subject as being unrecognized by others and unsettled in its faith, and thus enables us better to understand the fiduciary lack as a narrative mechanism. The autonomy of this dimension of vengeance, on the other hand, cannot be doubted. One need only glance at one of the deviations that *pardon* constitutes in order to recognize therein vengeance relieved of its pragmatic dimension, but containing nonetheless the liquidation of the fiduciary lack. The evaluation of the duel as a typical form of "moral reparation" is also quite instructive: Having reached the point of exhaustion, the Léon Blum type of duel (in which the injury is replaced by a "mark") has practically become a desemanticized ritual in which "honor" alone prevents it from being dispensed with.

However, we can say that the duel survives insofar as it remains an affronting, with fiduciary stakes, and does not end in a "tie" as long as, following the duel, the hero and the villain are recognized as such. For this pair of hero and villain, subject and anti-subject, is the result not of a categorical binary articulation but of a reciprocal proposition that makes them inseparable; the one never appears without the concomitant presence of the other. The opposition between this pair, at once united and antagonistic, the figurative manifestations of which often are based on the exploitation of the semantic universals *life* vs. *death*—there is a lot of killing in children's stories and in mythical narratives—may be considered at the same time, without much risk, as both "the affirmation of self and the destruction of the other."

Two Deviant Forms: Justice and Sadism

The fact that vengeance is the *NP* of the subject of doing and that it is constituted, as we have seen, only as a consequence of the emergence of the /being-able-to-do/, provides a very good account of the primordial role the handling of this component of the subject's competence is called on to play. It is indeed the delegation of being-able-to-do that installs the sender-judge and transforms vengeance into justice.

Whether it is God who proclaims vengeance as His, or a lord who strives to obtain the right to dispense "high justice," we are dealing here with a displacement of power that we will continue to call *delegation*, even though it is *superative*, that is, oriented from low to high, and not *inferative* as is so often the case. Orientation, in this case, seems moreover to be only a question of point of view.

Delegation has as its effect to establish a distance between the domains of the subject and of the sender-judge, between wanting-to-do and being-able-to-do, which can be overcome only by the modalization of *knowing*: *knowing* about the suffering that the sender inflicts on the anti-subject, a pleasure that the subject experiences thanks only to *knowing* about the other's punishment.

This intellectualizing of pains and pleasures explains for the most part the *depassioning* of vengeance that characterizes its socialization. It is not surprising that the disappearance of the immediacy that the somatic doing, carried out in the context of intersubjective relations, confers on passion leads progressively to the desemanticizing of the structure of vengeance and to its withering away. As for whether other structures for regulating the passions—for example, class struggle—can be effectively substituted for it, this is a question that concerns sociologists.

In opposition, in appearance at least, to this passional loss is the emotional gain we identify as sadistic behavior. We have already been struck by the syntagmatic arrangement

suffering —> *causing to suffer* —> *experiencing pleasure*,

which appears common to both vengeance and sadism. The more rigorous formulation in terms of actantial structures and narrative programs only confirms this initial impression. And yet the recognition of comparable syntactic structures only accentuates the differences of which the principal one appears to us to be the *phrastic* and nondiscursive character of sadistic syntax. Thus, as we can see, if the syntagmatic units constitutive of the sequence are common to both "passions," what is lacking in sadistic discourse—as in machine translation—is its power of *anaphorization*, by turning them both into "disordered" discourses. Each phrase-unit of sadistic discourse is correct, but the syntactic actants of the different units (such as the frustrating subject S_2 and the anti-subject S_2) are not integrated within a single, syncretic character. The sadistic subject S_1 feels indeed frustrated by S_2. It is nonetheless the case that the subject that S_1 will cause to suffer and the suffering that will cause S_1 pleasure, is not the same as the frustrating subject. Aimlessness is the result, an absence of a life project that only the integration of this syntax within the general narrative schema could mitigate.

Anger

The study of anger, which was initially undertaken in a logically sequential manner, has developed in other directions because we have taken into account different syntagmatic forms of the passions that appeared capable of being related to it. This has been done for two reasons: to inscribe anger within a paradigm of comparable forms and to develop choleric discourse to its ultimate consequence. Within this second perspective, the examination of vengeance appears particularly interesting to us. At the point of "contained anger"—and this is the point of differentiation—passional behavior develops, thanks to the acquired being-able-to-do, into a narrative program of "vengeance," a complex and complete *NP*. This regular development of passional discourse can then serve as a background for a better understanding of the troubling phenomenon of anger.

It seems at first sight that it is the violent character, the intensity of discontent, that can explain in part the fact that "passion" while developing borrows the trajectory of anger at the expense of that of vengeance. It is true that we have here a twofold intensity: Anger presupposes a violent disappointment but also the immediacy of the disappointed subject's reaction. This explanation, however, is not entirely satisfactory, for we see very well that the same characteristics may preside over the development of vengeance. We then speak not only of brusqueness but also of the rapidity of the offended party's reflexes. As a consequence, we are indeed obliged to have recourse to a typological interpretation, by attributing the distinctive characters of anger and vengeance either to innateness or to cultural particularism. What we have here is an option that concerns the theory of passions in its totality.

If every causal explanation appears unsatisfactory, the semantic description of the two trajectories is easy. We see that the crucial moment is constituted here by the emergence of the subject in terms of being-able-to do: In the case of vengeance, this modality is integrated within the totality of the modal competence of the subject ready to produce a suitable *NP*. In the case of anger, by contrast, the exacerbated being-able-to-do entirely dominates the subject and moves on to the *doing* before a program of action is definitely elaborated, being capable of using only the scattered elements that can ground this program, elements put together under the rubric of oriented aggressiveness (affirmation of self and destruction of the other). The *NP* of anger thus appears to be a *syncopated program*, employing the term *syncope* in its grammatical sense. Whatever the use may be, the distinction between vengeance and anger clearly makes us aware of the difference between *discourse about passion* and *passionate discourse* moved by "passion."

Chapter 10
Knowing and Believing:
A Single Cognitive Universe

Introduction

The preoccupation of semioticians with attempting to account fully for the modalization of discourses is not a recent phenomenon. Semioticians have long been aware of the importance of modalities. Indeed, for a long time the construction of a semio-narrative grammar was seen as a development of modal grammar. However, the way in which the concept of modal competence, followed by that of modal existence, has actually opened the way for using the modalities of /knowing-how-to-do/ and /knowing-how-to-be/ is what concerns us here.

Nonetheless, a deeper analysis of problems related to the cognitive dimension of discourses has had as a corollary the appearance of what, perhaps incorrectly, is called the modality of /believing/. Indeed, for a semiotician it has been difficult to support the view that communication is no more than a simple transfer of /knowing/. Familiarity with "paper" subjects encountered in texts has led to the awareness that subjects in a situation of communication are not neutral but rather endowed with variable modal competence. Given this, /causing-to-know/, which governs communication, has become a persuasive doing that has a corresponding and opposed interpretative doing at the other end of the chain. The change in perspective this has brought about can be summed up by saying that *persuading*, if it remains a part of *causing-to-know*, is first and foremost a *causing-to-believe*. Henceforth, all progress in our thinking about the conditions under which we know can only widen the domain of belief.

For example, we have seen that when we want to exteriorize "I think that," which serves as a support for the subject's interior discourse, it then becomes not an "I know" but rather an "I believe." We should note that "they say that," which is the principal source of communicated knowing, signifies only the absence of certitude and confidence. We should also note that our knowledge of the world rests in the first instance on "they say" (the rumor, *on-dit*). Thus we can ask whether, when speaking of the cognitive dimension of discourses and the modalities that articulate them, we are not essentially dealing with the dimension and the modalities of our beliefs whose knowledge, when scientifically expressed, would be no more than a parenthesis or even a meaning effect coming into being under as yet to be determined circumstances.

It is, rather out of frustration, that we tend to bring knowing and believing together as one entity by considering the usual categorical distinction between them as a false dichotomy. Yet we should at least recognize that in the natural languages the two terms not only can overlap without being confused with each other, but indeed can end up in diametric opposition. When we say, "We all know that we will die, but we don't believe it," or if we repeat, as Miguel de Unamuno was one of the last to do, the medieval "Credo quia absurdum," we are obliged to note not only that the thus instituted knowing does not succeed in expelling belief, but that belief indeed rests on, and is even consolidated by, the negation of knowing. It is as if knowing and believing justify an elastic structure that under extreme tension, through polarization, produces a categorical opposition, but that, as the tension is relaxed, can go so far as to make us confuse one of the terms with the other.

These "anomalies" are troubling and they make us long for the good old days when things were clearer. Georges Dumézil helpfully brought to our attention the fact that formerly the Latin *credere* at the same time covered the now separated domains of signification of belief and confidence. This means that an established and maintained trust between persons founded a trust in their speech about things and, finally, in things themselves.

This unseemly turning back to ancient sources teaches us at least one thing: If we want to found our certitudes, then before seeking an adequation between words and things we should examine open communication between human beings.

Cognitive Processes

Knowing Precedes Believing

If we follow the now classical procedure, we can grasp the specificity of the believing phenomenon within the framework of intersubjective communication. As we said earlier, the first thing to do in this case is to substitute loci for the exercise of persuasive doing and interpretative doing for the "neutral" instances of sender and receiver. Persuasive and interpretative doing are cognitive procedures that, in the first case, end up as causing-to-believe and, in the second, as an act of believing, that is, as an epistemic act. At the deep and abstract level of language the preceding explicative model can be reduced to a small number of simple operations. However, at the semio-narrative level, it can undergo syntagmatic expansions that allow us to establish the homologation of persuasive doing and narrative *manipulation*, as well as that of interpretative doing and narrative sanction. Also, if they are well formulated, we can conceive of these trajectories as being cognitive algorithms.

To illustrate this further it is convenient to take an example from a natural language, from French in this instance. By choosing, among the parasynonyms of persuasion, the verb *convaincre* (to convince), we can immediately try to make use of its definition as given in current dictionaries:

(a) "To lead someone //
(b)   // to recognize the truth   //
(c)   // of a proposition
                                                 (or of a fact)."

If we designate S_1 as the subject of manipulation and S_2 as the subject of sanction, we can view segment (a) as representing the persuasive doing of S_1, segment (b) as the interpretative doing of S_2, leading to the epistemic act, and segment (c) as the utterance-object (the "proposition") submitted to S_2 by S_1.

If we postpone until later the examination of S_1's persuasive procedures (a) which accompany the transmission of the utterance-object (c), it is because we need further clarification of segment (b), *recognizing the truth*. This is because we consider it to be a miniature version of the procedures of interpretation. Once again taking up our dictionaries, we find two new definitions of *recognizing (the truth)*:

"Admitting to be true //
                      // after having *denied* or
                      // after having *doubted*."
"Accepting   // despite *reservations*."

These rather trivial definitions lead us to make a certain number of observations, which we will attempt to catalogue.

The Epistemic Act Is a Transformation. The second series of definitions shows that the epistemic act, situated within the cognitive dimension of discourse, is indeed a transformation, that is, the categorical movement from one "state of belief" to another:

From what is *negated* to what is *accepted*,
From what one *doubts* to what one *accepts*, etc.

This simply means that following the transformation, the *epistemic status* of the utterance that is subjected to the judgment of S_2 will no longer be the same for that S_2.

The Epistemic Act Can Be Converted into an Interpretative Doing and into a Discoursive Process. The transformations we are speaking about are situated at the level of *deep syntax*. Thus, in our example, the movement from the *negated* to the *accepted* can be localized as an operation on the epistemic square (no matter what the terms of its four points). This is enough for us to be able to envisage a "narrativization" of these transformations. We can apply the general principle of the conversion of structures to them as we move from one level to the other. Thus, a cognitive operation of the logicosemantic type can, at the level of *surface syntax*, show a series of narrative programs organized hierarchically. We must not forget that it is at this anthropomorphic level that we find the interpretative doing of the subject whom we wish to convince.

Finally, at the discoursive level, interpretation programs will take the form of aspectualized processes. The epistemic act, which is categorical on the semio-narrative level, will be perceived as *punctual* on the discoursive level. The observer will read it either as *inchoative*, prolonged in a *durative* state (= *state* of belief, and no longer an *act*), or as *terminative* (of a belief—or of a doubt—that is of the past and has been outstripped).

Interpretation Is Recognition and Identification. If interpretative doing, because it must deal with a great variety of persuasion procedures (argumentation, demonstration, etc.), covers a vast area, we can nonetheless in the end reduce it to an operation of recognition (of the truth). Now recognition, as opposed to cognition (the French is *reconnaissance* and *connaissance*), is an *operation of comparison*. What is "proposed" (= the logical proposition, with *proposition* meaning a suggestion or offer), is compared to what is already known or believed. Recognition as comparison necessarily includes the *identification*, in the offered utterance, of the totality or of scraps of the "truth" one already possesses.

The epistemic act is an identification, because it uses the knowing/believing universe of the judging subject. Recognition of "truth," which, up to and including Einstein, was defined in terms of adequation with referential "reality," is now defined in terms of adequation vis-à-vis our own cognitive universe.

The Epistemic Act Is the Control for Adequation. We can see that "recognition" is initially a control on the adequation of the new and unknown vis-à-vis the old and known. We can also see that the truth or falsity of the proposition submitted for judgment is no more than a secondary effect. The results of this control can be positive or negative; the adequation can be recognized or rejected.

The epistemic act can be represented now in terms of its two sides. It is an affirmation or a refusal, and this in turn permits us to set it up on the square.

Note: We use the square suggested by Claude Zilberberg although we have replaced one of his terms, *believing*, with *to admit*. This is done to avoid problems of polysemy.

The Epistemic Act Is a Junctive Operation. After having considered the epistemic act as an operation, that is, as a "pure" cognitive doing, we can interpret the operations that try to identify the utterance subjected to epistemic judgment with such and such a fragment of the cognitive universe of the judging subject, as resulting either in *conjunction* (in the case of success) or in *disjunction* (in the case of failure) of the two objects considered.

Nonetheless, since epistemic modalizations are gradual and not categorical (as is the case, for example, with alethic modalizations), /to affirm/ and /to refuse/ can be considered only as extreme polarizations of junctive operations. The successful ones are conjunctions and the unsuccessful ones are disjunctions. The square on which these can be projected will have the peculiarity of presenting the schemas s_1 vs. $\bar{s}_1$ and s_2 vs. $\bar{s}_2$ *not* as *contradictions* but as *gradations*:

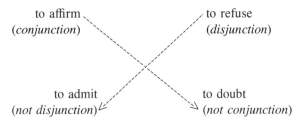

Thus one can more or less /doubt/ and more or less /admit/, but not more or less /affirm/ or /refuse/.

> *Note*: The axis /affirm/ vs. /refuse/, once binarized, becomes the fundamental category of logic: /assertion/ vs. /negation/ (with the restriction according to which $\bar{S}_2 = \bar{S}_1$, and $\bar{S}_1 = S_2$). The elementary syntactic trajectories — with all the necessary mediating passages, from refusal to affirmation via admission and from affirmation to refusal via doubt — account for the *semiotic* functioning of discourse.

The Epistemic Act Produces Epistemic Modalities. Up to now, we have spoken only of epistemic *modalizations*. We have identified them with epistemic acts and defined them as junctive operations. We thus view them as dynamic forms belonging to the order of "doing" and not "being." They can still easily be "substantivized"—and logic readily does this—by representing them no longer as modalizations but rather as *modalities* that indicate the modal status of utterances considered after the modalizing act. This amounts to saying that the epistemic act produces a "modal charge" that modally "colors" the utterance submitted to judgment.

Consequently we can add a new series of designations for the four points of the square that has already been established. Three kinds of designations referring to their definitions as *modalities*, as *modalizations*, or as *junctive operations* can thus be homologated:

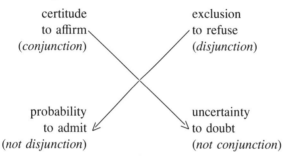

certitude   exclusion
to affirm   to refuse
(*conjunction*)   (*disjunction*)

probability   uncertainty
to admit   to doubt
(*not disjunction*)   (*not conjunction*)

The Subject Operator Is a Competent Subject. The operation that takes place within the cognitive dimension of discourse is of the order of *doing* and, as a necessary precondition for moving on to an act, presupposes a certain modal competence on the part of the subject. A more detailed examination of that competence is beyond the limits of our present study. We will simply say that this competence is probably made up of two modalities, one virtualizing and the other actualizing: /wanting-to-do/ and /knowing-how-to-do/.

Now we can imagine that at the discoursive level such a subject operator, linked by iteration to the preferential actualization of one or other of the epistemic modalities in a given cultural context, can be transformed into a stereotyped role. Thus, to the recurring exercise of judgments of certitude there would correspond, keeping in mind any complementary qualifying determinations, a "credulous person" or a "fanatic," and the habit of doubting would give rise to the role of "skeptic," etc.

Believing Precedes Knowing

The Proposition. In order to speak of the epistemic act, we have deliberately chosen to situate the locus of the epistemic subject's activity at the extreme limits of the interpretative trajectory. We have at the same time identified that subject with the judging receiver of the global narrative schema. Such a choice is, of course, only tactic. Nonetheless, thanks to the dramatization thus obtained, it allows for a "purer" grasp of the phenomenon we are considering and by that very fact allows us to construct a simulacrum of its functioning that ultimately could serve as a model for epistemic judgment. This model in turn will be integrated within semio-narrative syntax. It will be independent of ideological schemata and able to account for cognitive operations, whatever their position on the subject's trajectory.

It would be useful to remind ourselves that all human communication, all transactions, even if they are not verbal, require minimal mutual trust and engage the protagonists in what we have called the fiduciary contract. It is of little importance whether this contract precedes any act of communication or instead is instituted at first contact. This is a chicken-and-egg problem. In practice, all the analyst needs is the appropriate situation and an epistemic act that engages communication.

Whether we have an assertive "I think" that is sure of itself or an hesitant "I know," whether they are uttered aloud or are implicit, the engagement they bring about can be called a *contract proposition*. The two meanings of the word proposition — utterance (which involves the sender) and suggestion, invitation (to travel together a bit) — are not irreconcilable. The first above all involves the sender, the second addresses the receiver. And both definitions make evident the fiduciary relation that "personalizes" bipolar communication.

Manipulation According to Knowing. The preceding discussion means that any proposition formulated by the sender is founded on an epistemic base that moves from affirmation to doubt and from refutation to admission (dozens of verbs such as *to claim*, to *presume*, *to suppose*, *to suspect*, *to admit*, and *to conjecture* attest to this). However, this epistemic act, which serves as a prelude to communication, is not just a simple affirmation of the self. It is a reaching out, a seeking of consensus, of a contract, which the receiver will either accept or refuse. Between these two instances and these two position takings there is a cognitive space of persuasion and interpretation that, on the level of semio-narrative structures, corresponds to the vast structures of manipulation and sanction.

Recently we studied the problems of manipulation. Two principal forms, each definable in terms of the modality it privileges, merited special attention: manipulation *according to wanting*, which, for example, is manifested by temptation or seduction, and manipulation *according to being able*, which we recognize in threats and provocations. In both cases we have factitive operations that create montages of simulacra that, thanks to the "influenced" interpretative doing, are able to bring about the agreement or adhesion on the part of the manipulated subject. Thus, what we have are procedures that account for the meaning effects of "causing-to-believe" and "believing".

Now we can ask ourselves if the cognitive space thus identified can be considered as the locus for the exercise of another kind of manipulation, a manipulation *according to knowing* in which factitivity would take on the varied forms of logical argumentation and of scientific demonstration as well. For the epistemic subject, this manipulation represents a proposition of reasoning that is alethic and veridictory. "You can convince others using your own reasons, but you can persuade them only by using theirs" (Joseph Joubert, translated from French). The procedures that the sender uses in order to "convince" the receiver would thus specify the mode of manipulation according to knowing by distinguishing it from the other forms of persuasion that would directly (or rather, more directly) appeal to the "reasons" of the receiver.

It is as if the operation of "con-vincing" (French, "con-vaincre"), if we can re-coin the word a bit, consists of a series of steps on the cognitive level, steps that seek to produce a victory. But it is a complete victory, accepted and shared by the conquered person (French, *vaincu*), who is thus transformed into a convinced person. We thus have a *cognitive test* that can be organized into a series of programs that seek to produce tests and submit them to the judging epistemic instance. If such is the case, "learned discourse" would be no more than a particular kind of persuasive doing that, between two epistemic instances, develops a syntagmatic knowing-how-to-do that is of the order of logic.

Cognitive Systems

The Universe of Knowing and Believing

When, in analyzing a Maupassant story, we recognized the considerable difficulties the interpretation of figurative discourse encounters when it needs more than just the semantic data contained in the manifested discourse itself, we proposed a complementary reading procedure that consisted in confronting the received message with the receiver's *referential universe of knowing*. Whether we call this procedure reading, decoding, or deciphering is of no consequence. We still have the same phenomenon by which the unknown is integrated within the known and by which the known authenticates the unknown.

This universe of knowing is sometimes loosely designated as an *encyclopedia*. In effect, such a designation, even when interpreted as constituting a definition, teaches us nothing about the mode of organization of that universe because, of course, an encyclopedia is characterized by the absence of any intrinsic order. We can say the same for the "experience data" that come to the aid of the reader. Here we encounter another admission of defeat because we get rid of a given troublesome problem by referring it to sister disciplines that only our ignorance permits us to consider more competent.

The confrontation described earlier, which is indispensable at the stage of semantic interpretation, is still confrontation even when we reach the level of recognizing the validity of paradigmatic or syntagmatic *relations* between the molecular or molar units of discourse. The epistemic activity of the subjects defines itself as validation of these relations. This is especially so when that activity is conceived as being an "intimate and total adhesion." This amounts to saying that it is as a depository of "valid" forms of organization that the cognitive universe engages the epistemic instance that is integrated within the process of communication.

However, to be of any use to us this concept of universe must be relativized in two ways. The existence of collective universes characterized by different types of "mentalities," "systems of thought," or "beliefs" must be recognized. Individual universes that have been assumed by individuals but that have undergone a more or less coherent "deformation" must be recognized as such.

These distinctions, however, teach us nothing about the deep schism that seems to characterize European civilization. It has been there since the first oppositions were set up, in the Middle Ages, between the *profane* and the *sacred*. Even more, this schism separates two irreconcilable *universes of knowing and believing* whose existence is confirmed by dichotomies taking place within a cultural context and that oppose *reason* to *faith*.

We have seen the extent to which these secondary cultural developments (situated at the surface level of the Sapir-Whorf categories) do not hold up when the processes of intersubjective communication—where the fiduciary relation, even in strictly cognitive programs, seems to predominate—are carefully examined. Yet, as an intracultural phenomenon, this schism truly exists. As a collective phenomenon, what could be more suggestive than the appearance, side by side, in the nineteenth century, of scientism and symbolic poetry, which is just a particular form of sacred discourse? At the individual level, how could we fail to take seriously the testimony of a former Stalinist, who, when speaking of his "split personality" said, "From that moment on there was a me who *knew* and another who *believed*. The circuit between the two was broken. Their memories could not even communicate" (translated from J. Cathala, *Sans fleur ni fusil*, p. 347)? Likewise, would the theory of *possible worlds* not have taken another form had it not depended on an a priori postulation of a positivistic "real world"?

These clear oppositions raise one last question: Do there exist privileged semantic domains that—exclusively or in part—are covered by fiduciary networks of beliefs and others reserved for the sciences? At first sight, at least in the Western world, believing is situated within a domain that *grosso modo* corresponds to religion, philosophy, and poetry and is principally concerned with "our primary and final ends." Nevertheless, taking up once again the example of symbolism, we note that it developed at the very time when science claimed it had the answers to metaphysical problems, that is, when the two domains of knowing and believing intersected and overlapped. So it is with Marxist-Stalinist sociology, which, in its areas of application and in the answers it offered, corresponded exactly to the practical and "real" problems posed between the individual and society. In other words it is not the substance of the content that determines the cognitive relation the subject will have with it, but, on the contrary, the form of the content. It is only the examination of the forms of organization of the cognitive universe that can teach us about the role of knowing and believing in all this.

Thus, in referring to systems of belief and of knowledge, as well as to the processes they give rise to or sanction, we will speak of distinct types of rationality rather than of reason, which excludes faith. In so doing we are in agreement with Jean-Pierre Vernant (*Divination et Rationalité*).

Paradigmatic Rationality

Our hypothesis consists in claiming that sanction – or the epistemic presupposition in the case of the instance producing the utterance – must be interpreted as an adhesion of the proposed utterance to that portion of the cognitive universe to which it formally corresponds. Further, this sanction will choose the "fiduciary" or "logical" variant of its structure within this formal locus. Such an affirmation has to be made more explicit and must be further illustrated. To do so we will begin with the basics, that is, with the elementary structure of signification.

Binarism and Complex Terms. Without being drawn into the ontological debate (that is, the debate as to whether binary structures are "truer" and more "fundamental" than ternary ones, or vice versa), and also without taking a position as to the opportuneness or efficacy of their use, we still have to recognize the existence of an opposition between logical binarism and the "mixed structure" of pre-Socratic philosophy. This structure can still be seen in mythological studies, where it is manifested as the "coexistence of contraries." This last example is a unique formal locus that can have distinct articulations.

Now, to give a diachronic dimension to these same articulations, we should refer to the work of Vigo Brøndal, a linguist who belonged to an era that still believed in the progress of the human mind, an era that relied on extensive research and affirmed that the natural languages of societies at the leading edge of progress tended to be binary as to their grammatical categories.

However, as far as we are concerned, we have tried to respond to this twofold requirement by making use of the "semiotic square." This interpretation of the elementary structure of signification, while maintaining the principle of binarism, allows for the generation of neutral and complex terms. The elementary structure we have proposed can therefore accept the utterances of scientific, as well as religious and poetic, discourse.

The Categorical and the Gradual. The difference between the structural status of alethic modalities (*necessity, possibility,* for example) and epistemic modalities (*certitude, probability*) can only be disquieting for the semiotician. The first modalities seem to be articulated according to neat and categorical oppositions and their various linguistic expressions can be categorized. The second, on the contrary, are gradual and gradable.

This difference (which seems to accentuate the dichotomy between knowing and believing) is not limited to the modalities alone, that is, to just the qualities of the utterances and their actants. It is found in natural languages, alongside logical quantifiers, in the form of "indefinite quantitatives" (*a few*, *a little*, *a lot*, etc.), and at the level of subcontraries (*some*, *certain*) it is part of logical squares. The inventory can be widened if we add temporal (*early*, *late*) and spatial expressions (*near*, *far*). This brings together the principal axes of discoursive production. Regarding the latter, and emphasizing the role of the subject, we can speak of appreciation and evaluation. If we keep in mind the nature of the evaluated object, we can even speak of the tensiveness of the utterance produced. We have sought to account for this by means of the twofold procedure of objectivizing disengagement and subjectivizing engagement. At the same time we should keep in mind that in the final analysis, these problems have to do with basic options concerning the continuous or discontinuous character of the knowable object.

The Measurable and the Approximative. It is by means of tensiveness – and no longer gradualness – that we should try to interpret a particular type of production of signification Lévi-Strauss considered to be characteristic of mythical rationality. We refer here to the preference mythical discourse shows for categorization, that is, organizing according to significative opposition as well as the mode of *excess* and *insufficiency* (*too much*, *almost*). This way of thinking is opposed not only to the hard and fast categorizations of binary logic: Each excess or insufficiency refers to one or other of the terms of the binary category, which without being made explicit is considered the limit or norm. This means that it is not surprising if this presupposed category becomes the *measure* of everything else and if, moving from the quantitative to the qualitative, it serves as the foundation for ideology – and morality – and also as the *measure* we find, for example, in all Indo-European mythologies. Evaluation according to Cartesian "common sense" and the parallel transformation of the rational into the "reasonable" are illustrations of this found in our immediate cultural context. They show how these two forms of rationality can be successively confused and then distinguished from each other.

Syntagmatic Rationality.

The interest we have just shown in elementary structures comes from the fact that they constitute the topical loci where signification is apprehended. In those loci the epistemic act, as identification, will find some differential articulation or other that will allow it to "add faith" to new utterances that have been recorded. However, we must not lose sight of the fact that it is within these structures (which we can call constitutive) that the fundamental operation that can serve as the basis for a typology of syntactic relations is carried out and apprehended. Because the problems raised have gone beyond the framework of our present study, it is important to note, if not examine, some particularly striking cases of articulations of discursive syntax in order to see how they are recognized and interpreted through the epistemic instance.

Causal Thinking. The first of these cases takes on the frequent form known as "syntagmatic intelligence" and is better known by the term *causal reasoning.* It allows us to inquire into the role that such reasoning plays in recognizing and evaluating discursive truth-saying. Whereas logic, in its own way, has been particularly interested in interpropositional relations, most semioticians, following Propp's example, have given the role of the organizing principle of narrativity to temporality. They have interpreted the consecutive relations between functions (= the actions or events described) according to the famous *post hoc, ergo propter hoc,* as a causal series. This would be correct if causality were not thereby considered as a given of logical reasoning, capable, according to some, even of becoming the foundation of the linear description of history. But, of course, only a fiduciary status can be recognized in that relation. This is even more true given that such causal relations are particularly common, that they characterize mythical thinking ("the Gods are angry; we will suffer for it") as well as practical thinking ("clouds are moving in; it's going to rain"), that they organize sacred rituals as well as profane ones.

It is only if we inquire into the constitutive relations of discursive strings and if we follow natural causal linking, instead of moving "downstream" from "upstream," that initially we can remark the unexpected fact that only some discursive sequences have twofold interphrastic relations. What can be read as "causality" if we move from left to right, can also be read as "logical presupposition" if we move from right to left. On the other hand, most syntagmatic strings do not have this implicit foundation of a logical nature.

Thus we can identify two major types of *syntagmatic rationality* that are identical at the surface level: a *technical thinking* of an algorithmic nature and whose articulations are founded on objective modal necessity (= on a /*not-being-able-to-not-be*/), and *practical thinking* of a stereotypical nature. The latter depends on the co-occurrence, in temporal contiguity, of acts—or the utterances that describe them—whose successivity can be considered predictable and therefore plausible or even necessary ("subjectively," according to the mode of /having-to-be/).

This new distinction between knowing and believing, which appears to be categorical, is nonetheless still fragile. The algorithmic programs of technical rationality risk being overwhelmed at any moment by the omnipresence of daily practical thinking, which guides us in using all our "normal-people" habits and forces us to interpret everyday life in terms of social roles and pathemic or cogni-

tive stereotypes. Whether we like it or not, this normality (which we find in almost all individual or collective judgments), as we have seen, is linked to that
measure on which deviations of mythical thinking are based.

Parallel Thinking. A brief return to Latin sources—we are thinking here of the
twofold meaning of *credere*—has allowed us to grasp the quasi-natural semantic
pairing of trust in others and trust in what they say. Since knowing something to
be true and certain is no more than a question of trust, another lexical pairing,
trust/confidence, is equally suggestive. It is as though one of the guarantees, and
not the least important one, of the efficacy of *trustworthy discourse*, could be
found in its *confidential* character. It is as though the veracity of discourse were
confirmed by the communication of its implied and hidden contents.

This phenomenon is much more extensive than the simple technique of propa-
gating rumors or lies. In the privileged domains in which the fiduciary relation
is manifested, discourses such as those of religion, poetry, and philosophy are
placed under the rubric of *secret*. Moreover, modern substitutes for the sacred
word, such as the uncertain sermons of country priests seeking a new discourse
of faith, strongly suggest that we must "look for those things that are hidden behind other things."

Nonetheless, we can ask whether recognition of the bi-isotopic nature of discourse, whereby *seeming* hides and at the same time suggests an eventual *being*,
is not generalizable. For example, can our present-day concerns with the *implicit*,
the implied, the presupposed, be considered the same types of phenomena, even
though they have different articulations? We can go even further and say that from
this perspective, science can be interpreted as an effort to pierce and see through
the seeming of common sense in order to reach its being-true. This view presents
science as a victory of immanence over manifestation.

Now, the seeming of the natural world, just as the seeming of our discourses,
is most often of a figurative nature. The figures of the world have a twofold function: As the seeming of "reality" they are used by us as intra- or extradiscoursive
referents; as figures of language, they exist to say something other than themselves. It is this second figurative dimension that interests us. Figurative discourse, once dereferentialized, becomes available and able to launch out in the
search of other significations, anagogic ones. This bringing into play of the
figurative level succeeds in creating, under yet to be determined conditions, a new
"referent," the thematic level.

However, it is not so much the syntagmatic articulation of figurative discourse
that deserves our attention since that articulation is "causal," logical, or fiduciary
according to the specific case. Rather it is its ability to project a double reference,
one that *moves deeper* and creates a more abstract thematic isotopy, and one that
moves laterally and develops a new parallel figurative isotopy. We can think of
Alfred de Vigny's *Moïse*, the first "mythical" poem in French literature. In that

text, if Moses' misery and grandeur can produce a parallel reading of the poet's same misery and grandeur, this is due to the mediation of a *tertium comparationis* made up of the shared thematic level the poet identifies when he emphasizes the "power" and "solitude" of the hero.

This ability to extrapolate allows us to endow implicit parallel discourse with an original syntagmatic articulation. The latter can be considered as a form of discoursive rationality at least as important as the "syntagmatic intelligence" that organizes transphrastic strings. However, the epistemic sanction of such parallel discourse remains a problem.

Coming back to the discoursive mechanisms of *allegory* and *parable* can be of some help. For example, let us take the well-known parable of the prodigal son. Against a narrative and thematic background of lack and the liquidation of lack is superimposed a series of figurative isotopies that tell us of the loss of a piece of silver, of a lamb, of a son, etc. However, if we look more closely we see that this superimposition of isotopies is only an apparent one: Although they overlap they articulate and privilege such and such a sequence of the overall story. Even more, each of the parables almost imperceptibly changes the underlying theme so that, starting with disphoric or euphoric meaning effects linked to the loss of money, we end up with the Christian theology of repentance and salvation. This is undeniably a case of *discoursive progress*, a mode of figurative reasoning that, to a large extent, depends on the fact that there is no term-on-term homologation of the actants or functions of the different isotopies. From this point of view parabolic discourse is different from allegorical discourse, which is characterized by correspondence — resemblance or even identity — between the discrete elements of parallel isotopies.

We can thus see that parabolic discourse contains the embryo of the whole problematics of *figurative models* of reasoning, models that are essentially suggestive and allusive in nature and whose projection by the sender organizes and in part determines the unfolding of discourse. Such a model is obviously fiduciary and is of the order of subjective /having-to-be/. We have already had occasion to emphasize the importance of the "chess" model in the development of the theory of language, a model used by Saussure, Husserl, Wittgenstein, and Hjelmslev. Nonetheless, the same figurative model gave rise to four different theoretical discourses.

This figurative reasoning, whose use and validity go beyond the privileged domains in which the fiduciary relation is at play, unexpectedly reveals the role of believing in innovative discourses. In relation to figurative reasoning, analogic reasoning, originally considered to be of a logical nature, through use has been weakened to the point where it now designates not only reasoning through resemblance, much like allegory, but also practical thinking founded on plausibility. The concept of *homologation*, which has been substituted for analogy of old, introduces mathematical proportion into the evaluation of the relations between isotopies that are presumed to be parallel. As opposed to prospective and hypothetical figurative models, homological formulations have to do with the interpretative reading of discourses and with their verification. However, what most neatly contrasts fiduciary parabolic thinking with logical, homologizing thinking is, in the case of the first, the presence – or the construction – of discrete elements and of neat categories that are presupposed by homologation, but whose discreteness is not taken into account by parabolic thinking nor, as we saw when examining its paradigmatic mechanisms, by mythical thinking.

Conclusions

While trying to understand and reconstitute the procedures that lead to the epistemic act, we have postulated the existence of a cognitive universe of reference that alone can allow us to evaluate and assert the adequation between any new utterance and semiotic forms already in place. This universe is not some kind of encyclopedia filled with images of the world. It is a network of formal semiotic relations from among which the epistemic subject selects the equivalences needed to receive veridictory discourse. We have tried to show that these formal loci can receive distinct articulations in which we can recognize the respective importance of the fiduciary and the logical. Believing and knowing thus are part of the same cognitive universe.

Chapter 11
Semiotics and Social Communication

In Search of a Name

This discipline, which has grown immensely since the early 1950s, has actually taken on a name that is strange and difficult to transpose from one language to another. And indeed this unusual designation has not succeeded in finding a niche today in the terminology of the social sciences. Yet, it could be argued that it is in fact of no importance whether we are talking about social communication, mass communication, or even *mass media*, as long as the configuration of the object to be explored is clearly delineated by name and the body of investigators studying this object manage to treat it with discourses that are methodologically coherent or at least comparable. In short, the search for a name, far from signaling confusion or inconsistency, on the contrary can be the sign of originality.

Nonexplicit Content

Whether it is implicit, like something patently obvious, or willfully clouded over, a term seems to be missing in these complex and variable designations. The missing term happens to be the one referring to the contents, or the object of communication, which is normally considered only from the point of view of its means. In fact, the term in question could well be designated by the word *culture*, a vague term generally used to evoke the entire spectrum of valorized contents specific to a community. Moreover, whether one likes it or not, common usage implies the presence of the term *elite* when the word *mass* occurs. Thus, the opposition *mass culture/elite culture* appears to be the first dichotomy that, as an initial approach, can define negatively the area of study particular to the discipline being investigated. The outmoded and ideologically dangerous echoes set off by this dichotomy should not prevent us from asking if there do not, in fact, exist objective criteria, of a structural nature, on which it could be based. If this were the case, then new, neutral, or arbitrary designations would easily be able to dispel what is socially offensive in this terminology for both parties concerned. This is all the more so since a straightforward investigation into the specificity of the contents forming the subject of social communications would be preferable to the discreet attitude that attempts to conceal them for reasons unknown.

Communication

In European languages the term *communication* has replaced *media*, and this usage already implies the choice of a model that, for want of a more coherent methodology, organizes research. Edgar Morin has shown that this model consists in dividing the area of assigned research into three constituents, according to the canonical structure of communication. The transmission channels and the codes making communication possible are situated between the two poles, sender and receiver.

Without underestimating the principal advantage of this model, which is to assign various tasks to investigators in a practical and unambiguous manner, one has to recognize that it does not offer the proper guarantees of methodological homogeneity that would warrant the creation of an autonomous discipline. Indeed, if the description of the transmission channels and codes, undertaken under the aegis of information theory, could have seemed promising during the 1950s, the disappointing results of quantitative methods, due to premature utilization, readily dissipated all illusions. On the other hand, mass communication specialists then borrowed linguistic or semiotic procedures, and although they acquired a methodology, in return they sacrificed the specificity of their approach.

Although the setting up of the two autonomous instances of sender and receiver did give rise to partial analyses of a sociological or psychological nature having a real interest, the definition of these instances remained metaphorical and therefore hardly operational. On the social level, the extrapolation and utilization of the structure of interpersonal communication, as precondition, presuppose, at both ends of the communication chain, the epistemological elaboration of two *collective subjects* — the sender and receiver — endowed with emissive and receptive competencies that subsequently could be described and whose performances could be controlled. As a matter of fact, semiotics is just beginning to get a glimpse of these very problems.

The complexification brought to this schema by cybernetics, for example in Abraham Moles's work, does not seem to add any decisive methodological dimension to it. Rather, the apparent scientificity of this methodology comes from the confusion frequently encountered between schematization and structuration procedures. It does not really matter if, in drawing elegant charts, one multiplies the various instances of communication and encloses them nicely in balloons or squares, then inks in a good number of arrows indicating the same number of suggested trajectories and circuits; the diagram so obtained is nothing more than a visualized *aide-mémoire* of the problems that still need to be solved. The least one can say is that the establishment of levels of homogeneous articulations and the interdefinition of the elements to be subjected to logical operations remain a precondition to structuration.

It is not at all surprising that semioticians such as Yuri Lotman, who attempted to establish a connection between *communication* and *culture* and to found a semiotics of culture on information theory, soon abandoned this route. Although it can be tempting to consider culture as the totality of all the messages received by a society that then in turn is envisaged as an infinite text, it is extremely difficult to see where such a promising beginning could possibly lead, simply because there exist no intrinsic criteria to segment such a text. This is certainly the case for Lotman's typology of culture, which does not dwell on the initial definitions established. On the contrary, his typology is worked out starting from the problematics of semiosis and actually seeks to define cultural variables as metasemiotic connotations of signs that are specific to each culture and/or to each cultural state. Thus, cultures are defined somewhat like Michel Foucault's epistemes, that is, by the "attitudes" they adopt toward their own signs, and not toward their cultural texts, and even less so, as might have been expected, toward the communication codes used.

The Media

The last term that enters into the heterogeneous composition of the designators referring to this discipline concerns the *mediating means* used in the process of communication. Generally the accent put on the material means, while indicating a behaviorist approach that has greatly inspired these types of studies, clearly designates the general intent of this procedure, which consists in considering only the external features of the communication processes and in concentrating only on signifiers, to the exclusion of the transmitted significations. The *media* specialist acts in much the same way as a zoosemiotician, for example, who being a specialist in porcine language, tries to find out how pigs communicate among themselves and does not worry about what they say.

Such an attitude, in fact, corresponds to attaching importance to the transmission channels and in the final analysis to considering them as sufficient criteria for the classification of languages and cultures. Even more so, following Marshall McLuhan, such and such a channel would seem to help characterize and specify such and such a cultural entity. To say the least, it is strange to note that the notion of *importance*—the most generally and most often used term in the human sciences—which is simply a reiterated admission of a fundamental inability to attribute a precise determination to this phenomenon or to subject it to a quantitative evaluation, is sometimes established as the founding principle for an entire discipline.

Of course, after McLuhan's demonstration, who would dare deny the importance of printing in Western civilization? Yet, it would have to be shown exactly what importance we are talking about here, and what agent is being affected by this coefficient, during social communication. If, for example, it is the way in which information is received, then it can be claimed, not without reason, that olfactory communication is the most important one. To prove this, one really does not need to consult sexologists; all one needs to do is open Michel de Certeau's excellent book, *Les Possédés de Loudon*, to find that possession by the devil, the most efficient and most compelling of all communication, takes place through the olfactory channel.

A final remark cautions against approaching communication from the angle of the media used. The simple fact remains that these signs, which taken as a whole could account for a given cultural universe, in addition to being produced by different semiotic grammars, on the one hand vary in dimension and complexity, and on the other are signifying objects that are often extremely heterogeneous as to the plane of expression utilized. A film or a street scene, although each depends on several codes at the same time and involves a number of communication channels, is nonetheless a molar cultural object having a unique global signification. If it is undeniable that these complex languages of manifestation must be subjected to the type of analysis that seeks to untangle the complexity of the codes and to describe them separately one by one, it is only by positing the unicity of the signification manifested through all of the codes used that one can hope to confer a homogeneous status on research bearing on the cultural dimension of societies.

The Semiotic Dimension of Society

The somewhat exaggerated image of the approaches used in studying social communication arrived at by analyzing its elusive designation should not make us lose sight of the fact that the basic essentials, that is, the entire reason for this research, the interests, and the questions raised, do not fall under the foregoing criticism. Indeed, this problematics touches the core of complex industrial societies and remains central to our attempt to understand and to interpret an autonomous dimension of these societies, that is, the significant dimension by which a society exists as meaning for the individuals and groups that make it up, also by the way, for other societies that consider and recognize it as different. From a historical point of view it would be advisable to see, based on the remnants of ancient organizations of community life (to which we sometimes look back in nostalgia), if new forms of "sociability" have been worked out and how new and uncertain social cohesions and coherences have developed. In short, it is necessary to find an approach that can help us understand and describe how, in this new context, individuals succeed in transcending themselves and in meeting others, how they become integrated into social groups and live this integration within these groups. And, finally, this approach should be able to explain what these new "collective representations," both restrictive and assumed, are that make social beings of them. One can now understand—and our faltering attempts are proof of this—the difficulties in designating this dimension of social research, as well as the difficulty of the starting point from which it would be possible to speak about eminently social phenomena in terms of *communication*, by adapting the interpersonal verbal exchange model to the social dimension of semiotic phenomena.

Society and Individual

It is well known that a major Western tradition, which is both sociological and linguistic, rests on the implicit acceptance of the dichotomy *society* vs. *individual*. This tradition, moreover, claims to be able to reconcile the polarized terms by accounting for both the individual's insertion into society and the mode of existence of society as such. Indeed, "language," because it transcends individuals, is this autonomous organization that can be considered as a "social fact" constituting one of the forms of the existence of society, whereas speech is individual because it is assumed by the speaking subject who becomes the locus where the linguistic system and its programming as communicable discourse are taken up. This particular schema, setting up two autonomous semiotic instances and establishing their common meeting place to produce meaning effectively on the pragmatic level, does in fact account quite well for the functioning of the linguistic "machine" within the framework of restricted archaic communities, such as they are generally summarily represented. Yet, when applied to industrial societies this schema clearly shows the considerable gap separating the collective from the individual instance of semiotic existence, since it has not made provision for either social speech or individual sociolectal codes.

A Common Language

While remaining at the surface of semiotic phenomena, that is, at the level of signs and their organization, it is tempting to exploit a little more fully the opposition between language and speech, by pointing out that apparently the concept of *language* can easily be identified with the *concept* of grammar, which seems to be the only true system of constraint for the individual participating in communication and which, for this reason, appears to be coextensive to a given linguistic community. On the other hand, speech, which is characterized by the free use of the lexical *thesaurus*, creates zones of specific communication. In use, speech has a tendency to become fixed in set phrases and, through redundancy and successive association, to give rise to discursive configurations and lexical stereotypes that can be interpreted as just so many forms of the "socialization" of language. From this perspective, only grammatical forms, by definition, would be social, whereas vocabularies related to cultural contents would come from *second-degree socialization*, whose degree of integration can be evaluated only in terms of frequency and probability.

Such an interpretation, no matter how obvious it might seem, nonetheless comes up against the undeniable existence of a "common language," even if the problem of its delimitation raises new difficulties. The fact that the speakers of the same natural language understand each other – or at least have the impression that they do – presupposes a common semantic order. Whether one proceeds negatively by eliminating what belongs to technical language and specialized vocabulary, or positively by recording frequency of word use in a sufficiently representative corpus of texts, one will end up with an inventory of lexemes of no more than a thousand words. This "basic vocabulary," moreover, will be made up of grammatical words, a hundred or so adjectives, several hundred verbs, and several dozen adverbs. The list of frequencies, established in decreasing order, then falls off suddenly, indicating a very great dispersal of the substantives.

In short, these are roughly the semantic tools of social communication available *in a natural language*, the system of communication with the most extensive and greatest possibilities. These raw data must be kept in mind when speaking about sociolinguistics and, in general, about the way social communication takes place. In a way this points to an obvious weakness of "media," which however does not distinguish the "masses" or any other social class, but all of the social classes of an advanced society and all of those who partake in community communication. Moreover, this stock of lexemes is not as poor as it might seem at first sight. The words that make it up are highly polysemic; they can be combined syntagmatically in numerous ways. And if the significations of particular meanings called sememes are taken as unit of measure, then quantitatively this stock is comparable to the lists of terms making up technical, scientific, or aesthetic languages, which have an upper limit of roughly three thousand words. In addition, we note that this inventory is made up essentially of verbs and adjectives, in short, of predication tools (linguistic means of determination) for qualification and evaluation. It is therefore easy to see that this is indeed a fairly powerful store that enables its users to come to grips with the aggression of objects and the list of situations that are part of a much more extensive vocabulary inscribed in a "memory" that at every moment conjures up possible subjects with a view to their predication.

From this brief pragmatic overview we should retain the existence of a thesaurus common to all the members of a broad linguistic-cultural community. This thesaurus would be characterized mainly by (1) its relative quantitative narrowness; (2) the polysemic nature of the lexemes denoting a strong tendency to *metaphorization*; (3) its predicative aspect, which makes it particularly suited for producing value judgments and for transforming these series of terms into *axio-logical systems*; and (4) the disproportion between the emissive performances and the receptive performances of the users.

Sociolects and Semiotic Groups

The observation that in a linguistic community, there does exist, along with a socially restrictive grammar, a common lexical tool, which, in a manner of speaking, can be assimilated with linguistic *media*, already gives us a rough idea both of the semantic locus where the network of generalized social communications can be situated, and the forms and modes it assumes. That being the case, having basically taken care of the social semiotic status of individuals, it then becomes easy to think of their subsequent acculturation as a more or less successful apprenticeship in a certain number of specialized "languages" that involve them not in actual social groups but in restricted "language communities." The communities are made up of semiotic groups characterized by the competence that all of the individuals who are part of the group share in order to emit and to receive a certain type of discourse. From a semiotic point of view, a certain type of social differentiation can be defined not by initially considering social groups constituted by common socioeconomic practices but by considering a typology of semantic universes and socialized discourses. The same individual can participate in several *semiotic groups* and take on as many *sociosemiotic roles* as there are groups into which he or she is integrated.

The concept of semiotic group permits us to set on an equal footing all secondary sociolects: technical, scientific, aesthetic, ethical, etc. Yet, other characteristics highlight the comparability of these specialized "languages": first of all their size, which, on the average, does not exceed three thousand lexemes, and then the accentuated and statistically confirmed monosemic nature of the lexemes comprising them. It appears that these sociolects were only developments of meaning, dependent on the overarticulation of such and such a selected semantic universe. These overarticulations appear because of the quantitative increase in the lexematic labels, which following this analytic enterprise replacing polysemy, end up sharing the same quantity of information.

Although individuals might be integrated within the processes of generalized social communication and at the same time could participate in a certain number of groups using restricted networks of communication, they nonetheless are excluded from an extremely large number of other semiotic groups from which muted sounds and snatches of conversation can be heard periodically. For example, if we examine technical vocabulary as close to the preoccupations of everyday life as is the vocabulary of electricity, it is obvious that in extrasociolectal use only twenty or so words are used. The many remaining terms of the vocabulary are used only within a restricted network of communication. These lexical crumbs that each semiotic group lets fall into the public domain, however, are simply *commonplaces* in both senses of the word; that is, they make up the auxiliary stock of all "basic vocabulary" for a large part composed of denominations. It is an available memory that permits the user of a common language to speak of the world. At the same time, however, it represents the commonplaces, the banalities, of each and every microuniverse of knowledge.

In a general way these simple observations can be applied to all semantic configurations, lexicalized, and treated by technical managers, scientific clubs, and exclusive circles. For example, psychoanalysis, where the elaboration of an autonomous cognitive universe was accompanied by the diffusion of lexical bits outside the circles that practice this restricted communication, illustrates in an exemplary fashion the phenomenon we have just studied, where popularization appears to be accompanied by loss of subtle distinctions, by the overshadowing of differences that create meaning. In short, the progressive desemantization of a domain of knowledge whose existence, although kept out of the reach of the general public, nonetheless is present in memory much like a connotative object, much like a reassuring or terrifying certitude.

From this it becomes quite clear that the many facets of a hidden and briefly glimpsed semantic reality, whose presence is allusively demonstrated by some lexical remnants, seem to be just so many potential voids at the surface of a language. These voids in turn will be filled by surviving, resurgent, or new mythical and magical representations. Therefore research into the representations of electricity would quickly bring to the fore ideas of magical force, of supernatural power, ready to take on various figurative forms. In the same way the semantic void covered over by the term *complex* would inevitably make age-old images crop up of crabs or octopuses eating away at our soul. In this way the ancient figurative representations of illness would be conjured up.

We do remain skeptical of the importance attributed to these semantic voids and their mythical function. Yet we have to admit that the collective lexical apparatus a linguistic community has at its disposal, because of the concrete, polysemic, and valorizing nature of its predicates, admirably lends itself to the preferential institution of a *figurative dimension* in the countless discourses it can use. If we broaden somewhat the problematics, we can then ask if it would not be possible to consider the figurative form of communication as one of the principal characteristics of the semiotic dimension of a given society, by which the general involvement of the individuals making up the value systems defining "culture" expresses itself.

Toward A Discursive Sociosemiotics

The preceding reflections were deliberately situated within the framework of linguistic communication and at the level of those simple but vaguely determined signs that words happen to be. Although the lexical distributions and groupings can be established only by means of approximate statistics, which yield results that are only probabilities, they do permit us to posit the existence of a fundamental semantics whose lexicalizations give certain significative characteristics. This semantics on the one hand appears as coextensive to the entire linguistic community and thus in this way as making up an autonomous sociosemiotic dimension. On the other hand it takes on sort of sprawling characteristics since it extends its ramifications, in the guise of clusters of diversified denominations of the objects of the cultural world, toward all the sociolects with which it is able to mesh and integrate, by means of possible figurative and mythical discourses that can crop up in this stead.

Preconditions

Indeed, when one wishes to speak about the forms and contents that are the subject of generalized social communication, the main difficulty encountered is not in the multiplicity and the variety of their manifestations, which at first glance appear to be limitless. From this very point of view, Roland Barthes's *Mythologies* have long been a relatively extensive inventory but in fact these essays actually should be considered as determining a common semantic place that gives a social basis and founds the internal coherence of a semiotic universe, thus accounting for social discourse, which is both complex and simple. This is more or less taken for granted when we speak about *ethnoliterature*. Although it is possible to situate it within the framework of archaic or archaistic societies, the concept cannot be transposed and mechanically applied to industrial societies (if only for the simple reason that the latter's dimensions and complexity are much greater than the former's) in order to justify the existence of *socioliterature*. It is only if we recognize the existence of a semiotic sociability that is coextensive to such societies—and this is not at all obvious—that it becomes possible to postulate a signified that is collective in nature. This signified is unique even though it happens to take the form of a great number of languages of manifestation, which in turn adopt various communication channels and codes and use *media* that are often heterogeneous. Only on this condition can a *folklore* (that is, knowledge about the culture of a people—and not about popular culture—directed toward the cultures of macrosocieties) become possible.

One can now understand our concern, even if only from an empirical point of view, with attempting to lay the groundwork for such a fundamental semantics and also to determine the dominant features of this lexicon, that is, its metaphorical and axiological nature. Because, if we accept the distinction between two major forms of linguistic communication, the dialogical and discursive, and if we keep in mind what was previously said about the first of these two forms (its interpretation from a social point of view made us envisage the implicit existence of a *sociosemiotic grammar* understood as the semiotic connotation of our social behaviors; see chapter 12), then a *discoursive sociosemiotics* could account for the general manifestations of this second discursive form of widespread social communication. In addition, if we admit that the dichotomy *system* vs. *process* can account for the two principal modes of existence of any semiotic system (and not only of natural languages), it becomes clear that such a sociosemiotics should be able to take on all social discourses, independently of the substances, the channels, or *media* through which they appear (television, film, collective sports, entertainment, picture books, etc.), if only because they all refer back to the very same signifying universe and because their forms of discursive organization are comparable.

In addition, the metaphorical and axiological nature we discovered as being inherent to the lexicon of a commonly shared natural language leads us to believe — and this is by way of strong hypothesis — that the social discourses therein inscribed appear as *narrative and figurative discourses*. Everyone is aware of the role and impact of figurative narrativity, for example, as it appears in children's books (the apprenticeship of social structures), in those open-air museums that posters and display cases happen to be (the conditioning of sensitivities and collective tastes), right up to the psychoanalyst's couch, where it constitutes one of the major means for the establishment of effective communication. Therefore, it is only normal to expect to find the fundamental articulations of the value systems that are, so to speak, unwittingly assumed by society, under this figurative cover.

Specificity Criteria

The elaboration of discursive sociosemiotics, that is, of an area of research aware of its particular homogeneity, of its configurations, and its tasks, is rendered difficult by the very existence of an ambient ideology, a sort of implicit elitism that considers productions that have a social receiver as secondary subcategories. At the same time this ideology reluctantly admits and sometimes accuses the postulate of a single semiotic dimension underlying social stratification as having conservative ulterior motives, as if those who watch football games or western movies, or who read detective stories and comic strips, do not represent a valid sampling of all levels of society.

And yet, curiously enough, no matter how relative they might happen to be, the criteria that were progressively derived to distinguish ethnoliterature from the literature of specialized semiotic groups without any difficulties, also seem to apply to narrative objects produced by social discourse.

The first of these criteria happens to be the relative nonintervention of a narrator in productions having a social vocation, unlike the interest shown for itself and for the implied reader ("Mon semblable, mon frère"), by the subject of enunciation of literary texts displaying its intrusive presence. It is as though, when passing from ethnoliterature to socioliterature, a *de facto* state was transformed into a *de jure* state, sanctioned by success or failure. In the first case, the subject of enunciation is not known or is simply designated as a collective subject, whereas in the second case, where the mechanisms of production functioning before us can be laid bare and analyzed, the instance of enunciation must be concealed and its manifestations excluded from the text, because they hamper the social consumption of the products.

The second criterion, along the same lines as the first one, is the absence of semantic codes in social texts, which is quite contrary to their explicit and even often displayed inscription in comparable literary texts. Yet it should be said that the absence of semantic investment in the first case is more apparent than real, since, as a matter of fact, social texts are strewn with referential indexes that are just so many "directions for use" in the text explaining the correct way of reading it. From this perspective, the comparison between ethnic and social literature is very enlightening. Just as archaic or rural society (limited numerically), before the actual performance of oral discourse takes place, possesses the entire set of necessary reading codes, modern society finds gratification not in decoding new information or in acquiring supplementary knowledge, but in recognizing its own self in texts passing before it that can be deciphered without difficulty. Whether it is a question of riddles, the answers of which are already known and which are asked endlessly from one evening gathering to another, or of a child, who, before falling asleep, asks to hear last night's story and not a new one, or of a crowd of fans who want to watch the same games with the same players, the pleasure of meeting up with what is already known and experienced remains the same everywhere.

This redundancy of contents that are appreciated because they reflect a valorized image of ourselves is also complemented by the recurrence of forms. In contrast with the myth of creative originality that governs restricted semiotic groups of writers, ethno- and socioliteratures are characterized by the fixedness of forms and genres. The explanation according to which the fixedness of forms is necessary for the preservation of oral discourses, though it might be justified as far as ethnoliterature is concerned, is not sufficient when examining social discourses in modern societies that have writing at their disposal. Yet what can be more constraining than the rules governing collective sports or the demands imposed on the producers of so-called commercial films, or which they impose on themselves? It becomes obvious from this that a theory of generalized social communication must be placed not under the aegis of information but under that of signification.

Final Comments

One gets a curious impression when thinking about the progress made in "mass communication" over the last few years. It is as though an immanent reason, a sort of algorithmic logic, governed the strategy ordering the development of the social sciences. A nameless discipline having an ill-defined object and an embryonic methodology circulates, spreads out, and sprawls in every direction, and almost imposes itself. Yet, at the very moment when it interrogates itself and attempts to question its postulates and its manner of proceeding alongside the parallel and often contradictory development of other areas of research, it suddenly becomes apparent that this discipline covers a domain of unexplored scientific curiosity and that it does in fact correspond to a real need, that of undertaking semiotic research into the significative dimensions and articulations of present-day macrosocieties.

This discipline's global project is taking shape from a semiotic perspective. Indeed, it seems that the problematics can be confined to the following major themes:

1. Insofar as one takes up the problem of social communication from an *interpersonal* level, a sociosemiotic grammar should be able to provide models that are sufficiently general to be able to account for its organization and its functioning.
2. The recognition of the existence of semiotic groups using sociolects and producing social discourse for internal use establishes a domain of research that can focus on restricted social communication, taking place *within and between the semiotic groups* of a given society.
3. *Generalized* social communication involving society as a whole leads us to suggest the possibility of a *discoursive sociosemiotics* and to envisage the specific conditions for its elaboration.

Chapter 12
On Theoretical Models
in Sociolinguistics

Introduction

Inquiry in the area called *sociolinguistics*, which is part of the problematics of interdisciplinary research, is still badly defined, but because of the support it receives from a large number of investigators this discipline continues to demand its place under the sun. This is obviously desirable and even sometimes necessary from a theoretical point of view, yet in practice it comes up against major difficulties. It can even be claimed that it is impossible to bring together two scientific disciplines without one ending up dominating the other, without the methodological approach of one imposing itself on the other. Thus experience shows that the area of investigation staked out by sociolinguistics is, in fact, embraced by two types of quasi-independent research that share the same reviews and the same journals. Indeed, the use of sociological methods can only lead to the elaboration of a *sociology of natural languages*, whereas the establishment of the linguistic method heralds the development of a *sociological linguistics* (sociolinguistics).

A second point that bears on the distinction between *sociolinguistics* and *ethnolinguistics* should be underscored. The external criteria used to distinguish between these two disciplines do not seem pertinent on the theoretical plane, and they seem doubtful in practice. If, for example, we wish to exploit the opposition between developed societies and underdeveloped societies and say that we are doing sociolinguistics with respect to the former and ethnolinguistics with respect to the latter, then the concept of development is presupposed as having been defined. Now, in fact this is far from true and economists are the first ones to query this. Consequently perhaps we could reverse the problematics and distinguish between these two disciplines.

The third point concerns relations between language and society. If, on a world scale, we can identify a great diversity of natural languages, we also know that sociolinguistic preoccupations, which in fact consist in explaining the breakup of human language into thousands of particular languages, are one of the characteristic themes of mythology on the origins of language. What is called the Tower of Babel problem is present in almost all mythologies. All sociolinguistics does here is take up an old problem using terms that it attempts to modernize. In both cases an attempt is made to account for the diversity of languages by explaining the diversity of human societies at the very same time. The explanatory principle remains the same: Social significations must be sought in natural languages. In other words, natural languages become the signifiers enabling us to identify and contrast social groups regarding their sense of whether they belong to linguistic communities. In this case, sociolinguistic significations are the signified whose signifier is made up of natural languages and their articulations. Thus, the following provisional definition could be proposed according to which sociolinguistics would be the *study of languages having social connotations*.

This last point comes from the very fact that natural languages are not the only system of significations articulating and differentiating human societies. Other semiotics, the nonlinguistic ones, also converge on the same goal. For example, it has been noted that in certain African societies, characterized by the absence of myths on the origin of language, myths on the origins of the culture of dress (clothing, tattoos) are, so to speak, hypostatized. Thus, connotations of dress, just as those of natural languages, can serve to create both differences between linguistic communities and a feeling of identity, of cohesion, consolidating social groups. From this perspective sociolinguistics belongs to a much wider discipline that could be called *sociosemiotics*, which would include the study of the connotations of gestural, alimentary, dress semiotics, etc. It could very well be that dialectal differentiation in Italy is at the root of the diversification of the Italian people into regional communities. But it does seem that the dialectal articulations of a natural language do not suffice to account for the typology of "characters" making up the Italian people. For example, when it is said that the people from Gubbio are melancholic, this dialectal melancholia cannot be explained solely by linguistic particularities, since numerous semiotics contribute to producing a global meaning effect.

The Anthropological Approach

Defining a natural language is the major problem faced by sociolinguistics. On the one hand linguists do have the impression that they know what linguistics is (a knowledge based mainly on results from the description of the internal mechanisms of a language); yet, on the other hand, the concept of natural language is for the most part a sociolinguistic concept. Indeed, if we were to ask what a so-called national language, a dialect, or a patois is, linguistics would be unable to answer the question.

The concept of natural language can be taken to illustrate the possibility of very different theoretical approaches. For example, the typology of natural languages can be conceived of in at least three different ways.

First of all the problem of scientific taxonomy, strictly speaking, must be distinguished from sociolinguistic approaches and treated separately. Without having to refer back to the very large number of scientific projects in this domain, elaborated during the nineteenth century, it is possible to represent a more or less complete typology of natural language based on Louis Hjelmslev's or Noam Chomsky's recent theories. By positing that a language can be described either as a hierarchical system or as an organization of operational or transformational rules, one possesses the necessary objective criteria (that is, hierarchical or logical sequences of rules) to establish the structural correlations between different languages. Such a structural typology (scientific) obviously has nothing in common either with the sociology of languages or with sociolinguistics per se, since it does not take into account how languages are introduced in their social context. This typology is in more or less the same situation as, for example, so-called botanical taxonomy in relation to ethnobotanical taxonomies.

What ethnologists attempt to establish in describing botanical and zoological taxonomies, or others, are the articulations of meaning within specific societies, which, with what Claude Lévi-Strauss calls the categories of concrete logic within a given culture, determine the organization of the semantic microuniverse embracing the flora or the fauna. The description of a particular botanical taxonomy in a particular society is not what interests anthropologists, but rather it is the typology of these taxonomies that can account for, to use somewhat pretentious words, the functioning of the human mind as it is manifested throughout the diversity of linguistic communities. Thus what really is interesting in an ethnological taxonomy, first of all, is the categories used to establish the taxonomy and, then, the hierarchical relations between the categories employed. The comparison of the concrete logics that are specific to various linguistic communities constitute a given cultural typology.

In this same perspective, it would perhaps be possible to conceive of a typology of natural languages, by interpreting the genetic typology of languages, which is the major legacy of the nineteenth century, in the same way as ethnotaxonomies do. Within the framework of this typology we know that the criteria chosen to determine dialectal or linguistic dialects are extremely varied. For example, linguists do not agree as to the number of Romance languages making up Latinity, and differences in opinion are considerable since the number varies from five to fifty-six (Klaus Heger). Moreover, it should be said that administrative authorities do not understand anything either. For example, the Swiss government has declared Rhetoromanic as the country's fourth official national language. As a matter of fact, what is considered here as a single language is made up of at least two irreducible dialects, from which we can establish no grammatical koine.

The same holds true for the criterion of comprehension used to distinguish between languages: Scandinavian languages are considered to be three distinct languages, and yet the speakers understand each other, whereas, in the case of Italian or French patois, the speakers of the various patois do not understand each other, yet they do consider themselves Italian or French. The often evoked criterion of linguistic sentiment is no more pertinent then anything else. All one has to do is to refer to the Lithuanian example where the word *gudas* (cf. etym. *goth*) designates at the same time the neighboring nation, the Byelorussians, and any other person speaking a related Lithuanian dialect, as well as a child who does not speak yet, who only mutters. This final example very clearly illustrates the relativity of the concept of comprehension. In the final analysis, it is easy to see that we are dealing not with comprehension but with the recognition of the identity and the alterity of the speaking subjects. Every language has its own internal criteria and distinct elements that can generate attitudes of identification and exclusion toward those who take part in real or imagined communication.

To return to the typology of cultures, we know that one of the main scientific criteria generally used to divide Latinity into occidental Romania and oriental Romania, is a morphological criterion based on the two distinct modes the formation of the plural takes. In the Gallo-Roman area, the division of spoken languages in Gaul into *langue d'oc* and *langue d'oïl* is founded on a phonetic criterion, that is, on the opposition of *a* and of *e* in open accentuated syllables (*canta* vs. *chanter*). We can see that these criteria are atomistic concepts and that they are not situated at the same level of linguistic structure. That being the case, we should perhaps attempt to consider Latinity as a taxonomy and study the criteria and discriminatory categories that enable Latinity to take on the form of a family of languages. Such a taxonomic model of Romance languages considered from the point of view of their constituent categories and of their hierarchical organization could then be compared to another model of the same type, representing the typology of Germanic languages. In this instance we would be dealing with a type of research that would no longer be linguistic but rather ethno- or sociolinguistic.

The third type of possible typology is that of cultural spheres. Human societies use space to live and spread in: This criterion of space use, or the proxemic criterion, can be utilized to account for linguistic or dialectal differentiation. And so, research on isoglosses and how they are established, which can be represented by means of cartographic methods, is indeed the starting point for a typology of cultural spheres. The same map can represent the superimposition of several lines of configurations corresponding to distributions in space of data belonging to a political, historical, or linguistic order. A certain number of these concomitant lines would then enable us to circumscribe what could be called cultural spheres. An example, taken from the French, will better illustrate the methods. As a matter of fact, we note that on the map of France, isoglosses represent French dialects corresponding to the borders of the former provinces of the Roman Empire of the third century. There are as many dialects as there are former provinces. From this, we could say that certain sociological or historical factors can determine diachronically the present synchronic distribution of dialects or languages.

We can clearly see that such an approach does not come under sociolinguistics but rather under what can be called the sociology (or history) of languages. It proceeds by establishing multiple causalities that are very different in nature (historical, geographical, economical, etc.) and ends by determining linguistic facts considered as effects of these extralinguistic causes.

Sociolinguistic Taxonomies

Certain research methods that are specifically sociolinguistic can be contrasted with these sociological and ethnological approaches. We do not wish to deny the relevance of extralinguistic methods or to question the entire range of the extremely important works that illustrate them, but rather, for greater clarity, to establish the methodological boundaries within a singular domain of investigation. The sociolinguistic approach should be understood in terms of the description of the significative differentiations and articulations of human societies, that is, a description founded on the notation of the significant gaps at the level of natural languages. It is only insofar as small or great gaps can be registered at the level of natural languages considered as a social signifier that they can be given a social signified made up of the totality of social connotations. In other words, the sociolinguistic procedures of discovery and description must be situated on a unique and homogeneous level, and they do not consist in the establishment, on the one hand, of comparisons between linguistic categories and, on the other, of sociological categories. This is the criticism that can be made about the work done by Ferguson, one of the founders of current sociolinguistics, who uses a nonlinguistic distribution (which is even sometimes aprioristic) of the social classes of American society in order to compare it with Anglo-American social connotations. It is not a question here of denying the possibility or the appropriateness of the description of social structures. Quite the contrary, it would be wise even to envisage that these social structures, at the level of their praxis and their manifestation, can lay bare social connotations other than those that appear at the level of linguistic signification. Before attempting to undertake a synthesis that is necessary but also utopian, given the actual state of research in this domain, it seems essential first of all to assert the need for a homogeneous level of research and description.

A second point I would like to insist on is that sociolinguistics be considered as a scientific project of a general nature. Far from being satisfied with the description of specific linguistic communities, it should attempt to establish itself as a general theory of the manifestation and production of social significations in all sorts of human societies. It is clear that the study of natural languages as a spec̄fic corpus is useful and necessary, but it also seems obvious that this inductive approach must be accompanied by attempts to generalize and to formalize, that is, to construct general models that are hypothetical but operational and that could serve as working hypotheses for research in sociolinguistics. As Camillo Pezzi recently said, deductive and inductive approaches must focus on the same goals and be carried out simultaneously. In taking up the deductive approach, I would like to propose three types of *connotative categories* and *taxonomical models* that could embrace the domain of sociolinguistics.

Proxemic Categories and Models

We saw that none of the previously mentioned typologies could satisfactorily account for the imbrication of concepts such as language, dialect, and patois. We also noted that constant relations do not exist between the properties of natural languages considered as a signified, and their social signifiers, since the relation constituting "social signs" is arbitrary. A minimal gap between two local forms of speech (some vocabulary or intonation differences, for example) suffices to produce as a meaning effect the unanimous opinion that we are dealing with two different dialects. On the other hand, the existence of a maximal gap (for example, Breton, Picardy, or Alsatian), that is, the fact that these speeches are actually part of different languages, as far as the noninitiated user is concerned generates the feeling that these speeches are simply dialects all situated in the same way in relation to French, the national language.

We are thus obliged to admit that natural languages as signifiers of a social signified produce only *nondescript gaps* and that these gaps create only *negative*, purely *discriminatory* differences of meaning, according to the category *other* vs. *self*.

By taking account of implicitly recognized linguistic gaps we can thus see that such a subject excludes a class of individuals as others, different from self, and at the same time includes self in another class of individuals recognized as being the same, identical to the subject in this respect. It is a question here of a very simple linguistic model, functioning according to the binary principle of exclusion and inclusion and able to take on several hierarchical levels in relation to the complexity of societies. The general signification of such a formal model is nonetheless perfectly clear since its functioning accounts for the way in which human society, while exploiting spatial contiguity, constitutes itself as signification, using an interplay of negations and affirmations of solidarity in order to accomplish this.

Morphological Categories and Models

The morphological model that, in contrast to the preceding one, accounts for the internal articulation of these societies, can be opposed to the relatively simple proxemic model that at the level of meaning, so to speak, sanctions the identity and solidarity of human societies.

In our present state of knowledge, it is impossible to establish a morphological model that would be both general and exhaustive. It does nonetheless seem that the number of categories utilized internally to articulate societies is extremely limited. Its provisional inventory is presented as follows:

MORPHOSOCIAL CATEGORIES

I . Centripetal Categories

    1. *Sex* criterion: *feminine* vs. *masculine.*
    2. *Age class* criterion: *childish* vs. *adult.*
    3. *Hierarchy* criterion: *inferior* vs. (*superior* vs.) neutral.

II. Centrifugal Categories

    1. Transsocial category: *sacred* vs. *profane.*
    2. Antisocial category: *secret* vs. *public.*
    3. Extrasocial category: *external* vs. *internal.*

If we consider this list a little more closely, several comments should be made.

1. The set of enumerated categories should be considered as the inventory of the elements of a *combinatory arrangement.* Indeed, it is through the absence or the presence of such a category (or of such a term belonging to a category) that the society being studied can be defined. It is obvious, however, that a more meticulous analysis can always be undertaken and that a categorial term can be specified later on.

2. The gap between two terms belonging to a category can be minimal (stylistic) or maximal (two different languages). For example, Latin can be used as a sacred language. It is therefore possible to say that the existence of a morphosocial category is certain if and only if one of the terms can be represented, in at least one clearly identified instance, by a language that is foreign to the society being envisaged.

3. If the terms situated to the left (feminine, etc.) making up the linguistic gaps are considered as *marked*, then the set of nonmarked terms, situated to the right (masculine, etc.), can be said to make up the *common language* of a society.

4. The languages of social groups considered as marked terms through the de-

rived categories can be opposed to the concept of a common language, which is at the very least understood, if not spoken, by all individuals belonging to the same society. As a result, *every linguistic community* is (or can be to varying degrees) *plurilinguistic*.

5. We have said that the task of sociolinguistics is to study not only social connotations but also the linguistic signifiers that account for the presence of connotations. Thus, another typology, the typology of signifiers corresponding to the sociolinguistic categories studied here, is equally possible.

6. Moreover, certain sociolinguistic categories can be *axiologized*; that is, they can take on a connotation of valorization polarized into positive and negative terms. Thus, for example, sacred language is often valorized and considered superior to profane language.

7. Finally, it is necessary to underscore the cultural, significative, and nonnatural aspect of these sociolinguistic categories. The opposition between men and women as well as the different age classes can well rest on a certain referential reality; nonetheless here the distinction is essentially cultural. For example, a homosexual may be said to use feminine language. In the same way, the inaugurating myths of social order often attempt to justify the division of labor into masculine work and feminine work.

Functional Models and Categories

The two proposed models, the proxemic and the morphological, have a common characteristic: In societies that can be defined by the existence and praxis of these two models, the individuals making them up are categorized, once and for all, into fixed classes, for example, Sardinian and Italian, woman or priest. A third sociolinguistic model, the functional one, can be proposed, in opposition to the first two. It can be defined by the *mobility of individuals*, in relation to the sociolinguistic classes, and by their grouping together according to functional categories.

We could broadly say that this is simply a question of the transformation of the morphological classes into syntactic classes and that on the sociolinguistic level this transformation corresponds to *the replacing of class languages by classes of discourse*. Thus, in the Middle Ages Latin was a class language, used by clerics as a language of communication. In the nineteenth century, Latin was solely a sacred discourse.

Although at this time we cannot attempt to classify sociolinguistic discourses rigorously, we can, to elucidate our thought, nevertheless say that in a certain way the passage of a society from an underdeveloped state to a developed state corresponds in fact to the functionalization of the morphological categories. A sociolinguistic criterion could therefore be added to the dossier of the typology of societies.

In considering morphosocial categories such as *sacred* vs. *profane*, *secret* vs.

public, or *external* vs. *internal*, during the passage of so-called archaic societies to so-called modern societies, we witness the functionalization of entire areas of language and of their greater specification. Sacred language is transformed and develops into religious, philosophical, poetic discourses, etc., making possible a new typology of discourses and the construction of models that can account for their production. In the same way, secret language, represented, for example, in certain African societies in the guise of a private language of blacksmiths, develops and is subsequently transformed into scientific discourse, into a great number of scientific discourses. In turn, the external language often takes the form of politico-administrative discourses. In short, this is the *Vatersprache*, which is opposed to the *Muttersprache*, that is, the father's language, the language of administration, of politics, as opposed to the maternal language.

The criterion of the substitution of languages that we have proposed to introduce into sociolinguistics seems equally valid with regard to the function model: Functional discourse can take place in foreign languages, without the homogeneity of society being affected. This is the case concerning Latin used as a sacred language. We can also cite the example of French legal language used in England until the sixteenth century. In the same way, in African societies, scientific discourses very often take place in English as well as in French.

Starting with these observations we could perhaps begin to define the concept of the language of a culture. In this case the *language of a culture* would be a plurilinguistic state characterized by the fact that all the functional discourses take place in a single language (defined as *a* language by means of linguistic criteria and not sociolinguistic ones). It is obvious that no value judgment is attached to the concept of the language of a culture so defined. This is simply a question of a typological definition of an extreme, polarized state.

A characteristic feature of functional discourses should be underscored. These discourses often have complementary axiological connotations, which seem to be more frequent than in the case of morphosocial connotations. Thus, for example, we can apply the connotation of "sacred terror" not only to religious languages but also to scientific discourses. This implicit exercise of terrorism often takes place in the human sciences where linguists are "terrorized" by discourses held by mathematicians, but they often act in the same way with regard to sociologists, for example. A certain scientificity of discourse sets off a sort of complex of incomprehension of this language that is no more than its social "terrorizing" connotation. The same can be said for philosophical discourses or poetic discourses, which have connotations of "truth" or of "beauty." A parallel typology of discourses based on the analysis of axiological connotations could thus be envisaged.

From this we can attempt to propose sociolinguistic criteria that can enable us to establish distinctions between different types of societies. We can thus say that proxemic and morphological models, by characterizing so-called archaic societies, generally account for them, whereas the presence of morphological and functional models characterizes the so-called modern or industrial societies. Be that as it may, such a distinction, in the final analysis, has only a theoretical value.

Sociolinguistic Syntax

If we now shift our point of view, and if, instead of considering sociolinguistic connotations as constituting a society through a set of significant articulations and differentiations, we investigate the *use* an individual belonging to such a society can make (and actually does make) of these connotations, we move from a socio-linguistic morphology of a taxonomic nature to a sociolinguistic syntax. Indeed if, within the framework of interpersonal communication, the social connotations underlie the messages exchanged, they also serve as implicit criteria of recognition and classification of the speaker. We can say that each of the speakers is constantly interpreted by the other and globally recognized as a combination of sociolinguistic features. For example, normally after a brief conversation between two strangers the speakers have already carried out, each on his own behalf, their reciprocal, implicit sociolinguistic reconnaissances, and each knows more or less what to expect from his vis-à-vis.

However, things are more complicated because the speakers engaged in communication are not only readers, or *interpreters of the discourse* of the other, who at a given moment decode it as a specific configuration of semic features resulting from the combination of sociolinguistic categories. Speakers are at the same time *producers of discourse*: The recognition, in the other, of a specific sociolinguistic configuration automatically produces the phenomenon of self-correction, an adjustment of one's own discourse. Thus, if speaker L_1 connotes her discourse as a woman's discourse, then speaker L_2 will attempt to redeploy his discourse as discourse addressed to a woman. In the same way, having implicitly recognized in speaker L_1's words, discourse from a hierarchical superior, speaker L_2 will adapt his discourse by transforming it into either discourse addressed to a superior, discourse addressed to an equal, or discourse addressed to an inferior, ostentatiously denying in this last instance the other's superiority. A final example would be the appearance in an adult of a sort of false childish language, of baby speech that, although an adaptation to the child-speaker, most often produces in the latter a sentiment of superiority and condescension. In any case, these examples demonstrate just how complex and flexible such a sociolinguistic syntax can be.

We can therefore say that by taking as a base the three suggested taxonomies (the proxemic, morphological, and functional models), by including a small number of axiological categories, and by considering the set of these categories as being the morphology of a sociolinguistic grammar, from this morphology we should be able to work out a syntax of sociolinguistic communication. Such a syntax must necessarily take on the form of a *strategy of communication*, and the model that at first glance comes to mind is the one that could be extrapolated, for example, from game theory.

It seems useful here to insist on the autonomy of sociolinguistic grammar in relation to the natural languages it connotes. A syntax of social connotations is not implicit and subjacent to exchanged messages and discourses. It functions in a quasi-independent manner from the semantic contents invested in the messages and discourses. In spite of its implicit nature the existence of such a grammar is certain, if only because it accounts for a large number of diverse, dispersed, and badly explained phenomena.

The existence of an implicit sociolinguistic grammar explains, for example, the impossibility of learning a foreign language in adulthood. We think we speak English and Italian well; everyone compliments us on this, but it would be a mistake to ignore the mental restrictions accompanying these compliments. We speak Italian well precisely because we are foreigners, that is, sociolinguistically neutral; we are not concerned by the interplay of sociolinguistic categories. Let us take another example. We sometimes make fun of the English by saying that they speak only about the weather. Nonetheless, this type of communication where the quantity of information exchanged is often next to zero is the best proof we have that the semantic content is immaterial with respect to the adequate functioning of sociolinguistic communication. A conversation held in a salon, as we well know, can often be a nonverbal massacre. The refinement of French classical literature, from *La Princesse de Clèves* to Stendhal's novels, can be explained in large part by the minute observance of the rules of this implicit syntax. On the other hand, the establishment of closed circles and clubs can be explained by the desire of their members to do away with sociolinguistic grammars and not to have to put up with the endless decoding of social connotations. If the French worker has an aversion to mingling with the middle classes — even the lower middle classes — it is because such social communication, putting into play a different sociolinguistic code, sets off, in much the same way as with the English club member, a feeling of malaise of which he is not always conscious. Finally, the affirmation by recent immigrants that American society is homogeneous and does not have the distinctions of social classes is rather touching and shows their attachment to their new country. It can be explained, however, by the insensitivity of this class of Americans to the sociolinguistic codes and rules in use.

Important research continues to be undertaken in this domain. We could mention those studies that bear on the sociolinguistic use of a specific linguistic subcode, that of the personal pronouns, which, although extremely complex, takes on important variations from one linguistic community to another. Another domain, somewhat related, concerns research, which has assumed a certain importance in the United States, on what can be called the system of address. Both of these domains have a common feature: They are privileged areas of investigation, because the linguistic signifier by which the social signified can be analyzed, at the level of natural languages, is made up of quasi-autonomous codes. Because of the homogeneity of the corpora, this approach has undeniable advantages and guarantees with respect to rigor. However, the number of such autonomous codes is very limited in natural languages, and sociolinguistics, by confining itself to their study, runs the risk, as has already happened in the study of kinship terminologies, of focusing on methodological refinements and forgetting the actual scope of its scientific project.

It is necessary to come back to our initial remarks: Social connotations are not linked to the particular articulations of the linguistic signifier; the relationship between gaps in the signifier and those of the social signified they engender is arbitrary. Linguistic phenomena of all sorts, linguistic units of all dimensions, situated at all the levels of language, can be socially connoted. Hence we can see that it is this very absence of the motivation of sociolinguistic connotations that prevents us from undertaking their study starting from a single signifier, tnat is, from the description of natural language. It is the arbitrariness of the "sociolinguistic sign" that obliges us to elaborate, during the ongoing description, working hypotheses of a general nature taking the form of the sociolinguistic models we have attempted to bring to the fore. Only scientific praxis can validate them.

Conclusion

The limits of this work as well as the author's areas of competence have been decisive as to the choice of themes and to the exclusion of other problems that today are being raised in sociolinguistics. While justifying the necessity for theoretization, it nonetheless has seemed important for us to show one of the possible shapes sociolinguistic theory can take. Indeed, it can take the form of a general sociolinguistic grammar, having a morphology of a taxonomic nature and a syntax of sociolinguistic communication. Such a grammar should be of a general nature and therefore provide models and procedures for description that enable us to highlight, in the form of specific performance, the manifestations of social connotations in each given linguistic community.

Chapter 13
On Evenemential History

Introductory Remarks

History and Literature

The same can be said of semiotics as of any other discipline that becomes "topical" at a given historical moment because of short-term epistemic fluctuations. The discipline is invested with an almost transcendental power allowing it to lavish opinions and advice on all problems related to humanistic knowledge. Although they are aware of the artificiality and lack of seriousness of such a position, semioticians cannot (and even should not) avoid the problem if only because, when asked to reflect on unfamiliar objects, they can test the solidity of their enterprise and especially the general applicability of models that are so difficult to construct.

To speak about history, those archives of human knowledge constituted by endless words of generations of historians, does seem more difficult than to study literature, where semioticians have been trained in investigating the rules governing figurative discourses. Yet these two disciplines have much in common. Among other things they share the responsibility, at different levels of education, of transmitting cultural experience and presumably of training future scholars. It is all the more curious to note that in spite of this dominant position, neither discipline has felt the need to establish a terminological distinction between their denomination and the object of their study. It is as though the immanent existence of historical structures and of literary structures were of the order of evidence, as though the contents manipulated were real because sanctioned by their universality.

We must admit, though, that from a strictly semiotic point of view, neither history nor literature deals only with content, although in appearance their task does in fact seem to be the reification of contents and the assurance of their effective transmission. Because they are not limited to any specific area of knowledge, these disciplines are "totalitarian" and their projected content is the totality of human significations.

However, their nature as formal disciplines can define them positively much better than the negative term *totalitarian*. They can thus be compared with linguistics, but also, in a certain way, with logic and mathematics since these disciplines all appear as specific modes of information, of the formulation and organization of contents.

Resemblances stop there. For the science of literature can consider that its task is to uncover the formal organization implicit in literary discourses and, beginning with known rules, to elaborate models that can account for the production of such texts. Yet the science of history cannot be content with this type of explanation, which, in the best of cases, would simply end up establishing a historiographic typology, that is, models accounting for the "stories" historians tell and not for the production of history. Such a typological description obviously is an aspect of the historian's scientific doing, just as typologies of the philosophies of language or of the history of linguistics can become the object of the linguist's investigations; yet when all is said and done the history of linguistics is not linguistics.

Historical Dimensions

It would be presumptuous to believe that historians are not aware of these ambiguities. Indeed they seek, if not to suppress, at least to circumvent the difficulties of postulating a historical knowledge, and, especially, of a historical knowing-how-to-do, which would be scientific in nature. The best proof of this can be found in what is conventionally called the French *Annales* school, whose principal task is to establish and ensure a fundamental dimension of history at which the deep historical structures can be situated, independently of the conjectural fluctuations of historicity.

This fundamental dimension, which is where taxonomic organizations and structural transformations of social phenomena take place, can then be opposed to historical appearances, a surface dimension where historicity is manifested. The latter is characterized by an infinite number of microevents happening together at each moment and everywhere, thousands at a time, and which because of this cannot be exhaustively or systematically described.

It is undeniable, however, that in practice, one starts from this multiplicity of microfacts when selecting those events that, because they are deemed significant, acquire the dignity of historical events and, strung together, make up the series of events that can be integrated into historical discourse. It does thus seem necessary to posit an intermediary dimension, or a dimension of events of history situated between the levels of deep history and surface historicity.

The concept of selection was just used to account for the apparition of the historical event. The problem of decisional authority, setting up the criteria for selecting and making choices, must of course be raised. The answer, already known to us, is twofold. If one considers that structures are inscribed in things, deep history, by selecting its events, will announce its historical project at another level and trace step by step its evenemential trajectory. If one considers that structures are inscribed in minds, it is historians, who taking on an ambient or sometimes explicit ideology from which they extract their criteria of selection, will seek to give a correct interpretation of events and their sequence.

It can be seen that both attitudes are equally "ideological" and do not leave room for elaborating scientific discourse. The latter is essentially a praxis, which can inscribe this multidimensionality of history within its theoretical component while, in practice, seeking to validate its own hypotheses either through the coherence of its constructs or through the necessary equivalences that set in place the structures facilitating the passage from one dimension to the other. For it is obvious that to speak of history—no matter what meaning it already has or the interpretation it will be given—it is necessary to construct a language that permits one to do so.

Fundamental Structures

The Plurality of Structures

Nowadays two types of discourse are commonly held when dealing with the fundamental dimension of historical societies. The first type, opposing structures to events as two modes of distinct semiotic existence, establishes the fundamental dimension—because it is structurally organized—as a deeper structure than the one at which the strings of events occur. The second discourse, which is not seen as contradicting the former, takes this fundamental dimension into consideration and gives it a layered structure. This structure is then unfolded into superimposable, autonomous levels according to the degree of depth or fundamentality of each level in relation to the other. For example, economic structures are deeper than social structures, which in turn are deeper than cultural structures, and so forth.

At first glance this analysis seems perfectly legitimate since by decomposing the fundamental dimension of societies into subcategories it makes them more intelligible. However, difficulties arise when we attempt to represent the type of relations between history's different deep structures and its dimension of events. Whether we admit that, in a certain way and within certain limits, the fundamental structures generate historical events, or, on the contrary, that the events produce the structures, the problem of their interrelations inevitably crops up. Three distinct possibilities can be envisaged.

First, the fundamental level made up of superimposed levels presupposing each other, communicates, so to speak, with the dimension of events through its most superficial level. This would satisfy logic, but appears absurd since only the superstructures would have a direct relation with events.

Second, the deep structures, whether economic, social, etc., would each separately have direct relations with the level of events. To remain faithful to the chosen model we would then have to admit not only that there exist distinct economic events, social events, etc., but that history's dimension of events must itself be decomposed into as many levels and as many programs of events as there are deep structural levels. We can see that we need only to substitute the term *exchange* for *event* to meet up with, almost as is, the notion of global social structure proposed by Lévi-Strauss.

Third, a historical event (or a series of events), when it takes place, ends up having relations with several structural levels at the same time, and it does not matter whether it is produced by their convergence or is reflected on several levels. This seems to be the explanation given by Jacques Berque, for example.

No matter what interpretation we adopt—and the last two do not seem incompatible—it does appear that the graphic representation of such a model laying out the levels of depth and indicating their interrelations on a flat surface would be difficult to imagine. It would seem as though two sorts of commonly accepted hierarchies rest on a twofold conception of "depth."

A Simulacrum of Organization

It is our purpose not to question the global notion of social structures but to inquire into the possibility of using them as models for a science of history. It is both curious and regrettable to note that in spite of the already honorable age attained by Marxist social stratification theory, broadly speaking, history continues to be written in much the same way as in the past and that no serious effort has been made to work out homogeneous and comparable descriptions of the different structural levels of societies.

And yet Marx's legacy includes the description, in a way exemplary, of the economic structure called capitalism, and this description, independent of its intrinsic value, has the merit of being a constructed model and an achronological model at that. These two characteristics do seem specific to every model that could claim to be operational. Because it has a certain number of invariants and variables, the model can be applied to any society of the sort mentioned, independently of the spatiotemporal coordinates in which it is inscribed.

The constructed and therefore achronological nature of the models of global social structures enables us to account for an important phenomenon, namely, the often noted inadequacy between described structures and their particular historical realization. This phenomenon can be observed in the various domains where the semiotician's doing is exercised: Just as there exists no pure state capitalism, there exists no Gothic cathedral exactly reproducing the concept of the Gothic, nor any novel that conforms to the exact definition of the novel in every way.

Different explanations can be given for this phenomenon. We shall retain only two of them. If an economic structure cannot be found in a pure state it is because the moment in which it happens at the same time incorporates manifestations of surviving structures corresponding to the model governing the previous structural state, and as well as structures that already foreshadow the future that the model will simply elaborate. If such an event or such a string of events cannot be interpreted within the framework of a single model, probably it is because several models corresponding to as many deep structural levels were present when it was produced.

If for the time being we set aside the important problem of the retroaction of events on structures and accept the simple theoretical schema according to which several models belonging, first of all to the different states and, especially, to the different levels of deep history, converge to produce a historical object or event, we can immediately come to a certain number of conclusions. If several structures exist that converge to produce the same factual object, they can have a number of incompatibilities. That is, they can exclude each other: Certain elements can exclude other elements, they can also have vast areas of compatibilities. It is within these zones of structural compatibilities that humanity's historical freedom seems to be situated. That is where the original choices of history are made. Indeed, it is because they are inscribed within the vast network of incompatibilities and compatibilities, of exclusions and inclusions, that historical events can be said to be significant and distinguished from the infinity of daily microevents.

If such a representation has any value whatsoever we can then imagine that the deep structures are part of a kind of grammar of history and governed by it, all the while constituting the taxonomic component. This grammar is composed of a certain number of restrictive rules that progressively limit the possibilities of manifestation, but also, probably, the rules governing the organization of the syntactic strings that can be inscribed in historical discourse.

Surface Syntax

The Parameters

Marxist tradition and works emanating from the *Annales* school give us an idea of the general outlines and internal organization of the deep structures of fundamental history, yet the same does not hold true for a history of events. The latter, which has been epistemologically devalorized for a long time, has nonetheless enjoyed renewed favor thanks to Raymond Aron's inquiry, for example, into the status of political history, whose structural nature he denies, and to studies carried out by neopositivistic logicians attempting to apply their own practice to historical descriptions. Consequently we can say that today preoccupations with the theoretical foundations of the history of events are expressed only through rather unconvincing questioning or weak examples.

At first glance, it does not seem that the establishment of an autonomous dimension of historical descriptions on which the series of events should be situated necessarily implies abandoning or denying the fundamental dimension of history. On the contrary, linguistics today shows the operative effectiveness of maintaining distinctions between autonomous levels and domains, even though problems related to their interrelations are more and more complicated. Positing the existence of a dimension of events in history could even provide the pretext for proposing the seemingly opposite task, which would attempt to see if it is possible to establish procedures for recognizing historical events at the level of the countless manifestations of daily facts.

Historiographic tradition, dating back to the beginning of this discipline, has a tendency to confuse history and historicity, to consider the inscription of events in their spatiotemporal coordinates as granting them the status of historical events, the procedure of their inscription as being the criterion of the historian's scientific doing. Yet it is evident that if these coordinates are used to inscribe events, for this reason they cannot be considered as constituting these same events. To use a linguistic term, space and time are simply parameters of these events and, because of this fact, can be either totally absent or often imprecise. Although in certain cases it is possible to measure events quantitatively with the help of constructed chronometric time, this is not at all the case with the measurement of space (in latitudes or longitudes), since any topological indications bearing on a street, a town, or a country refer to sociological entities and not to abstract spatial coordinates. It seems necessary to maintain the distinction between historical events and their rooting in historicity.

The Historical Referent

Another positivistic tradition continues to claim that the historical fact can be defined as a denotation of reality, precisely because it is a fact. Things are far from being that simple, however.

For example, in linguistics the problem of reality, reduced to a minimal epistemological necessity, is linked to the presence of a certain "being there" of something, which we call the substance of the signifier, and then it is immediately bracketed off. If we attempt to apply the same line of reasoning to history, we see then that the historical manifestation is not present for historians, that instead of constructing a description starting from this manifestation, historians simply project their hypothetical construct onto the past and pompously call it reality.

As a matter of fact, history can be written only through linguistic mediation, by substituting historical texts—their true referent—for strings of "real" events, which are afterward reconstituted as a referential projection. In the best of cases, historians use documents and chronicles from the period studied which in themselves are already free translations in natural languages of somatic programs carried out by real subjects. Here historical and archaeological monuments play a role that is only comparable to the role of the extralinguistic context of discourse.

Such a situation is not exceptional in the social sciences, and historians aware of the mediation of natural languages could easily assume its consequences. Here two attitudes are possible: First, we can consider all the ways of writing history as syntagmatic forms—which vary from one historian to another, from one society to another—part and parcel of discourses called historical discourses; second, we can turn to historical semiotics, comparable to literary semiotics, whose task would be to establish a typology of the historiographic narrative structures. However, such a project runs the risk of not satisfying whoever would want to investigate the conditions of a science of history, that is, of a scientific discourse that would no longer bear on the historian's doing but on the "doing" of history. It is obvious that such a discourse must be a continuously evolving discourse, which, while exploring its object, must attempt to work out another operative language, distinct from the natural language whose mediation enables approaching the object studied.

Historical Utterances

Regarding a history of events it would be appropriate—and logicians interested in problems of history have not let the opportunity go by—to consider historical discourse as being made up of utterances describing "facts" strung together according to rules to be worked out. Constructed historical utterances, corresponding to described events, would be characterized by their limited number of canonical forms and would thus constitute a manageable, operative, methodological apparatus.

In our opinion, one possible way of proceeding would be to start from the purely semantic and non-"realistic" definition of the historical fact. From this definition, which is the past participle of the verb *doing* (in French, *faire* and *fait*), we can, by first bracketing off the reference to the past that it enfolds, take a canonical utterance of a logical nature as a linguistic simulacrum of the historical fact. We would then consider *doing* as a function of this utterance and posit a subject and an object of this doing as "proper names" linked by the function relation. The formal utterance

$$F \text{ doing } (S \longrightarrow O)$$

(which simply means that someone does something) nevertheless permits us to formulate all historical events univocally, while leaving the possibility of envisaging, through the investment of specified semantic contents, the development of a typology of historical utterances.

These semantic restrictions play a considerable role not only in the elaboration of the formal language but also and especially in the definition of the very object of historical investigation. By simply investing the function F with a restrictive content *doing*, we automatically exclude from the historian's consideration utterances—and the contents they are supposed to enfold—having the function *being*; "the sky is blue" or "the general is energetic" are not historical utterances. The same is true when, for example, we decide to restrict the semantic definition of the historical utterance. If we decide to consider as subjects of historical utterances only human subjects, in order to distinguish human history from natural history, then, for example, an earthquake cannot be considered a historical fact. Obviously the restrictions introduced are not real propositions, and they are suggested only as examples of metalinguistic constructions.

Collective Subjects

Yet the problem of the historical subject forces us immediately to go beyond the limits of the utterance and to examine its role within the framework of a string of utterances. For example, in a sequence that would describe the production of cars at Renault factories, the subject of doing, while in principle human, can be interchanged. In certain manufacturing subprograms, one worker can be substituted for another; in other segments of the program, a machine can replace a human being. This is merely a question of the syntagmatic substitution of subjects having a hypotactic status. Throughout the stringing of the utterances the permanence of a unique subject is guaranteed by the unity of the programmed doing, that is, oriented in such a way as to attain a specific object. Under the figurative covering of their designations, "The Renault Factories," in the natural language of French, can be considered as representing a syntagmatic type of collective subject or a subject that is the subject not of a single utterance but of a programmed string of historical utterances. It is to be understood that the subject of such a series of utterances is not the "factory" but the group of persons insofar as they participate in a common doing. The syntagmatic subject is therefore not the group of concrete persons, in the flesh, but a group of persons considered only as agents of a programmed doing. We can thus foresee the possibility of specifying the subjects and the programs of historical doing according to structural levels corresponding to their activities.

The problem is rather different when it is question of a collective subject of a different order, when, for example, we speak of the crowd demonstrating in the streets. In order to get beyond the narrow notion according to which the crowd is only a simple numerical collection of individuals, we need to set into place more complex mechanisms that have already been tested by narrative semiotics and that show how a collective subject is constituted by the integration of a wanting-to-do shared by all and by the constitution of a collective being-able-to-do. It is the common assumption of the constituent modalities of competence of a subject that transforms the individuals composing a crowd – insofar as they partake in this common wanting and being-able-to and not otherwise – into a collective subject able to undertake a collective doing that cannot be broken down into successive individual doings. We can then see how the broadening of the problematics of the subject leads us once again beyond the framework of the utterance and, at the level of its logical presupposition, to project its inscription in a program of utterances governing the institution of the collective subject.

In addition, one could always object that the collective doing of a crowd, even if it can be canonically described by means of a program of utterances, is not necessarily a historic doing. Indeed, what makes the Fall of the Bastille a historic event is not its collective program, which can be formalized, or even the consequences of this doing, but rather its significant nature, which it takes on only because the "crowd" is not a collective actant as such, but a hyponymic subject representing a collective actant – a social class, for example, whose representative it happens to be. It can be seen that the definition of such collective subjects (which we would like to designate as paradigmatic, in opposition to the syntagmatic subjects already examined) is taxonomic in nature and, ultimately, falls within the province of social structures. Moreover, the typology of the former is situated at a deeper level than that of the history of events.

Toward a Historical Syntax

These brief observations on the possibility of formulating the events of surface history by means of canonical descriptive utterances are motivated by the actual preoccupations of discursive semiotics, yet their thrust on the whole corresponds to efforts by certain logicians who would like to give scientific status to historical descriptions. However, it does seem obvious that these efforts will not bear fruit as long as (1) they remain tainted by naive positivistic presuppositions and claim to describe a ready-made preorganized reality (which in fact is simply a lexematic categorization of the world subjected to sociocultural relativism), and (2) a continuous and explicit reference is maintained between the two levels – fundamental and evenemential – of historical development.

These remarks, nevertheless, bear only on the construction of historical utterances. We have seen that each time we attempt to analyze in greater detail the constituent elements of these utterances, the problem of their organization into sequences and programs inevitably arises. Indeed, the real object of the history of events is to become a historical discourse able to manipulate canonical historical utterances by means of a discursive syntax satisfying scientific criteria.

Semioticians have noted that the insertion, in an otherwise coherent discourse, of an utterance denoting an isolated fact produces what is called an illusion of reality. However, the succession of isolated utterances, without identifiable relations between them, as a connotation produces an absurd meaning effect. Thus two successive utterances are generally interpreted as being linked, according to the ancient principle of *post hoc, ergo propter hoc*, by a "causal" relation. When examined more closely, this type of syntagmatic stringing, which seems essential to account for historical developments, covers all sorts of badly defined relations (causality, probability, verisimilitude, belief, etc.) whose typology has not even been established yet. Under these conditions it does seem difficult to begin with the chronological stringing of events, as currently done by historians, before transforming them into a syntax organizing causal-type relations between utterances. The orientation of such a syntax in the direction of decisional logic, making subjects of utterances and historical programs responsible for their doing, would give the historical project an intentional ideology.

For these reasons, to us the cautiously utilized model of interpretation found in biology, presented in the mode of an "a posteriori finality" seems to be the most neutral one in use today. From this perspective, the meaning of history would be readable only after the fact, and the construction of historical discourse would indeed be a reconstruction of history, by authenticating in this way the historians' true procedures, which have always been to start from their own instances of enunciation and penetrate backward into the depths of history. Historical syntax attempting to establish strings of utterances, starting from the ends and not the beginnings of historical programs, would have at its disposal a logic of presuppositions that could found the constituent relations of the strings of historical utterances. Nonetheless historians would still maintain the chronological order of exposition for didactic discourse.

Chapter 14
Reflections on Ethnosemiotic Objects

Ambiguities of the European Ethnological Project

To speak of poetic, musical, and gestural languages together, even if one chooses to consider them only as systems of communication within the framework offered by the European ethnology project, might appear rash. The example of omnipresent gestuality organizing and programming all human behaviors, by connoting them each time with distinctive indexes that relativize and specify them as belonging to such and such a cultural community or such and such a social class, is a case in point. For example, in the gesticulation of the human body, we quickly lose sight of the criteria permitting us to distinguish not only the role of communication from that of doing but also the categories defining ethnological gestuality. All of our gestures bear the traces of social connotations. If it is true, as Koechlin[1] has noted, that in France there exist two very distinct ways—masculine and feminine—of taking off a sweater, then it can be said that a gestural program as insignificant as *making a bed* would yield, on a European scale, an extremely rich and suggestive cultural typology.

Yet it is true that *making a bed* is not communication but the carrying out of an operation. However, even in carrying out pure practical operations, people betray their cultural status and, by this very fact, signify at the very least their belonging to a social group. The bringing together of cultures, one of the favorite themes of sociolinguistics today, is consequently a particular form of communication, which is certainly not interpersonal but social.

As a hypothesis, if European ethnology were to endorse this project of explor-

214

ing intercultural communication, it would still have to specify first what cultures it meant to concentrate on, what sociocultural series it hoped to bring together, in order to spark significations that could define them precisely as cultural totalities.

The question is far from trivial since it naively raises the problem of the very object of European ethnology. Actually, what is the aim of European ethnology or, as it called in North America, "folklore studies"? Is the goal to bring out their originality while describing certain social classes that are dying out by being progressively integrated into dominant industrial societies? In this case ethnology would be part of European *sociology* studying the internal articulations of existing macrosocieties. Should ethnology not rather seek to reconstitute – much as the collections of cultural objects and archives of oral traditions deposited in our ethnographic museums would lead us to believe – the cultural specialities of agricultural societies between the fifteenth and nineteenth centuries, societies dominated by pockets of urban civilizations, but which nevertheless lived in a sort of cultural and economical autarky? This would clearly be the task of *historical ethnology*.

Ethnology can also be given a third objective. Starting from the idea of the cultural autarky of agricultural societies, but also taking into account the sort of suspension of history that characterizes them (recent excavations in Anatolia have uncovered sixth and seventh millennia B.C. dwellings comparable to the present-day homes of Turkish peasants), much like archaeologists we could be tempted to try and identify structural indexes within historically determined cultural data, permitting the reconstruction of a lost culture, covered over by easily restorable layers. Could this then not be the object of a truly European ethnology?

An example will suffice to illustrate the ethnologic approach in the European domain. Of the three possible isotopies, which one would an ethnologist choose in order to carry out a structural analysis of the feasts taking place at the end of the year in an agricultural East European community: the New Year feasts organized in a collective farm, the Christian customs at Christmas, or the reconstruction of the "pagan" ceremonies and rituals underlying these two manifestations?

The Semiotic Approach

These questions concerning the very project of European ethnology and the ambiguity of its approach would be fully justified in light of the disorders created by the heterogeneity of research perspectives encountered in general theoretical works as well as in anthologies on European folklore. For us, however, they arise only within the problematics we hope to deal with here.

Different approaches are indeed possible when in an overview we wish to bring together poetic, musical, and gestural facts in order to discover the elements of their compatibility.

Within the framework of a general methodological reflection, we can attempt to bring together folklore facts by noting, in each language considered, similar facts of the same order. For example, we could examine popular song in the light of results obtained by recent scholarship in poetics or by using methods just now being worked out in ethnomusicology, in this way integrating folk gestuality within the problematics of visual semiotics in general.

Within a more strictly semiotic perspective, we can attempt to situate these facts on a more narrow isotopy, by considering them only from the point of view of their signifier. It then becomes evident that these are three cases of discoursive phenomena having iterative regularities. Because of this, each of these phenomena can therefore be analyzed and described separately as grammars and therefore be compared.

But it is possible to skip the intermediate stages and, instead of considering each language separately, focus more particularly on the phenomenon of their syncretism. One is free to see that languages, which in other respects can have an autonomous existence, can also function as languages of manifestation combining several codes of expression to produce a global signification. We shall mainly focus our attention on these complex semiotic objects.

Ethnosemiotics and Sociosemiotics

Two sorts of examples crop up that could illustrate our notion of complex semiotic objects. They can be found within the framework of archaic societies (the sung dance of warriors preparing for a punitive expedition) and within the cultural context of our societies (comic opera). The bringing together of the sacred and the profane is not at all surprising and history is there to explain this since we do know, for example, that opera was created and developed precisely during the sixteenth century, the period when the Western world was definitely desacralized.

However, what distinguishes a mythical object from an aesthetic one is the specific form of the cultural connotation underlying both phenomena. When attempting to establish a typology of literary texts, the Soviet semiotician Yuri Lotman indeed showed that in the end what determines the sacred, didactic, or literary nature of any text are not necessarily the intrinsic properties of the text in question but rather the connotative attitudes of the reader, who is inscribed within a given cultural context.

Previously, when investigating the nature of the sociolinguistic categories underlying natural languages,[2] we thought we could distinguish two distinct modes in which social connotations functioned, corresponding to two types of societies—archaic and industrial—that they helped to articulate into signification. In archaic-type societies the natural language defining a given cultural community is articulated into different morphologically stable "languages": Sacred language is opposed to profane language, women's language to men's, language used outside a society to that used within, etc. Passing from an old to a new cultural type happens not only by the breaking up and multiplication of these "social languages" into multiple discourses (philosophical, religious, poetic discourses, etc., will correspond to sacred language), but also through the appearance of a sort of mobile sociolinguistic syntax, permitting each member of the collectivity, by successively taking up different discourses and modes of speech, to behave much like a chameleon. A relatively stable sociolinguistic morphology gives way to a syntax of polysemic social communication.

Starting from observations on natural languages it is easy to extrapolate this constructed schema and to apply it to all the manifested languages of a given culture, while inscribing sociolinguistic facts within the wider framework of sociosemiotics. By applying the same principle of transformation, we can see how complex semiotic objects, recognizable at the level of ethnosemiotics, break apart and give rise to a stylistics of multiple variation at the sociosemiotic level.

This passage from ethnosemiotics to sociosemiotics can be recognized in several different ways:

1. A global mythical phenomenon (that is, a semiotic object whose signification is expressed at the same time by poetic, musical, and gestural codes) is broken down and to a degree appears in what are called developed societies, as disjoined and autonomous discourses: poetry, music, dance.

2. Instead of being connoted as manifestations of the sacred, these various autonomous languages take on ludic or aesthetic functions in macrosocieties.

3. With regard to their production and use, instead of being collective manifestations, poetic, musical, or gestural expressions fall within the province of individual stylistics.

4. Instead of being collective productions of meaning, the semiotic objects generated by these languages essentially become objects of individual consumption.

European ethnologists must therefore choose between two possible structural explanations of the phenomena studied. An ethnosemiotic approach can be opposed to a sociosemiotic approach since they generate distinctive facts, not only through their modes of production and consumption but also through their very structures. Insofar as most of the data ethnologists have are typical of a transitional "folk" state, in other words of an ethnosociological syncretism, they cannot be described directly, but only by referring to one or another of the structurally defined models.

The Situation of the Folk Fact

From the point of view of history, the existence of periods of transition, far from being exceptional, appears as a normal state. Each culture, by the very fact that it is historical, among the infinite quantity of data used to represent it, at any given moment possesses structural elements, both of what it was and of what it will become. However, our models of interpretation of these data are, in a certain sense, ahistorical, if only because their construction demands an internal coherence that the simple presence of heterogeneous data cannot give them.

The analysis of folk facts must therefore refer back to either ethnosemiotic models, or sociosemiotic schemata for the organization and interpretation of these data.

Examples taken from research on narrativity over the last few years, by means of analogy and in a much more concrete way, will enable us to situate this methodological problem. We do know, for example, that to the *mythical narrative*, of an ethnosemiotic order, corresponds, at the folk level, *the magical tale*, characterized by a sort of loss of meaning, recognizable by the absence of an explicit semantic code in the narrative. We also know that *literary narrative*, which reappears at the sociosemiotic level, is marked by the reactivation of meaning, by the reintegration of semanticism within its formal structure, but obviously with the difference that literary narratives express individualized value systems, whereas myths are collective axiological expressions. We can therefore ask ourselves if the same type of typological trajectory starts from *sacred poetry*, of an ethnosemiotic nature, passes through *folk poetry*, in a certain way desemanticized, and ends up with the reappearance of what is called *modern poetry*, which is individualized and often hermetic. Modern languages do not have a word to designate complex mythical objects such as *songs danced* or *dances sung*, but the same does not hold true for what are called archaic societies. However, would it be wrong to see in certain forms of folk gestuality (work songs, danced and sung games, certain popular dances) degraded and desemantisized forms of former gestural ritual? Adopting the desemantisization hypothesis as characterizing folk phenomena, within the syncretism of poetic, musical, and gestural expressions of meanings, would have a twofold advantage: Not only would we find the complementary liturgical form of theology contained in mythical narrative, but, starting from cultural stereotypes encountered at the folk level, we also could attempt to elaborate procedures that would enable the reactivation of signification.

The Materiality of the Mythical

The identification of two sorts of poetic objects — some falling within the province of sacred language, others representing a modern form of personalized sacredness, objects that would be comparable because of their structural organization and differentiated only by the collective or individual nature of their semantic investments — permits us to use our knowledge of modern poetics to clarify certain aspects of sacred poetry. We know that the specificity of poetic language in the first place consists in the specific treatment this language gives to its plane of signifiers. Rhythm, rhyme, assonance, etc., in forms of diffuse poetry, are simply the dispersed elements of the organization of expression as it appears in its greatest density, in certain forms of modern poetry and in ancient forms of sacred poetry. In these borderline cases the poetic articulation of the signifier is defined by a set of structures that are in correlation with those of the signified and can be homologous to the latter. Thus poetic language is seen as a specific organization of *parole* that attempts to free itself from the arbitrary nature of linguistic signs and regain an original motivation such as those of onomatopoeic signs, or, in the extreme, of the human scream. This taking up of the signifier, which is thus brought closer to its signified, can be interpreted as an attempt by the subject of poetic discourse, beyond signs and symbols, to get back to the *materiality* of language, and as far as the receiver is concerned it takes on the meaning effect of creating an impression of truth, or reality of what is uttered.

It thus seems self-evident that the duplication or triplication of the plane of signification of language, when produced with the adjunction of complementary musical or gestural expression, can only further consolidate this illusion of the authenticity of speech, this certitude of true communication, endowing the mythical global object being examined with the greatest possible efficiency. Yet, it is obvious that if song, even at the folk level, appears as the near natural accompaniment of poetry, and is actually fused with it, dance, while being one of the forms of gestuality, is not its only form. Generally speaking, mythical gestuality is one of the strong forms of a human being's engagement in the production of meaning. Not only does it set into play the entire human body but it also, thanks to the body's mobility, enables establishing direct relations between a person and surrounding space. Hence a complementary dimension of signification, or proxemic dimension, appears. Whether it be in Lithuanian songs about the coming of spring where the poetic call is reinforced by the repeated swinging, as high as possible, of the singer perched on a swing, or in the Provençal farandole, where in an uninterrupted rhythmic movement a human chain explores the totality of communal space and mythically appropriates it, ritual gestuality appears as the human being's relation to the world.

Coherent Deformation

Another specific feature of poetic language — a feature that is fully shared with the sacred languages of archaic societies — resides in the distance, willingly posited, separating the enunciator from the natural language used to express oneself. If, up to a point, sacred language can be a language other than daily language (Latin, for example), this distance can be seen most often in the coherent deformation of natural language itself. If sacred language is used to communicate with the transhuman, it is normal then that it does represent a distortion in relation to the daily and the practical. This would seem to explain, for example, why sixteenth-century treatises on exorcism had worked out a complete phonetics that could account for the devil's discourse. Closer to us today, when the devil speaks through the possessed women of Loudon studied by M. de Certeau,[3] not only do the women express themselves in bad Latin but, in addition, their discourse is consolidated by gestuality having animal (that is, subhuman) characteristics. The same holds true for circus gestuality — a relic of former times — where the acrobat attempts to signify the superhuman, whereas the clown serves as counterpoint by producing the subhuman. The same could be said concerning the new gestural rituals that sports championships happen to be in modern-day society, where going beyond the limits of the human body has been granted the status of an absolute value that has given rise to the founding of a caste of demigods.

It is from this very perspective that we could ask to what degree the principle of voice determination and, more precisely, variations in the tone of voice, would be pertinent, among other criteria (melodic, functional), in the classification of popular songs.

We should note the deformation of signifiers introduced by rhythm as being one of the most apparent deformations in question. It is noteworthy to remark that songsters of Dogon hymns as well as of Rumanian ballads use the same distortion procedures, by imposing a musical rhythm contrary to the rules of accentuation and intonation of natural languages. We can take this a step further by proposing that the deformation of the signifier be considered no longer an end in itself, but an attempt to institute a new coherence, a signifying organization of the second degree whose rhythmic accompaniment underscored by dance would be only the emphatic affirmation. The same holds true when we consider the melodic aspect of poetry, and not just its rhythmic aspect. Recent research in popular Spanish poetry[4] at the level of the organization of verse, and in conjunction with the rhythmic schema characterizing it, seems to have brought out the existence of iterated vocalic schemata made up of vowel variations according to pitch. These schemata enable us to identify their geographic distribution according to variable structural properties. If further study of this type confirmed the initial results, by establishing more certain correlations between the melodic schemata (poetic and musical) and the rhythmic schemata (poetic and musical), we could perhaps one day better understand the entire poetic phenomenon. Taking into account both the deforming and regulating nature of the new governing principles of poetic language, in this way the problem of the refrain takes on a different light. Because of the desemantization of folk song and the substitutability of words, because of its very illegibility, the refrain appears as the possible guardian of the melodic and rhythmic schemata of forgotten sacred song.

Collective Efficacy

Even though the mythical object we are attempting to interpret happens to be a complex object, integrating several languages of expression, and defined in its specificity as having a secondary structural organization (more or less consolidated by the recurrences and superimposition of the signifiers), we still cannot ultimately see what distinguishes, for example, marriage ceremonies from Viennese operettas. This is all the more the case since consummate manipulators succeed admirably well in putting on folk shows that rival comic opera productions.

This is indeed precisely because the "folklorization" of this sort of collective popular taste begins with the showing of ethnosemiotic objects. The presence of a spectator diverts semiotic doing from its original function and, by making it an object of contemplation, transforms the authentic subject of this doing into a bad actor.

Insofar as semiotic activity is of the order of communication and takes place along the axis of *sending* vs. *receiving*, the mythical charge is necessarily on the side of the sender: The "true" message, contained within the sacred song, is addressed not to a public of human listeners but to a mythical receiver, and often attempts to establish contractual links with it. But it is especially in the form of mythical doing having an explicit finality that it seems to happen: Whether it is a question of mythical accompaniment of practical doing (e.g., sung rituals to make wheat grow), semiotic activity is never a making-to-see but a making-to-do. Communication or doing, a true message or a finalized program, the mythical act is always defined as an efficient operation.

Contrary to the passive, receptive attitude of the individual situated within the sociosemiotic context where poetry is recited, where music is heard and ballet seen, the relation between people and ethnosemiotic objects is one of participation. The first effect of this type of activity is to integrate the individual within the group and to establish the social group as a *collective subject*: We can see that societies defined by ethnosemiotic communication are strongly cohesive. Hence it is not surprising that macrosocieties such as French society, for example, have retained group songs in only two specific instances: in kindergarten, where social life is first experienced, and, in part, in the army, where individuals are subjected to norms having social finalities.

Extremely efficient social systems of communication therefore seem to be one of the characteristic features of European culture underlying various folk manifestations of interest to European ethnologists.

Notes

Notes

Foreword

1. Jean Petitot-Cocorda, *Morphogenèse du sens* (Paris: PUF, 1985), p. 273. This concept is taken by Greimas from Hjelmslev.

2. Forthcoming in English. John Benjamin's introduction and translation by Paul Perron.

3. Hayden White *Metahistory: The Historical Imagination in Nineteenth-Century Europe* (Baltimore: Johns Hopkins University Press, 1973). The interested reader will note some modifications of my own position on this classic work since the review article, "The Poetics of Historiography" (reprinted in *The Ideologies of Theory*, vol. I, in press).

4. See Jameson, *The Political Unconscious* (Ithaca, N.Y.: Cornell University Press, 1981), pp. 165ff. and 253ff. or "After Armageddon: Character Systems in *Dr. Bloodmoney,*" *Science-Fiction Studies 2* (March 1975):31–42.

5. Thus, for example: "Certainly the greatest philosophers . . . resist reduction to the archetypes provided by Pepper. If anything, their thought represents a mediation between two or more of the kinds of doctrinaire positions which Pepper outlines" (p. 13, n. 7); or: "The dialectical tension which characterizes the work of every master historian usually arises from an effort to wed a mode of employment with a mode of argument or of ideological implication which is inconsonant with it" (p. 29).

Introduction

1. Quoted in J.-C. Coquet, "Éléments de bio-bibliographie," in *Recueil d'hommages pour/Essays in honor of Algirdas Julien Greimas*, ed. H. Parret and H. G. Ruprecht (Amsterdam: John Benjamins, 1985), p. liv.

2. In their introduction to *Recueil d'hommages pour/Essays in honor of Algirdas Julien Greimas*, Parret and Ruprecht point out that Greimas transforms the stratificational concept of meaning into a transpositional one and enriches the relational concept of meaning inherited from Saussurian linguistics by means of a transpositional component. "Just as the *articulation* constitutes a supplement to *rela-*

tion, transposition constitutes a supplement to the *articulated relation*" (pp. xxvi–xxvii).

3. For definitions and interdefinitions of terms used both by Greimas and in this foreword, readers should consult A. J. Greimas and J. Courtés, *Semiotics and Language, An Analytical Dictionary* (Bloomington: Indiana University Press, 1982).

4. For a presentation of the basic theoretical model through its application to a biblical text, see D. Patte, "Greimas' Model for the Generative Trajectory of Meaning in Discourses," *American Journal of Semiotics* 1(1982):59–78.

5. It is on this very issue regarding the possibility of conceiving semantics as a science that J. Culler (1975) questions the viability of Greimas's undertaking. However, as R. Scheifler (1983) remarks, Culler's critique stems from the fact that the failure he sees in the method "takes *semiotics* (logic of signs) rather than *semiology* (problems of meaning) as its measure" (p. xiii). On the one hand, this amounts to conflating the differences that exist between the natural and human sciences, which are sciences of signification. On the other hand, Culler presupposes that the social sciences should be conceived of as a system and not as a process (or an ongoing scientific project), that is, as a "scientific doing which is manifested always in an incomplete and often defective way in the discourses it produces, which are recognizable, at first glance, only because of the socio-linguistic connotations of 'scientificness' with which they are endowed." See Greimas, *Sémiotique et sciences sociales* (Paris: Le Seuil, 1976), pp. 9–42.

6. In Ruprecht, "Ouvertures meta-sémiotiques: Entretien avec A. J. Greimas," *Recherches Sémiotiques/Semiotic Inquiry* 4(1984):1–23, Greimas elaborates on the hypothetico-deductive aspect of the theory. Initially local hypotheses are formulated, and when there seems to be incompatibility with the theory an attempt is made to integrate the phenomenon within the coherence of the system as a whole. Such a phenomenon must be analyzed not only as such but according to the rule of *pertinence*; that is, it is inscribed in a hierarchically superior level so that phenomena of a comparable nature can also be explained in terms of this hierarchical metalevel. "This is the deductive aspect of the hypothesis. You formulate it in terms of an acquired experience or semiotic *praxis*. Then you attempt to construct a model which is hierarchically superior, therefore more powerful, and this is where deduction has an effect, that you can test to find out if the coherence of the theory is not weakened" (p. 7).

7. Unedited paper, "Universaux et narrativité," given at a colloquium on the universals of narrativity held at the University of Toronto, June 1984.

8. Given the uncertain status of knowledge and the abuse of terminology such as formalization, and formal theories used in the social sciences, Greimas argues that the time is not ripe to formulate any theories in this domain in terms of formal language. For him it is essential, not only in semiotics but in the human and social sciences, to "construct a theory of a *conceptual* nature, that is to say a coherent theory where concepts are interdefined and hold together. It is only when such a theory is constructed that we should speak about its formalization, that is to say its transformation into formal language" (Ruprecht, "Ouvertures meta-sémiotiques," pp. 7–8).

9. For an analysis of various discourses in the social sciences see A. J. Greimas and E. Landowski, *Introduction à l'analyse du discours en sciences sociales* (Paris: Hachette, 1979).

10. "Universaux et narrativité."

Chapter 1. Comparative Mythology

1. It will be noted that this study, which goes back to 1962, precedes Lévi-Strauss's *Mythologiques*. Even though the procedures of its presentation might appear a little out of date, the text still has some didactic value.

2. Dumézil has clearly shown that the stories or fragments of stories that can be used by mythology are found in all contexts: in sacred texts, epic poems, descriptions of rituals and ceremonies,

historical works, the legends of folklore, etc. For the study of signification, it is irrelevant which of these forms the signifiers take.

3. Lévi-Strauss, "The Structural Study of Myth," *Journal of American Folklore* 68 (1955): 428–44.

4. We place between slashes (/ . . . /) any word or expression that has to do with the signified. We do this to make it clear that they belong not to the mythical story itself but rather to the "terminology" of mythological description. On this matter, see our clarification in the concluding pages of this chapter.

5. Since we wish to carry the description of distinctive features as far as possible, we will stick to the formulation of myth that results from an analysis devoted to Oedipus and will not refer to the generalized formula Lévi-Strauss proposes further on in his same study.

6. One can wonder whether it might not be possible to give an approximate date for myths from past societies by taking into account not the signifier, whose elements are incontestably old, but their global signification: A given political "ideology," for instance, is compatible with some historical contexts and not with others.

7. Mentioning only what is essential, we will not carry this analysis to the point where it would identify new oppositions, for example, /causing/ vs. /caused/, the first corresponding to the instigator of the fight, the second to the fight itself.

8. For a definition of this term, see the concluding passages of this chapter.

9. In the same way, at the comparative level: If the etymological relationship suggested by Dumézil is valid, it could be confirmed by the correlation between ritual and theological facts:

$$\frac{\text{Çams--}}{\text{cens-}} \approx \frac{\text{Prthu}}{\text{Fortuna}}$$

10. The present study was carried out before the publication of *La Pensée sauvage*. Some of Lévi-Strauss's observations (above all as found on pp. 46 and 47) would probably have helped in a more defined formulation of the problem of the ritual story.

11. Throughout this chapter we have underlined semes and *lexemes* in a different way. The term *lexeme* is replaced by *sememe* from our *Sémantique structurale* (Paris: Larousse, 1966).

Chapter 2. Toward a Semiotics of the Natural World

1. F. Rastier, "Comportements et signification," *Langages* 10(1968):76–86.

2. B. Koechlin, "Techniques corporelles et leur notation symbolique," *Langages* 10(1968): 45–46.

3. *Sémantique structurale* (Paris: Larousse, 1966), pp. 55 ff.

4. Here they are respectively studied in the order: (1) orientation, (2) support, and (3) displacement.

5. See V. Proca-Ciortea and A. Giurchescu, "Quelques aspects théoriques de l'analyse de la danse populaire," *Langages* 10(1968):87–93, and B. Koechlin, "Techniques corporelles et leur notation symbolique," *Langages* 10(1968):36–47.

6. See F. Rastier's study in *Langages* 10(1968) and "Gestural Communication," this chapter.

7. See "Gestural Communication," this chapter.

8. See J. Kristeva, "Le Geste, pratique ou communication?" *Langages* 10(1968):48–64.

9. See "Utterance and Enunciation," this chapter.

10. See R. Cresswell, "Le Geste manuel associé au langage," *Langages* 10(1968):119–27.

11. A relationship between gestural elements.

12. A difference of signification.

13. See P. Fabbri, "Considérations sur la proxémique," *Langages* 10(1968):65–75.

14. See C. Hutt, "Dictionnaire du langage gestuel chez les trappistes," *Langages* 10(1968): 107-18.

15. See C. Bremond, "Pour un gestuaire des bandes dessinées," *Langages* 10(1968):94-100.

16. See "The Presence of Meaning," this chapter.

17. *Sémantique structurale* (Paris: Larousse, 1966), p. 105.

Chapter 3. The Interaction of Semiotic Constraints

1. Although the existence of this type of relation seems undeniable, the problem of its orientation ($s_1 \longrightarrow s_2$ or $s_2 \longrightarrow s_1$) has not yet been settled. We shall not raise this issue here since its solution is not necessary for this demonstration.

2. In the same way as the term *seme* is employed to designate minimal distinctive features of content, we shall employ the term *pheme* to designate the distinctive feature of expression (it being understood that phemes, like semes, are semantic by nature).

3. M. Gross, "L'emploi des Modèles en linguistique," *Langages* 9(1968):3-8, 5: "In a modern linguistics article there are as many nongrammatical examples as acceptable examples."

4. Although facts of this type are frequently cited in Jakobson's *Selected Writings, 1: Phonological Studies* (The Hague: Mouton, 1970), we know of no scientific study of them; doubtless phonologists have preferred to eliminate the noninjunctions from the systems they have studied.

5. In the French *Code Civil*, the first paragraph of the chapter *Des moyens d'acquérir la propriété* (*On the Means of Acquiring Property*) is entitled "le Mariage."

Chapter 5. A Problem of Narrative Semiotics: Objects of Value

1. G. Dumézil, *Mythe et épopée* (Paris: Gallimard, 1968), pp. 541-42.

2. C. Calame-Griaule, quoted by Denise Paulme, "Échanges successifs," in *Alliés animaux*, p. 102.

3. D. Paulme, "Échanges successifs," p. 137.

4. See Aarne and Thompson's type 554, analyzed by D. Paulme, in "Échanges successifs."

5. *Structural Semantics*, trans. D. McDowell, R. Schleifer, and A. Velie (Lincoln and London: University of Nebraska Press, 1983), chapter 2, "The Elementary Structure of Signification."

6. Chapter 4, this volume, "Elements of a Narrative Grammar."

7. In order to simplify we are leaving aside all of the problematics of the subject by postponing its institution as a *wanting-to-be* in relation with the object considered as a *being-wanted*.

8. This was treated in a paper given as part of our annual research seminar held in Paris since 1965 at l'Ecole Pratique des Hautes Etudes.

9. Acts of the Palermo International Colloquium, *Structures et genres de la littérature ethnique*.

10. Chapter 3, this volume, "The Interaction of Semiotic Constraints," written in collaboration with François Rastier.

11. Notably the analysis of Denise Paulme, "Échanges successifs," in *Alliés animaux*.

Chapter 7. Toward a Theory of Modalities

1. [*Si* is the affirmative answer to a negative question or statement. – Trans.]

2. [Translators of Propp use the term *mandatory*. – Trans.]

3. See M. Rengstorf, "Pour une quatrième modalité narrative," *Langages* 43(1976):71-77.

Chapter 8. On the Modalization of Being

1. M. Rengstorf, "Pour une quatrième modalité narrative," *Langages* 43(1976):71-77.

2. Algirdas Julien Greimas, *Maupassant. La Sémiotique du texte: Exercices pratiques* (Paris: Le Seuil, 1976).

Chapter 9. On Anger: A Lexical Semantic Study

1. [*To wait* is French, *attendre*; French, *attente* is both *a wait* and *expectation*; the two are joined in the French verb *s'attendre à, to expect.* — Trans.]

2. [These verbs are "pronominal" in French: *to anger oneself, to put oneself into a state of being offended*, and so on. — Trans.]

3. Greimas, "Le défi," in *Du Sens II* (Paris: Le Seuil, 1983), pp. 213-23.

4. [*Se fâcher, s'offenser, se mettre en colère.* — Trans.]

Chapter 14. Reflections on Ethnosemiotic Objects

1. "Techniques corporelles et leur notation symbolique," in *Pratiques et langages gestuels*, special issue of *Langages* 10(1968):36-47.

2. See "On Theoretical Models in Sociolinguistics," chapter 12, this volume.

3. *Les Possédés de Loudon*, July 1970.

4. A. Lomax and E. Crowell Trayer, "Phonotactique du chant populaire," *L'Homme* (Jan.-April 1964):5-12.

Index

Index

Theory and History of Literature

Algirdas Julien Greimas, French semiotician of Lithuanian origin, is professor of general semiotics at the Ecole des Hautes Etudes en Sciences Sociales in Paris, where he has been director of studies since 1965. The essays in this book draw upon three of his works: *Du sens, Sémiotique et sciences sociales*, and *Du sens II*. Other books available in English are *Semiotics and Language: An Analytical Dictionary* (with J. Courtes), *Structural Semantics*, and — forthcoming — *On Gods and Men* and *Maupassant: The Semiotics of Text*.

Paul J. Perron and **Frank H. Collins** both teach at the University of Toronto. Collins is graduate coordinator for medieval studies and associate professor of French. Perron is a professor of French and co-author of *Balzac, Sémiotique du personnage romanesque*. He has also edited several volumes on semiotics.

Fredric Jameson teaches at Duke University. *The Political Unconscious* is his most recent book.

DATE DUE
